woman's own
365 Menu Cookbook
Marguerite Patten

Hamlyn
London . New York . Sydney . Toronto

Contents

Meals suitable for *Cold Weather* are Weeks 36 to 48.

Meals suitable for *Hot Weather* (using summer fruits, etc.) are Weeks 12 to 20.

The other weeks are suitable for most times of the year.

Jacket picture by Eric Carter

Colour photographs — Syndication International

Published by The Hamlyn Publishing Group Limited
London . New York . Sydney . Toronto
Astronaut House, Feltham, Middlesex, England
© The Hamlyn Publishing Group Limited 1973
Second Impression 1974
ISBN 0 600 36096 2

Printed in England by Cox and Wyman Limited, Fakenham

Introduction

Using your Menu Book

In this book you will find a menu for a main meal for every day of the week, i.e. 365 days. I would suggest that in order to get the very best value from this book you read through the entire week's menus; this will give you an idea if these fit in with a) the kind of food your family likes, b) your budget, c) the other meals you plan during the week, i.e. breakfast and either lunch or supper.

Shopping

Some of you will shop once a week because you have good storage facilities, a large refrigerator, a home freezer, etc., and therefore the shopping suggested on various days will not apply. You will be able to buy most of the food at one time.

Remember that not all vegetables are given in the recipes, for example potatoes are not mentioned with every meal. Probably you will not wish to serve them at each meal but I have listed them as a reminder. I have not listed green vegetables on each occasion as I thought you would probably prefer to use up some of the vegetables left over from other days, and to see which green vegetables are best and cheapest at the time.

On some days you will find a vegetable needed in cooking the dish is not mentioned in the shopping list, for example in Week 1 (Wednesday) I use celery in a recipe, but such a small amount is required that I have assumed you will have some left from earlier in the week.

I have not mentioned dry or canned foods in the shopping lists for most of us have a reasonable stock of canned food in the storecupboard, neither have I suggested frozen foods to be bought frequently. Many people store good supplies of frozen food in modern refrigerators, where the freezing compartment enables you to keep these for a long period. Home freezers enable food you freeze yourself or commercially frozen food to be stored for a long period. It is a good idea to replace cans of food and packets of frozen food as soon as possible after using them.

I have not listed the amount of butter, margarine, etc., required in recipes because most of us keep reasonable stocks of these, but since there is nothing more annoying than to be short of eggs when you want to make a dish I have given an indication of the amount of *eggs, milk* and *cheese* used for the recipes in each week. Cheese required for the end of a meal is not listed.

In order to minimise the time spent on shopping I have grouped the days together so you may shop for several days at one time. The weeks are not exactly the same, as the amount of perishable foods will be different for each week.

Storing Food

Sometimes I felt a little worried about storing very perishable foods such as minced meat, sausagemeat, fish, etc., and have emphasised 'careful storage' in the shopping lists. If you are storing these kinds of food, do keep them as near the freezing compartment of your refrigerator as possible.

Soft and perishable fruits can be stored in the refrigerator, although these should *NOT* be placed too near the freezing compartment, and should be used as soon as possible.

Salad ingredients are best if stored in the salad container in the refrigerator, or in polythene containers. Green and other vegetables should be kept in a cool place with adequate air circulation.

Planning Well-Balanced Meals

As you read the shopping lists and recipes consider the kind of foods mentioned.

If the week's shopping list gives a generous number of eggs or quantity of milk to be used in cooking, this means you can be rather more sparing with eggs and milk at other meals.

If the week's main meals are fairly high in carbohydrates, e.g. you have a generous amount of pastry, potatoes or sweet puddings or other substantial dishes, then make sure your other meals are lighter and avoid these foods which, while sustaining and popular, can cause overweight.

If the week's main meals are very economical then you can spend more on supper or lunch, but if you have more luxurious main dishes choose economical foods such as eggs, cheaper fish, etc., for the basis of lunch or supper.

Basic Sauces, etc.

You will find recipes for sauces on page 5. All recipes, unless stated to the contrary, serve 4, but some gâteaux, pies, etc., may produce rather more portions. Obviously these mean you can serve the dish for another meal. I like sponge-type gâteaux as desserts, for any left may be frozen and used as a teatime cake at some future date.

I hope this book will solve the ever-present problem of 'what shall we have today?'.

Marguerite Patten

Oven Temperatures

The following chart gives the conversions from degrees Fahrenheit to degrees Celsius (formerly known as Centigrade) recommended by the manufacturers of electric cookers.

Description	Electric Setting	Gas Mark
very cool	225°F.–110°C.	$\frac{1}{4}$
	250°F.–130°C.	$\frac{1}{2}$
cool	275°F.–140°C.	1
	300°F.–150°C.	2
very moderate	325°F.–170°C.	3
moderate	350°F.–180°C.	4
moderate *to*	375°F.–190°C.	5
moderately hot	400°F.–200°C.	6
hot	425°F.–220°C.	7
	450°F.–230°C.	8
very hot	475°F.–240°C.	9

Note: this table is an approximate guide only. Different makes of cooker vary and if you are in any doubt about the setting, it is as well to refer to the manufacturer's temperature chart.

Sometimes I suggest only the lower setting, e.g. 375°F. or Gas Mark 5 for Moderately hot. This is because the *whole menu*, as opposed to individual dishes within the menus, must be cooked very carefully to prevent over-heating or over-browning.

Bread Sauce 1 small onion, 2–3 cloves (optional), ½ pint (3 dl.) milk, 2 oz. (50 g.) soft white breadcrumbs, 1 oz. (25 g.) butter or margarine, seasoning, little thick cream (optional).
Peel the onion, stick the cloves into this. Put the onion into the milk with the other ingredients (except the cream), bring the milk to boiling point. Cover the pan and remove from the heat. Leave in a warm place until 5 minutes before serving. Remove onion with cloves, heat the sauce, stirring well. Add a small amount of cream if desired.

Custard Sauce Although a custard sauce can be made with eggs and milk, see page 88, it is assumed the custard powder type of sauce will be used where the recipe states 'serve with custard' and 1 pint (½ litre) of milk has been allocated for this. This gives a generous 4 portions. Follow the directions on the packet or tin for making this sauce but *do* cook the custard well and stir continually as it thickens. Remember custard becomes more 'solid' as it cools, so use less custard powder.
To vary: **Sweet White Sauce:** use cornflour instead of custard powder. Flavour sauce with a little vanilla essence or sweet sherry.

Brown Sauce 1 oz. (25 g.) fat or dripping (or a little more), 1 small onion, 1 small carrot, 1 oz. (25 g.) flour, ½ pint (3 dl.) brown stock*, seasoning.
*made by simmering beef or mutton or game bones. If not available use water and 1 beef stock cube.
Heat the fat or dripping, fry chopped onion and carrot for a few minutes. Stir in flour and cook for several minutes. Gradually blend in the stock. Bring to the boil and cook until thickened, sieve or emulsify in the liquidiser to give a smooth sauce. Season well.
Note: if a recipe states 'a thick brown sauce' it generally assumes ¼ pint (1½ dl.) stock only. This consistency, known as a panada, is used for binding ingredients together.
To vary: add a little sherry or port wine, or Madeira wine, or tomato purée to give a change of flavour.

Cranberry Sauce 8 oz. (200 g.) cranberries, 6 tablespoons water, 2 oz. (50 g.) sugar (or a little more), ½ oz. (15 g.) butter, 1 tablespoon port wine.
Simmer the ingredients together. Sieve or emulsify if you want a smooth sauce.

Cranberry Jelly 1 lb. (½ kilo) cranberries, ½ pint (3 dl.) water, sugar.
Simmer the fruit and water until a smooth purée. Put through a jelly bag. Allow 1 lb. (½ kilo) sugar to each 1 pint (6 dl.) juice. Stir the sugar with the juice until dissolved. Boil rapidly until set. Put into pots and seal down.

White Sauce 1 oz. (25 g.) butter or margarine, 1 oz. (25 g.) flour, ½ pint (3 dl.) milk, seasoning.
Heat the butter or margarine, stir in the flour, then cook this 'roux' for several minutes over a gentle heat. Stir in the milk, bring to the boil, stir until thickened. Season well.
Note: if preferred, blend the flour and milk. Put into a pan with the butter or margarine. Bring slowly to the boil, stir until thickened and smooth, season well. *A thick white sauce,* i.e. a panada, is made with ¼ pint (1½ dl.) milk only. This is used for binding ingredients together.
To vary: flavour the sauce with anchovy essence, grated cheese (see page 72), chopped parsley, beaten egg or egg yolk (do not boil after adding this), etc.

Sauces to make
In many cases the sauce ingredients are part of the recipe, but sometimes the recipe states '½ pint (3 dl.) white sauce' or simply 'make the sauce with margarine, flour, etc.'.
Here are some of the basic recipes you need, quantities are sufficient for 4 people.

WEEK 1

Chicken and bacon, plus good flavoured chicken stock, provide the basis for the main dishes for the first three days of this week.

For your shopping list the main meals need:
4–5 eggs, 2 pints (generous 1 litre) milk, about 12 oz. (300 g.) Cheddar or other cooking cheese.

Sunday, Monday and Tuesday need:
Boiling fowl (if not obtainable, buy roasting chicken and allow barely 20 minutes per lb. and 20 minutes over), piece of bacon (soak if cured).
Sponge cakes, thick cream, ice cream (optional).
Potatoes, onions, garlic (optional), tomatoes, green pepper, cauliflower, cabbage, carrots, celery, parsley, cooked beetroot, watercress, lemon, oranges, apples, fruit for pie (if not apples), blackberries.

Wednesday and Thursday need:
Lamb chops, liver, bacon rashers.
Parsnips, tomatoes, potatoes, onions, large cooking apples, lemon.

Friday and Saturday need:
Fresh haddock, minced beef or frozen beefburgers.
Thick cream or cream topping.
Onions, tomatoes, parsley and/or chives, potatoes, peas or root vegetables, lemon.

SUNDAY

Creamed Chicken boiling fowl, salt. For sauce: 1½ oz. (40 g.) butter, 1½ oz. (40 g.) flour, ½ pint (3 dl.) milk, ¼ pint (1½ dl.) stock, seasoning, 2 tablespoons cream, squeeze of lemon juice.
Simmer chicken in salted water, allowing 30 minutes per lb. (½ kilo) and 30 minutes over. When cooked, slice meat. Serve with sauce made with butter, flour, milk, stock, seasoning, cream and lemon juice.

Spanish Rice 1 chopped onion, 2 skinned tomatoes, little green pepper, 1 oz. (25 g.) fat, 1 pint (6 dl.) water, 4 oz. (100 g.) long grain rice, seasoning.
Fry onion, tomatoes and green pepper in the fat. Add the water, rice and seasoning; simmer 30 minutes, stir as it thickens.

Golden Cauliflower top a cooked cauliflower with a chopped hard-boiled egg and a little melted butter.

Orange Trifle sponge cakes, marmalade, fresh orange juice, 1 orange jelly, custard, whipped cream, orange slices.
Spread split sponge cakes with marmalade. Place in bowl. Moisten with orange juice and pour over hot orange jelly. When set, cover with custard. Decorate with whipped cream and orange slices.

WEDNESDAY

Stuffed Lamb Chops 4 thick loin lamb chops, 2 oz. (50 g.) breadcrumbs (brown are particularly good), 2 tablespoons chopped celery, 2 teaspoons chopped parsley or celery leaves, seasoning, 1 oz. (25 g.) chopped suet or melted margarine, 1 oz. (25 g.) sultanas, 1 egg yolk (cover white and save for Apricot Fluff on Saturday). Cut across flesh of chops to form pocket. Blend breadcrumbs with celery, parsley or celery leaves, seasoning, suet or melted margarine and sultanas. Bind with egg yolk. Press into chops, wrap each chop in greased foil, cook for 45 minutes in moderately hot oven, Gas Mark 6, 400°F. (200°C.).

Roast Parsnips parsnips, salt, fat.
Cut peeled parsnips into neat pieces, half cook in boiling salted water, strain, then roast in hot fat for 45 minutes.

Mincemeat Apples 4 large cooking apples, little butter, 2 tablespoons water, 1 tablespoon golden syrup, 1 tablespoon lemon juice, mincemeat.
Core apples, slit skins. Put into buttered dish with water, golden syrup and lemon juice. Fill centres with mincemeat. Cook in coolest part of moderately hot oven for approximately 1 hour. Serve liquid in dish as sauce.

THURSDAY

Liver, Bacon and Tomatoes 1 lb. lambs' or calves' liver, seasoning, flour, 2 oz. (50 g.) fat, few rashers bacon, halved, halved tomatoes.
Coat liver with little seasoned flour (too much coating hardens outside), fry for 3–4 minutes only on both sides in hot fat. Add bacon, then tomatoes. Lift on to hot serving dish, serve with *Tomato flavoured gravy:* leave 1 tablespoon fat and any meat residue in pan, stir in 1 oz. (25 g.) flour, cook for several minutes, gradually add ½ pint (3 dl.) stock (or water and a chicken stock cube), seasoning and a good tablespoon concentrated tomato purée. Bring to the boil and cook, stirring well, until thickened.

Lyonnaise Potatoes boil approximately 1 lb. (½ kilo) peeled potatoes. Slice thickly. Peel and thinly slice 8 oz. (¼ kilo) onions. Heat little fat in pan, put in onions and cook until tender. Add seasoning and the potatoes and continue cooking until lightly brown. If using same pan for liver, cook potatoes first and put in covered dish in oven. Top with chopped parsley.

Welsh Rarebit blend 4 oz. (100 g.) grated cheese, 1 teaspoon made-mustard, pinch salt, pepper, 2 tablespoons milk (or milk and brown ale). Spread on hot buttered toast, brown under the grill.

MONDAY

Boiled Bacon piece gammon, hock or collar.
Simmer bacon in water, allowing 35–40 minutes per lb. (½ kilo). (Soak overnight before cooking for heavily salted bacon.)

Spicy Tomato Sauce 1 onion, 1 apple, 1 oz. (25 g.) margarine, 2 teaspoons cornflour, seasoning, pinches of ginger, nutmeg, curry powder and sugar, 4 fresh skinned tomatoes and ¼ pint (1½ dl.) water or 1 medium can tomatoes.
Fry finely chopped onion and peeled and cored apple in margarine. Stir in cornflour, seasoning, ginger, nutmeg, curry powder and sugar. Cook for a few minutes. Add fresh tomatoes and water or canned tomatoes. Simmer 10 minutes. Sieve if wished.

Creamed Butter Beans soak beans overnight in cold water. Strain. Simmer in same pan with bacon for 1½ hours. Strain, toss in 2 tablespoons cream and chopped parsley.

Caramel Fingers 3 oz. (75 g.) brown sugar, 2 oz. (50 g.) butter, sponge fingers, ice cream or thick apple purée.
Heat sugar and butter in pan until sugar melts, stirring well. Lay sponge fingers in this mixture, turn once or twice so that they absorb caramel. Top with ice cream or thick apple purée.

TUESDAY

French Onion Soup 3 large onions, 2 oz. (50 g.) beef dripping, 1¼–1½ pints (7½–9 dl.) brown stock (chicken stock from earlier in week plus a beef stock cube gives excellent flavour), seasoning, toast or French bread, grated Gruyère or Cheddar cheese.
Cut peeled onions into thin rings, then neat pieces. Cook onions in beef dripping until golden. Add brown stock. Add plenty of seasoning, cook for 30–40 minutes. Pour soup over rounds of toast or French bread in ovenproof soup cups. Top with grated cheese, heat for *2–3 minutes only* under grill to melt cheese. For stronger flavour add one or two crushed cloves of garlic to onions.

Bacon and Chicken Salad 1 finely shredded cabbage, diced or sliced bacon and chicken left-overs, grated raw carrots, diced celery, diced apple, diced beetroot, diced gherkin, sprigs watercress.
Use cabbage as base of salad. Arrange bacon and chicken left-overs on this with carrots, celery, apple, beetroot, gherkin and sprigs of watercress.

Fruit Pie 6 oz. (150 g.) shortcrust pastry, page 10, 3–4 apples, medium can or 8–12 oz. (200–300 g.) fresh blackberries, sugar, water.
Make the fruit pie as page 46, filling the dish with sliced apples, the canned fruit plus a little syrup and sugar, or fresh fruit, water and sugar. Bake as page 46. If preferred use other fruit.

FRIDAY

Haddock Provençal 1–1½ lb. (½–¾ kilo) haddock or 4 haddock steaks, about 4 tablespoons milk, cider or white wine, onion, tomato, chopped parsley or chives, seasoning, little butter.
Divide haddock into 4 pieces, or use steaks. Put in dish with milk, cider or white wine. Top with few wafer-thin slices onion, thick slices tomato, parsley or chives. Season, cover with buttered paper or foil. Bake for 30 minutes in moderate oven.

Potato Nests 1–1½ lb. (½–¾ kilo) potatoes, seasoning, knob margarine, little butter, cooked peas or mixed vegetables.
Cook and mash potatoes, add seasoning, margarine, but no milk. Form into 4 nest shapes in buttered ovenproof dish. Bake for 25 minutes until brown. Fill nests with cooked peas or mixed vegetables.

Lemon Soufflé Pudding 2 oz. (50 g.) margarine, 2 oz. (50 g.) sugar, 2 eggs (separated), finely grated rind and juice of 1 lemon, 2 oz. (50 g.) self-raising flour, ⅓ pint (2 dl.) milk.
Cream margarine with sugar. Add egg yolks, lemon rind and juice, flour and milk. Don't worry if mixture curdles. Lastly fold in stiffly beaten egg whites. Pour into pie dish, stand in dish of cold water, cook for 40 minutes in coolest part of oven.

SATURDAY

Cheeseburgers 1 packet frozen ham or beefburgers *or* 12 oz. (300 g.) minced beef, seasoning, pinch mixed herbs, 2 oz. (50 g.) breadcrumbs, 1 egg, processed or Cheddar cheese.
Use frozen ham or beefburgers or make them by combining beef, seasoning, mixed herbs, breadcrumbs and egg. Form into 4 flat cakes. Fry or grill frozen or home-made meat cakes. Put into dish, top with sliced processed or Cheddar cheese, brown under grill.

Fried Onion Rings onions, milk, seasoned flour, 2–3 oz. (50–75 g.) fat.
Peel onions, cut into slices, dip in milk, then seasoned flour, fry until crisp and brown. Drain on absorbent paper.

Apricot Fluff a medium can apricots, ½ lemon jelly, 1 egg white, thick cream or packet cream topping.
Strain off syrup from can of apricots and, if necessary, add water to make ½ pint (3 dl.). Heat syrup and dissolve half a lemon jelly in it. Let stiffen slightly, fold in chopped apricots and stiffly beaten egg white. Put into glasses, cover with cream or cream topping.

Week 2

Topside is a comparatively economical roasting joint of beef and will appeal to those families who dislike excess fat. It can have a tendency to dry in cooking, so the method suggested below is ideal. Some left-over meat is minced and used with the ham for Monday.

For your shopping list the main meals need:
about 12 eggs, 4 pints (2¼ litres) milk, about 6 oz. (150 g.) Cheddar or other cooking cheese.
Sunday and Monday need:
Topside.
Potatoes, onions, tomatoes, carrots, fresh herbs — including parsley and chives, rhubarb.
Tuesday and Wednesday need:
Minute steaks, lambs' hearts.
Potatoes, watercress, tomatoes, carrots, swedes, onions (optional — depends on choice of stuffing), parsley, cooking apples.
Thursday, Friday and Saturday need:
Sausages, bacon rashers, chicken joints (keep frozen until Friday then thaw out gradually in the refrigerator or store fresh jointed chicken carefully).
Little cream (thick or thin).
Potatoes, onions, tomatoes, mushrooms, carrots, lettuce, watercress (store carefully or buy on Saturday), French beans, parsley, apples, other fresh fruit.

Sunday

Vegetable Topside 2 large onions, 4 tomatoes, 1 oz. (25 g.) fat, seasoning, 1 teaspoon fresh chopped herbs or pinch dried herbs, joint of topside, carrots.
Fry the thinly sliced onions and the thickly sliced tomatoes in the fat. Add seasoning and herbs. Put half the vegetables on to a large piece of foil, stand joint over this, put rest of vegetables on top of meat. Arrange small scraped seasoned carrots on the foil. Wrap meat and vegetables completely. Cook for 20 minutes per lb. (½ kilo) and 20 minutes over in centre of a hot oven, Gas Mark 6, 400°F. (200°C.).

Yorkshire Pudding make batter with 4 oz. flour, pinch salt, 1 egg, ½ pint (3 dl.) milk, add chopped parsley and chives to flavour. Bake in a knob of hot fat at the top of the oven for 25–30 minutes, raising heat to very hot for first 10 minutes cooking time.

Fondant Potatoes heat knob of fat in roasting tin, add peeled potatoes and 3 tablespoons stock or water. Roast in usual way. The liquid gives a very moist texture to the potatoes.

Rhubarb Crumble put 1 lb. (½ kilo) diced rhubarb, 2–3 oz. (50–75 g.) chopped dates or sultanas, 2 oz. (50 g.) sugar, 2 tablespoons water into a pie dish. Rub 1½ oz. (40 g.) margarine into 3 oz. (75 g.) flour, add 2 oz. (50 g.) brown sugar, sprinkle over the top of the rhubarb. Bake for 40 minutes in coolest part of hot oven.

Wednesday

Stuffed Hearts 8 small lambs' hearts, sage and onion or parsley stuffing (pages 10 and 24).
Clean and split hearts. Fill with stuffing. Wrap each heart in small square of greased foil. Bake for 1½ hours in a moderate oven, Gas Mark 4, 350°F. (180°C.). Unwrap, serve on a hot dish and use fat remaining in foil to make gravy.

Vegetable Medley put wafer-thin slices of potato, carrot and swede into a greased casserole. Season well and add a little water. Cover with a lid or foil. Bake as lambs' hearts.

Spiced Bread and Butter Pudding 4 thin slices of bread and butter, 2 oz. (50 g.) mixed dried fruit, 2 eggs, 1 oz. (25 g.) sugar, 1 teaspoon mixed spice, ¾ pint (4½ dl.) milk.
Put bread and butter into a pie dish, add dried fruit. Beat eggs with sugar and spice and add milk. Pour over the bread and butter and bake for 1 hour in the coolest part of a moderate oven.

Thursday

Piquant Sausages split sausages and spread with French mustard. Roll each sausage in bacon. Fry or grill steadily until crisp and serve with spaghetti, etc., below, or with canned spaghetti in tomato and cheese sauce.

Spaghetti in Tomato Sauce approximately 8 oz. (200 g.) spaghetti, salt. For sauce: 1 grated onion, 1 grated apple, 1 oz. (25 g.) margarine, 4 large skinned tomatoes, ¾ pint (4½ dl.) water, 1 level dessertspoon cornflour, seasoning.
Boil the spaghetti in plenty of salted water. Strain and top with the sauce. To make the sauce: fry onion and apple in margarine. Add tomatoes and ½ pint (3 dl.) of the water. Simmer until a pulp. Sieve if wished. Blend cornflour with remaining water and add to tomato mixture. Heat until clear and season well.

Golden Fritters 1 egg, 4 oz. (100 g.) self-raising flour, 2 oz. (50 g.) seedless raisins, 1 grated raw apple, just under ¼ pint (1½ dl.) milk, 2–3 oz. (50–75 g.) fat for frying, sugar.
Mix the egg with the flour, raisins and apple. Add the milk. Drop spoonfuls of thick batter into hot fat. Fry until crisp and golden brown. Dust with sugar.

MONDAY

Crumbled Ham Roll 8 oz. (200 g.) canned ham, 8 oz. (200 g.) left-over meat from Sunday, 1 oz. (25 g.) fat, 1 oz. (25 g.) flour, ¼ pint (1½ dl.) stock, 1 finely chopped onion, seasoning, 2 tablespoons soft breadcrumbs, 1 egg. To coat: 4–5 tablespoons soft breadcrumbs.
Mince ham and beef, stir into a thick sauce made with the fat, flour and stock, add onion, seasoning, breadcrumbs and egg. Form into a roll shape. Coat very thickly with crumbs. Put on to greased baking tray. Bake for 1–1¼ hours in centre of a very moderate oven, Gas Mark 4, 350°F. (180°C.). Serve with gravy, creamed potatoes and the following salad.

Tomato and Onion Salad 4–5 tomatoes, 1–2 onions, black olives, chopped parsley and chives, seasoning, little oil and vinegar.
Slice tomatoes and peeled onion thinly, arrange on dish or individual plates. Top with olives, chopped herbs and seasoned oil and vinegar (see picture, page 34).

Honey Rice 2 oz. (50 g.) pudding rice, 2 tablespoons honey, 1 pint (6 dl.) milk, grated nutmeg.
Put rice and honey into a pie dish, cover with milk, top with nutmeg. Cook for 1–1¼ hours in a very moderate oven. Picture page 27.

TUESDAY

Watercress Soup 1 good sized bunch watercress, 1 oz. (25 g.) butter, ½ pint (3 dl.) chicken stock or water and stock cube, 1 pint (6 dl.) milk, seasoning, 1 oz. (25 g.) flour.
Fry the watercress leaves in butter. Add chicken stock or water and stock cube, half the milk and seasoning. Simmer for 10 minutes. Blend flour with remaining milk, stir into soup, cook until thickened. Add extra seasoning, garnish with freshly chopped watercress leaves.

Minute Steaks fry 4 thin slices of rump steak (known as Minute Steaks) for 1 minute each side in a little hot butter. Cook halved, well seasoned tomatoes at the same time.

Sauté Potatoes fry thick slices of boiled potatoes in hot fat until golden. Toss in chopped parsley before serving.

Apple Castles approximately ½ pint (3 dl.) thick apple purée, 2 oz. (50 g.) margarine, 2 oz. (50 g.) castor sugar, 1 egg, 3 oz. (75 g.) sieved self-raising flour, ½ tablespoon milk, glacé cherries.
Make thick apple purée. Make sponge mixture by creaming margarine with sugar, beat in egg, fold in flour and milk. Put into 8 greased castle pudding tins. Cover with foil or greased paper, steam for 15 minutes. Turn out and top with hot apple purée and glacé cherries.

FRIDAY

Cheese and Mushroom Omelette fry sliced mushrooms until just tender. Make omelettes in the usual way and fill with grated cheese and the fried mushrooms.

Peas and Carrot Straws scrape or peel carrots, cut into very thin straws. Put into boiling salted water, simmer for 5 minutes, then add frozen peas. Continue cooking until both vegetables are tender.

Chocolate Sponge 3 oz. (75 g.) margarine, 3 oz. (75 g.) sugar, 2 eggs, 3 oz. (75 g.) self-raising flour sieved with 1 oz. (25 g.) chocolate powder.
Cream margarine with sugar. Gradually beat in eggs then fold in flour and chocolate powder. Steam in greased mould or basin for 1¼ hours. Serve with Chocolate Cream Sauce.
To make *Chocolate Cream Sauce:* 1 oz. (25 g.) chocolate powder, 1 tablespoon cornflour, ½ pint (3 dl.) milk, 1 oz. (25 g.) sugar, 4 tablespoons cream.
Add chocolate powder to cornflour and blend with milk. Put into a saucepan with sugar and cook until smooth and thickened. Take off the heat and whisk in cream.

SATURDAY

Crusted Chicken joints of young frying chicken, melted margarine or butter, breadcrumbs or crushed cornflakes.
Brush joints of chicken liberally with melted margarine or butter. Stand for a short time until this becomes a little set, then roll in rather coarse breadcrumbs or crushed cornflakes. Bake for ½ hour in a moderately hot oven, Gas Mark 5, 375°F. (190°C.).

Spring Salad lettuce, watercress, oil and vinegar, carrots, French beans, tomato, parsley, hard-boiled egg and gherkins.
Toss shredded lettuce, watercress in a well seasoned oil and vinegar dressing. Arrange on a flat dish. Add grated raw carrot, French beans tossed in oil and vinegar dressing, sliced tomato tossed in parsley, diced hard-boiled egg and gherkins.
Oil and Vinegar Dressing: it is a good idea to make up a large quantity of this and keep it in a screw-topped jar, then shake well before using.
Blend seasoning (including a little mustard), sugar, oil and vinegar together. Most people like 2 parts oil to 1 part vinegar.

Follow with a selection of cheeses, crisp biscuits and fresh fruit.

Week 3

Try to buy sufficient pork to make the Potato Pie on Monday, for this makes a very pleasant change from the more familiar beef.

For your shopping list the main meals need:
7 eggs, generous 4 pints (generous 2¼ litres) milk, 3–4 oz. (75–100 g.) cream cheese, 4–6 oz. (100–150 g.) Cheddar or other cooking cheese.

Sunday, Monday and Tuesday need:
Pork, lambs' kidneys (store carefully near freezer). Potatoes (some large for baking), onions, sage, tomatoes, cabbage, swede, dessert and cooking apples, dates, orange, prunes.

Wednesday and Thursday need:
Beef sausagemeat (store carefully near freezer). Cream (thick or thin), ice cream (optional). Mixed vegetables, tomatoes (some large), cucumber or gherkins, chives, watercress.

Friday and Saturday need:
White fish, middle neck of lamb. Potatoes, parsley, cauliflower, green pepper, onion, chives, lemon.

Sunday

Roast Pork cook in hot oven, Gas Mark 6, 400°F. (200°C.) allowing 25 minutes per lb. (½ kilo) and 25 minutes over. Rub fat or skin well with oil for crisp crackling.

Sage and Onion Stuffing 2 large onions, 4 oz. (100 g.) wholemeal or brown breadcrumbs, 2 oz. (50 g.) fat, 1–2 teaspoons chopped sage, seasoning.
Partially cook onions, chop finely. Mix with breadcrumbs, fat, sage and seasoning. Bake in separate dish or make 'pocket' in meat and insert stuffing. It will take 1 hour if baked separately.

Glazed Apples halve, peel and core dessert apples, put in meat tin 35 minutes before meat is fully cooked. Roll in the fat, then sprinkle lightly with brown sugar. Serve round joint, topped with stuffing.

Date Upside-down Pudding dates, 1 orange, 3 oz. (75 g.) margarine, 4 oz. (100 g.) flour, 3 oz. (75 g.) sugar, 1 egg, milk to mix.
Put thick layer of dates at bottom of ovenproof dish. Grate rind from orange and moisten dates with orange juice. Rub margarine into flour, add sugar, orange rind, beaten egg and milk to make a sticky consistency. Spread over dates and bake for ¾ hour in centre of oven.

Wednesday

Cheese and Vegetable Flan *shortcrust pastry flan:* 6 oz. (150 g.) plain flour, pinch salt, 3 oz. (75 g.) fat, water to mix. Filling: ½ pint (3 dl.) thick cheese sauce, page 5, 12 oz. (300 g.) canned or cooked vegetables.
To make a flan: sieve flour and salt, rub in fat and add enough water to bind. Roll out and line a 7–8-inch (18–20-cm.) flan ring on an upturned baking tray or a sandwich tin.
To bake a flan 'blind': fill the flan case with greased greaseproof paper or foil and crusts of bread or haricot beans, and bake for approximately 20–25 minutes above the centre of a hot oven, Gas Mark 6–7, 425°F. (220°C.), until crisp and golden brown.
Fill with hot cheese sauce mixed with hot well drained canned or cooked vegetables just before serving and put into a cool oven, Gas Mark 1, 275°F. (140°C.), to heat thoroughly.

Mocha Cup Custards 2 eggs, 1 oz. (25 g.) sugar, 1 oz. (25 g.) chocolate powder, ½ tablespoon coffee essence, ¾ pint (4½ dl.) warm milk. To serve: cream.
Beat eggs, sugar, chocolate powder and coffee essence together, add the warm milk. Strain into 4 small dishes. Stand in a baking tin of water. Bake for 50 minutes to 1 hour in a cool oven. Serve with cream.

Thursday

Beef Loaf ½ teaspoon salt, ½ teaspoon dry mustard, shake of pepper, 8 oz. (200 g.) self-raising flour, 2 oz. (50 g.) fat, milk to mix, 1 beaten egg, pinch mixed herbs, 1 lb. (½ kilo) beef sausagemeat.
Sieve salt, mustard, pepper and flour. Rub in fat, make to soft rolling consistency with milk. Roll dough to an oblong about ¼ inch (½ cm.) thick. Add half the egg and herbs to sausagemeat. Shape into an oblong a little smaller than the dough. Put on top of dough, turn in the side edges, roll dough and sausagemeat together to give a loaf shape. Put into greased and floured 2-lb. (1-kilo) loaf tin. Brush top with rest of egg. Bake in centre of hot oven, Gas Mark 7, 425°F. (220°C.) for 30 minutes, then lower heat to moderate, Gas Mark 4, 350°F. (180°C.) for 30 minutes. Serve hot or cold.

Tomato Cups halve large tomatoes, chop centre pulp and mix with diced cucumber or gherkin, chopped chives and chopped watercress. Pile back into tomato cases.

Pineapple Sponge dissolve pineapple jelly in 1 pint (6 dl.) boiling water made up with syrup from small can pineapple rings. Arrange pineapple in base of 6-inch (15-cm.) sponge case, placed in a deep dish. Slowly pour over cooled jelly and leave to set. Turn out.

MONDAY

Potato Pie 3 skinned, sliced tomatoes, thinly sliced or diced pork (left over from the joint) *or* canned chopped pork could be used, sage and onion stuffing *or* thinly sliced onions with sprinkling of chopped sage, seasoning, few tablespoons stock, creamed potatoes.
Put tomatoes at the bottom of a dish. Cover with pork, then a layer of stuffing or the sliced onions with sage and seasoning. Moisten with the stock and top with potatoes. Bake for 30 minutes in a moderately hot oven, Gas Mark 5, 375°F. (190°C.).

Cabbage Delmonico cabbage, ½ pint (3 dl.) white sauce, see page 5, rolled oats and crumbs.
Strain lightly cooked cabbage and blend with sauce. Put in hot dish, top with a layer of rolled oats and crumbs. Brown in oven.

Baked Apples apples, golden syrup, sultanas.
Fill cored apples with golden syrup and sultanas before baking.
To bake apples: allow approximately 1 hour for really large apples in the centre of the moderately hot oven setting as Potato Pie above, but 1¼ hours if you bake these at a slightly lower setting; picture page 35.

TUESDAY

Scotch Hotpot 1 medium swede, 2 large onions, 8 oz. (¼ kilo) tomatoes, 1 oz. (25 g.) fat, seasoning, 2–3 tablespoons stock, little margarine.
Cut swede, onions and tomatoes into thin slices. Fry onion in fat. Arrange well seasoned layers of vegetables in greased casserole ending with onions. Cover with stock and little margarine. Put lid on casserole. Cook for 1½ hours in centre of a very moderate oven, Gas Mark 3, 325°F. (170°C.). Take lid off for last 30 minutes.

Stuffed Potatoes large potatoes, seasoning, kidneys.
Scrub potatoes. Make hole in centre of each and put in a well seasoned kidney. Cook for 1½ hours in greased dish in oven.

Cheese Fingers thick slices of fresh bread, cream cheese, chopped nuts, prunes.
Spread sides and top of sliced bread with cream cheese. Roll in nuts. Top with well drained prunes. Cut into neat fingers just before serving.

FRIDAY

Fish Creams 1 lb. (½ kilo) white fish, 1 oz. (25 g.) margarine, 1 oz. (25 g.) flour, ¼ pint (1½ dl.) milk, 1 tablespoon lemon juice, few drops chilli or tabasco sauce, 2 egg yolks, 1 tablespoon chopped parsley, seasoning.
Stir flaked *lightly* cooked white fish into a thick white sauce made with the margarine, flour and milk. Add the lemon juice, chilli or tabasco sauce, egg yolks (save whites for Rice Meringue on Saturday) and chopped parsley. Season well. Put into 4 greased moulds or cups. Cover with greased paper or foil and steam for 30 minutes, or bake in dish of water for the same time.

Cauliflower Polonaise top cooked cauliflower with fried breadcrumbs, chopped hard-boiled egg and parsley.

Speedy Fruit Flan 6 oz. (150 g.) pastry (see details for Wednesday), can cherry pie filling (or other fruit pie filling), little desiccated coconut.
It would be sensible to make 2 flans on Wednesday, bake one and store in a tin until Friday. Spoon the pie filling into this. Decorate with dessicated coconut.

SATURDAY

Lamb Casserole 1 oz. (25 g.) fat, 8 pieces middle neck of lamb, 1 green pepper, 1 onion, 1 oz. (25 g.) flour, ¾ pint (4½ dl.) stock, seasoning, pinch dried rosemary, small can baked beans in tomato sauce.
Heat fat in pan, toss lamb in this, put in casserole. Toss diced pepper and chopped onion in fat, add to lamb. Stir flour into remaining fat in saucepan, then gradually blend in stock. When thickened add seasoning, pinch rosemary and baked beans. Pour over lamb. Cover casserole and cook for 1¾ hours in very moderate oven, Gas Mark 3, 325°F. (170°C.).

Fluffy Stuffed Potatoes cut slice from top of each jacket potato, scoop out pulp, mash with butter, milk, add seasoning, little chopped chives. Pile back into cases and heat.

Rice Meringue 2–3 oz. (50–75 g.) rice, 3 oz. (75 g.) castor sugar, 1 pint (6 dl.) milk, little jam or fruit purée, 2 egg whites (left over from Fish Creams).
Mix rice, 1 oz. (25 g.) sugar and milk and bake for 1¼ hours in coolest part of oven. Spread top with jam or fruit purée, then a meringue made by whisking the egg whites and folding in the remaining sugar. Return to the oven for 15 minutes. Instead of using jam or fruit purée the rice can be flavoured by adding 1–2 oz. (25–50 g.) chocolate powder or 1 tablespoon coffee essence to the milk.

WEEK 4

Ox liver is economical compared to lambs' or calves' liver. If cooked slowly (see Thursday) it is deliciously tender and it is an excellent source of iron.

For your shopping list the main meals need:
about 9 eggs, 3 pints (1¾ litres) milk, 8–12 oz. (200–300 g.) Cheddar or other cooking cheese.
Sunday and Monday need:
Roasting chicken, sausagemeat (store carefully near freezer), bacon rashers.
Sponge cakes, ice cream.
Potatoes, selection of spring vegetables, chives, mixed herbs, parsley, onion, fruit for Charlotte, fruit juice.
Tuesday, Wednesday and Thursday need:
Minced beef, sausagemeat, ox liver (store carefully), fresh haddock (store carefully – near freezer).
Potatoes, tomatoes, green salad, parsley, root vegetables, pears, lemon.
Friday and Saturday need:
Steak (preferably rump).
Cream (thick or thin – optional).
Spinach, onion, salad ingredients, rhubarb, lemon.

SUNDAY

Spring Soup simmer 1 lb. (½ kilo) diced spring vegetables in 1 pint (6 dl.) seasoned stock. Blend 1 oz. (25 g.) flour with ½ pint (3 dl.) milk, add to pan with 1 oz. (25 g.) butter. Stir until thickened and re-season. Top with chopped chives and croûtons of fried bread.

Roast Chicken chicken, 2 stuffings (see below), little butter or fat.
Sausagemeat stuffing: mix chopped cooked chicken's liver, ½ teaspoon mixed herbs and ½ lb. (¼ kilo) sausagemeat.
Raisin stuffing: mix 3 oz. (75 g.) breadcrumbs, 2 oz. (50 g.) seedless raisins, 1 tablespoon grated onion, 1½ oz. (40 g.) suet or melted margarine, 1 tablespoon chopped parsley and seasoning.
Put in stuffings and weigh chicken. Top with butter or fat. Roast for 15 minutes per lb. (½ kilo) and 15 minutes over in hot oven, Gas Mark 6, 400°F. (200°C.).

Fruit Charlotte 6 slices bread, 2–3 oz. (50–75 g.) margarine, 2–3 oz. (50–75 g.) brown sugar, about ¾ pint (4½ dl.) fruit purée.
Cut bread into fingers. Crisp in hot margarine. Line bottom of tin or dish with some bread fingers, add some sugar then a layer of fruit purée. Continue like this ending with a layer of bread and sugar. Cook for 45 minutes in coolest part of oven. Reduce heat to very moderate, Gas Mark 3, 325°F. (170°C.), after removing chicken.

WEDNESDAY

Baked Stuffed Haddock 2 skinned chopped tomatoes, 3 oz. (75 g.) breadcrumbs, 1 tablespoon chopped parsley, ½ teaspoon mixed herbs, 1 oz. (25 g.) melted margarine or suet, seasoning, 1 whole haddock (split) or 4 haddock cutlets.
Mix together the tomatoes, breadcrumbs, parsley, herbs, margarine or suet and seasoning. Spread on cutlets or in fish. Cook in greased covered dish for 35 minutes for whole fish, 20–25 minutes for cutlets, in a moderate oven, Gas Mark 4, 350°F. (180°C.).

Apricot Butterscotch Meringue 2 oz. (50 g.) brown sugar, 2 oz. (50 g.) margarine, 4 oz. (100 g.) rolled oats, small can apricots, 1 egg white, 1 oz. (25 g.) sugar.
Heat sugar and margarine in saucepan until golden brown. Stir in oats. Put well drained apricots at bottom of shallow dish. Press rolled oat mixture on top and bake for 25 minutes in centre of moderate oven. Top with border of meringue made with egg white and sugar, return to slow oven, Gas Mark 1, 275°F. (140°C.), for 15–20 minutes. Serve hot with apricot syrup. (Save egg yolk, covered with 1 tablespoon water, for use in Thursday's Cheese Straws.)

THURSDAY

Liver Rolls 12 oz.–1 lb. (⅜–½ kilo) ox liver, sage and onion stuffing, brown sauce.
Cut liver into thin slices. Spread with stuffing (page 10) and roll firmly. Put into casserole, pour over brown sauce and cover with a lid. Cook for 1½ hours in a very moderate oven, Gas Mark 3, 325°F. (170°C.). Another casserole of diced root vegetables can be cooked at the same time.

Hot Potato Salad cook 4 jacket potatoes at the same time as casserole. Skin while hot, dice and toss with 2 rashers, baked or fried, then chopped bacon, and chopped parsley.

Cheese Straws 2 oz. (50 g.) margarine, 4 oz. (100 g.) well seasoned flour, 2 oz. (50 g.) grated cheese, 1 egg yolk and a little water (left over from Wednesday).
Rub margarine into flour, add cheese, bind with egg yolk and water. Roll out, cut into thin fingers, put on greased tin. Bake in hot oven, Gas Mark 6, 400°C. (200°C.), for 10 minutes, before cooking casseroles of liver and vegetables.

MONDAY

Chicken Kromeskies 12 oz. (300 g.) cooked chicken, 2 oz. (50 g.) breadcrumbs, 1 oz. (25 g.) flour, 1 oz. (25 g.) fat, ¼ pint (1½ dl.) milk (or chicken stock), seasoning, 4 bacon rashers, egg and crumbs for coating or batter (see below).
Mince or chop pieces of chicken, blend with breadcrumbs and a sauce made with flour, fat and milk or stock. Season and cool. Form into 8 finger shapes. Wrap each in half rasher of bacon. Coat with beaten egg and crumbs or batter, then fry steadily. Any stuffing left over from Sunday can be heated and served with these.
To make a coating batter: sieve 4 oz. (100 g.) flour (plain or self-raising), pinch salt, add 1 egg, ¼ pint (1½ dl.) milk.

Savoury Potatoes beat chopped parsley into creamed potatoes.

Coffee Walnut Fingers 2 sponge cakes, fruit juice or sherry, coffee ice cream, chopped walnuts.
Split sponge cakes (the type used for trifles). Arrange on flat dish. Moisten with fruit juice or sherry, then top with slices of coffee ice cream and walnuts.

TUESDAY

Steak and Spaghetti Wedges 8 oz. (¼ kilo) minced beef, 8 oz. (¼ kilo) sausagemeat, 2 oz. (50 g.) breadcrumbs, 1 onion, 1 oz. (25 g.) fat, 1 rasher finely chopped bacon, seasoning, 4 oz. (100 g.) spaghetti, ½ pint (3 dl.) white, cheese or tomato sauce (or canned spaghetti in tomato sauce).
Blend beef and sausagemeat with breadcrumbs and chopped onion (fried in fat). Add bacon and seasoning. Form into neat round and fit into greased 7-inch (18-cm.) tin. Cover with greased foil or greaseproof paper and bake for 1 hour in the centre of a moderate oven, Gas Mark 4, 350°F. (180°C.). Cook spaghetti and mix with sauce, or heat canned spaghetti. Turn out meatround, top with spaghetti. Cut into wedges. Serve with green salad.

Ginger Pears 4 firm dessert pears, finely grated rind and juice of 1 lemon, ½ pint (3 dl.) water, 2 level teaspoons cornflour, 1 teaspoon powdered ginger.
Halve pears, core and peel. Put rind and juice of lemon and water, blended with cornflour and ginger, into a pan. Simmer until clear and smooth, stirring well. Pour over halved pears and leave until cold. Chopped preserved ginger could be added to this sweet if you wish.

FRIDAY

Eggs Florentine fresh or frozen spinach, hard-boiled or poached eggs, cheese sauce, grated cheese, breadcrumbs.
Arrange cooked spinach at the bottom of a dish, top with halved hard-boiled or poached eggs and cheese sauce. Cover with grated cheese and breadcrumbs and brown in a hot oven, Gas Mark 6, 400°F. (200°C.), for a few minutes only.

Choco-Nut Tarts 6 oz. (150 g.) shortcrust pastry*, ½ oz. (15 g.) cocoa, ½ oz. (15 g.) cornflour, ½ pint (3 dl.) milk, 2 oz. (50 g.) sugar, ½ oz. (15 g.) butter, 1 oz. (25 g.) chopped blanched almonds.
*make an extra 12 oz. (300 g.) pastry for the next day at the same time.
Line deep patty tins with pastry. Bake 'blind' until crisp. Blend cocoa, cornflour and milk. Put into saucepan and cook until thickened, adding sugar. Remove from heat, beat in butter and most of the almonds. Put into tart cases and top with the remaining almonds. Serve with cream if wished.
Note. When a recipe states 6 oz. (150 g.) pastry it means pastry made with 6 oz. flour, etc. For recipe, see page 10.

SATURDAY

Cornish Pasties 12 oz. (300 g.) shortcrust pastry, 1 large potato, 1 large onion, 8–12 oz. (200–300 g.) diced steak (preferably rump), seasoning, 1 tablespoon stock.
Roll out pastry and cut into 4 large rounds. Cut peeled potato and onion into tiny cubes, mix with the steak, seasoning and stock. Put on to pastry, damp the edges, and form into 4 pasty shapes. Seal edges. Bake for 20 minutes in hot oven, Gas Mark 7, 425°F. (220°C.), then lower oven to moderate, Gas Mark 4, 350°F. (180°C.) for a further 20 minutes. Serve hot or cold with a mixed salad. (Shortcrust pastry recipes, pages 10 and 108.)

Rhubarb Mould 1 lb. (½ kilo) rhubarb, ¾ pint (4½ dl.) water, 2–3 oz. (50–75 g.) sugar, ½ oz. (15 g.) powdered gelatine, juice of 1 lemon.
Cook rhubarb with water and sugar until a purée. Soften gelatine in lemon juice, add to hot purée and stir until dissolved. Pour into mould, leave to set.

WEEK 5

If you like lamb 'French-style', i.e. slightly underdone, allow just *under* 20 minutes per lb. (½ kilo) and 20 minutes over in a moderately hot to hot oven. When new potatoes are very small, scrub then dry them well and cook with the skins on.

For your shopping list the main meals need:
8 eggs*, 1¾–2¾ pints (1–1½ litres) milk (depending upon whether you make custard on Sunday), 3 oz. (75 g.) or 6 oz. (150 g.) Cheddar or other cooking cheese if making cheese pastry for Saturday, cream cheese spread (optional).
*more if making the sponge cake (Monday).

Sunday and Monday need:
Lamb.
Cream (thick or thin – optional), chocolate or plain sponge (unless baking this).
New potatoes, garlic or rosemary, parsley or mint, cucumber, ingredients for green salad, tomatoes, mint (or mint jelly).

Tuesday, Wednesday and Thursday need:
Lambs' kidneys, bacon rashers, veal chops, pork chops (store near freezer).
Potatoes, tomatoes, chives (optional), parsley, onions, mushrooms (optional), fresh fruit, dessert apples, cooked fruit for Thursday (optional).

Friday and Saturday need:
Fresh haddock, prawns, bacon rashers.
Potatoes, tomatoes, lemons, cooking apples.

SUNDAY

Roast Lamb lamb, garlic clove or rosemary.
For a new flavour, roast lamb with a garlic clove inserted under the skin, or a little chopped rosemary sprinkled over meat during cooking.

Crumbed New Potatoes cook potatoes, drain, then toss in fried crumbs and chopped parsley or chopped mint.

Fruit and Sherry Fingers *almond-flavoured pastry:*
2 oz. (50 g.) fat, 4 oz. (100 g.) flour, 2 oz. (50 g.) ground almonds, 1 oz. (25 g.) sugar (optional), 1 egg yolk and water (save white for Saturday in covered container), 2 tablespoons apricot jam, 2 oz. (50 g.) sultanas, 2 oz. (50 g.) chopped raisins, 2 oz. (50 g.) desiccated coconut, 1 oz. (25 g.) icing sugar, 1 tablespoon sherry. To dust: little extra icing sugar. To serve: cream or custard.
Rub fat into flour, add ground almonds, sugar, bind with egg yolk and water. Roll out to a flat oblong and bake until golden brown (see below). Mix jam with sultanas, raisins, coconut, icing sugar and sherry. Cut pastry into neat fingers, top with sherry and fruit mixture. Dust with icing sugar, serve with cream or custard.
To bake a sweet or nut-flavoured shortcrust: most shortcrust pastry may be baked in a hot oven. When sugar or nuts are added to the flour, etc., use only a moderately hot oven.

WEDNESDAY

Paprika Veal and Rice 1 oz. (25 g.) fat or 1 tablespoon oil, 4 veal chops, 2 rashers chopped bacon, 2 sliced onions, 2 oz. (50 g.) mushrooms (optional), 1 oz. (25 g.) flour, 2 level teaspoons paprika, ¾ pint (4½ dl.) stock or water and chicken stock cube, seasoning, rice*, 1 oz. (25 g.) margarine, 1 tablespoon chopped parsley.
Heat fat or oil in pan. Fry chops on either side with bacon, onions and mushrooms. Blend flour and paprika with stock or water and stock cube. Add to pan and bring to the boil, stirring until smooth. Season well, then cover pan, lower heat and cook for 30 minutes. Boil rice and when cooked toss in margarine and chopped parsley. Arrange in a border round the dish and put the chops in the centre, pour sauce on top. If veal is not obtainable, then use 2 thick slices topside beef cut into halves to make 4 portions. Simmer for 40 minutes.
To boil rice: allow at least 1 oz. (25 g.) uncooked rice per person. Put 4 oz. (100 g.) rice into a pan with 8 fl. oz. (nearly 2 dl.) cold water and salt to taste. Bring the water to the boil and stir briskly with a fork. Cover the pan, lower the heat and simmer gently for about 15 minutes, by which time the rice should be tender and the water absorbed.

Follow with cheese and biscuits and a fresh fruit salad served with cream cheese spread.

THURSDAY

Grilled Pork Chops with Apple Rings seasoning, flour, 4 pork chops, 2 large or 4 small dessert apples, little honey.
Season and lightly flour the chops, score the fat to encourage crispness. Cook on either side under a hot grill until golden brown, then lower heat slightly and cook through to the middle. Core, but do not peel the apples, cut into ¼-inch (½-cm.) rounds, brush with a little of the pork fat and with honey. Put under the grill for the last 10 minutes and cook with the chops. If space does not allow the chops and apple rings to be cooked together, heat a little margarine in the grill pan before cooking the chops, toss the apple rings in this, brush with honey. Put the chops on the grid and cook both chops and apples together.

Cornflake Flan cream 2 oz. (50 g.) margarine or butter with 2 oz. (50 g.) sugar, gradually work in 4 oz. (100 g.) crushed cornflakes. Form into a flan shape. Either allow to stand in a cool place for several hours, or bake in a moderately hot oven, Gas Mark 5, 375°F. (190°C.) for 10 minutes. Many fillings may be used – cooked fruit, fruit salad or jelly cream. To make the jelly cream, melt a 1 pint (6 dl.) jelly in ½ pint (3 dl.) water. When cold, add ½ pint (3 dl.) evaporated milk. Allow to set slightly, whisk vigorously and pile into flan.

MONDAY

Lamb and Potato Salad cooked lamb, boiled potatoes, mayonnaise or salad cream, diced cucumber or gherkins, few capers, green salad. To garnish: tomatoes and cucumber. To serve: mint sauce or mint jelly.
Dice lamb and potatoes, blend together with mayonnaise or salad cream, cucumber or gherkins and a few capers. Pile neatly on a bed of green salad and garnish with tomatoes and cucumber. Serve with mint sauce or mint jelly.

Jamaican Chocolate Sponge chocolate or plain sponge cake, 2 oz. (50 g.) butter or margarine, 3 oz. (75 g.) icing sugar, 2 oz. (50 g.) melted plain chocolate, few drops of rum essence.
Make or buy a chocolate or plain sponge cake. Split and fill with butter or margarine creamed with icing sugar, melted chocolate and rum essence.
To make a chocolate or plain sponge: cream 4 oz. (100 g.) margarine with 4 oz. (100 g.) castor sugar. Gradually beat in 2 eggs and then fold in $3\frac{1}{2}$ oz. (90 g.) self-raising flour (or plain flour and 1 teaspoon baking powder) sieved with 1 tablespoon cocoa; or use 4 oz. (100 g.) flour. Divide between two 6–7-inch (15–18-cm.) sandwich tins and bake for approximately 18 minutes in a moderate oven.

TUESDAY

Kidneys and Bacon lambs' kidneys, flour, pinch salt, mustard, cayenne pepper, fat for frying, rashers of bacon. Split kidneys into halves and roll in flour seasoned with pinch salt, mustard, cayenne pepper. Fry in hot fat until tender, adding rashers of bacon for last few minutes.

Spiced Tomatoes fry halved or sliced tomatoes until tender, sprinkle with seasoning, pinch sugar and mixed spice. Top with chives or parsley.

Walnut Pancakes 4 oz. (100 g.) flour, pinch salt, 1 egg, $\frac{1}{2}$ pint (3 dl.) milk and water mixed, 2 oz. (50 g.) finely chopped walnuts, golden syrup.
Make pancake batter with flour, salt, egg, milk and water. Add walnuts. Fry in the usual way, roll and serve with hot golden syrup.

FRIDAY

Prawn and Haddock Mould 1 lb. ($\frac{1}{2}$ kilo) fresh skinned haddock fillet, $\frac{1}{2}$ pint (3 dl.) water, seasoning, 1 tablespoon lemon juice, 1 oz. (25 g.) margarine, 1 oz. (25 g.) flour, $\frac{1}{4}$ pint ($1\frac{1}{2}$ dl.) milk, $\frac{1}{4}$ pint ($1\frac{1}{2}$ dl.) fish stock, 2 oz. (50 g.) each soft *and* crisp breadcrumbs, 2 hard-boiled eggs, 2 oz. (50 g.) prawns. To garnish: lemon.
Cook haddock in water for 5 minutes, adding seasoning and lemon juice. Break into large flakes. Make a sauce with margarine, flour, milk, strained fish stock, seasoning. Add haddock and *soft* breadcrumbs. Grease a loaf tin, coat with crisp breadcrumbs, spread half fish mixture at bottom, cover with sliced eggs, nearly all the shelled prawns, then rest of fish mixture. Stand the tin in a dish of cold water, cover with greased paper or foil. Bake for 45 minutes in a very moderate oven, Gas Mark 3, 325°F. (170°C.). Turn out, garnish with lemon and remaining prawns. Serve with Scalloped Potatoes, page 95 and 111.

Queen of Puddings beat 2 egg yolks with 1 oz. (25 g.) sugar, add $\frac{1}{2}$ pint (3 dl.) warm milk and 1 teaspoon finely grated lemon rind.
Pour over 2 oz. (50 g.) fine cake or breadcrumbs and mix well. Spread a thin layer of jam at the bottom of a buttered pie dish, add crumb mixture and bake for 35–40 minutes in a very moderate oven until the pudding is just set. Spread top with jam, then cover with meringue made with 2 stiffly beaten egg whites and 2 oz. (50 g.) sugar. Return to oven for 20 minutes. Serve hot.

SATURDAY

Bacon and Cheese Pie 10 oz. shortcrust or cheese crust pastry, see pages 10 and 25, 4 or 5 rashers bacon, 3 skinned sliced tomatoes, 2 egg yolks, 3 oz. (75 g.) grated cheese, seasoning, milk.
Line pie plate with pastry. Cover with diced and lightly fried bacon, tomatoes, beaten egg yolks mixed with grated cheese. Season well and cover with more shortcrust or cheese crust pastry. Brush with milk to glaze and bake in the centre of a moderately hot oven, Gas Mark 5–6, 375–400°F. (190–200°C.) for approximately 40 minutes, after 20 minutes reducing heat to moderate. Serve hot or cold with vegetables or salad.
To vary: make the mixture into small pies as picture page 83, and bake for only 20–25 minutes.

Apple Fluff 1 lb. ($\frac{1}{2}$ kilo) apples, little water, sugar, 2 egg whites.
Cook apples with minimum of water and sugar to taste until a soft purée. Add the stiffly beaten egg whites.
To vary: to make an even lighter mixture use the egg white left from Sunday. Whisk the 3 egg whites then fold into the apple mixture.

WEEK 6

The method of cooking steak in foil, as described in the menu for Sunday, means the meat may be left to cook without attention.

Extra root vegetables and rings of red and green pepper may be cooked with the meat, and the meat can be flavoured with crushed peppercorns to make Steak au Poivre, but the sprouts, shown in the picture page 18, must be cooked in the usual way, to retain colour, texture and vitamins.

For your shopping list the main meals need:
11 eggs, 1¾ pints (1 litre) milk, 8 oz. (200 g.) cream cheese.

Sunday and Monday need:
Steak, bacon rashers.
Red wine (optional).
Potatoes, onions, parsley, sprouts or other green vegetable, peppers, carrots, mushrooms, tomatoes, lemons.

Tuesday, Wednesday and Thursday need:
Pork chops, cooked tongue, boiling chicken.
Small quantity cream (thick or thin).
Potatoes, onions, peas, sweet corn, potato crisps, oranges and selection of fresh fruit.

Friday and Saturday need:
Cutlets cod, cooked ham.
Ice cream, cream (thick *and* thin).
Potatoes, onions, tomatoes, carrot, herbs, rhubarb.

SUNDAY

Foil-Baked Steak 1¼ lb. (⅝ kilo) rump steak, butter or oil, 2 tablespoons red wine or brown stock (optional), 1 large very thinly sliced onion (optional), 2 teaspoons chopped parsley (optional), seasoning.
Buy steak in one large slice about ¾ inch (2 cm.) thick. Brush large piece of foil with butter or oil. The steak can be wrapped in this and cooked without garnish, but for extra flavour add wine or good brown stock, thinly sliced onion, chopped parsley and seasoning. Put 'parcel' into roasting tin. Allow 35 minutes cooking time for well done steak without garnish, but 40–45 minutes with wine and other flavourings; 25–35 minutes for medium cooked steak; 15–25 minutes for underdone steak, Gas Mark 7, 425°F. (220°C.).

Lemon Cheesecake little butter, digestive biscuits or cornflakes, 2 oz. (50 g.) butter, 3 oz. (75 g.) sugar, 2 teaspoons grated lemon rind, 2 eggs, 1 oz. (25 g.) cornflour, 8 oz. (200 g.) cream cheese, 3 tablespoons lemon juice.
Use ovenproof dish about 9 inches (23 cm.) wide, 1½ inches (3½ cm.) deep. Spread bottom and sides with little butter and coat with crushed biscuits or cornflakes. Cream butter with sugar and grated lemon rind. Add beaten eggs, cornflour, cream cheese and lemon juice. Put into dish and bake in centre of oven at Gas Mark 2, 300°F. (150°C.) for 1 hour. Allow to cool in oven with heat turned off.

WEDNESDAY

Braised Tongue 1 oz. (25 g.) fat, 1 oz. (25 g.) flour, just over ½ pint (3 dl.) well flavoured brown stock, seasoning, 1 tablespoon sherry or lemon juice, cooked tongue, cooked peas, sweetcorn, potato crisps.
Make brown sauce with fat, flour and stock. Season and add sherry or lemon juice. Put fairly thick slices of tongue into this and heat for 5 minutes only. Serve in a border of peas, sweet corn and potato crisps.

Coconut Peaches 8 canned halved peaches, 1 oz. (25 g.) butter or margarine, 1 oz. (25 g.) brown sugar, 1 egg, 2 oz. (50 g.) chopped raisins, 2 oz. (50 g.) desiccated coconut.
Fill peach halves with coconut mixture made by creaming butter or margarine, brown sugar, then adding egg, raisins and coconut. Brown under a low grill.

THURSDAY

Creamed Curry of Chicken 1 boiling chicken, 1½ oz. (40 g.) butter, 1½ oz. (40 g.) flour, seasoning, 2 teaspoons curry powder, ½ pint (3 dl.) milk, ¼ pint (1½ dl.) chicken stock, 2 tablespoons cream. To serve: cooked rice, hard-boiled egg, lemon.
Steam chicken until tender. Cut leg joints and wings away from body, leave breast to be used in patties on Saturday. Make ¾ pint (4½ dl.) creamy white sauce with butter, flour, seasoning, curry powder, milk, chicken stock and cream. Add chicken joints, heat gently. Serve in border of cooked rice, garnished with hard-boiled egg and lemon.

Custard Tarts 6 oz. shortcrust pastry, see page 10, 1 egg white, 2 whole eggs, 1 oz. (25 g.) sugar, ½ pint (3 dl.) milk, grated nutmeg.
Line 8 or 9 deep patty tins with pastry, brush with egg white. Fill with custard made by mixing 2 eggs, sugar and milk. Top with grated nutmeg and cook for 20–25 minutes in centre of hot oven, Gas Mark 6, 400°F. (200°C.).

MONDAY

Mushroom Rolls 4 large rashers bacon, 4 oz. (100 g.) chopped mushrooms, 1 chopped onion, 1 oz. (25 g.) fat, 2 oz. (50 g.) breadcrumbs, 2 teaspoons chopped parsley, seasoning, 1 egg, crisp breadcrumbs.
Cut bacon into halves. Fry chopped mushrooms and onion in fat, add breadcrumbs, parsley and seasoning. Cool mixture. Form into 8 finger shapes then wrap in bacon, forming neat rolls. Dip in beaten egg, roll in crisp breadcrumbs, secure with wooden cocktail sticks or tie with cotton. Cook for 30 minutes towards top of oven, Gas Mark 4, 350°F. (180°C.). Remove cotton. Serve with baked tomatoes.

Golden Cap Pudding golden syrup or apricot jam, 3 oz. (75 g.) margarine, 3 oz. (75 g.) sugar, 1 egg, 4 oz. (100 g.) self-raising flour (or plain flour and 1 level teaspoon baking powder), 2 tablespoons milk.
Put syrup or jam at the bottom of a basin. Cover with sponge made from margarine creamed with sugar, egg, flour (or flour and baking powder) and milk. Oven-steam. To do this, stand covered basin in deep tin or larger basin filled with water and cook for 1¼ hours in moderate oven.

TUESDAY

Casserole of Pork 4 pork chops, seasoning, flour, 1 oz. (25 g.) fat, 1 onion, sprinkling sage, large can tomato soup.
Coat pork chops in seasoned flour, fry for few minutes in fat, transfer to casserole. Fry sliced onion in fat, add to casserole with sprinkling sage and canned tomato soup. Cover the casserole and cook in moderate oven, Gas Mark 4, 350°F. (180°C.) for 1¼ hours.

Baked Onions peel small onions and brush with melted fat. Season lightly and bake for 1¼ hours.

Fresh Fruit Salad 2 oranges, 2–3 oz. (50–75 g.) sugar, ⅓ pint (2 dl.) water, 1 apple, 1 pear, 1 banana, pipped grapes, and any other fresh fruit in season.
Remove peel from oranges and cut away pith. Simmer orange 'zest' (outer peel) with sugar and water for 5 minutes. Pour over the sliced fresh fruit.

FRIDAY

Cod and Macaroni Bake 2 oz. (50 g.) macaroni, salt, 1 medium onion, 1 oz. (25 g.) fat, 4 skinned sliced tomatoes, seasoning, 4 portions cod, 1 egg, ½ pint (3 dl.) milk.
Cook the macaroni in boiling salted water until just soft, strain. Peel and slice the onion, fry in the hot fat for 5 minutes. Mix the onion, tomatoes and seasoning with the macaroni. Put at the bottom of a greased dish, top with the cod and season. Beat the egg, add seasoning and milk. Strain over the fish. Cover the dish with greased foil or paper and bake for 40 minutes in the centre of a moderately hot oven, Gas Mark 6, 400°F. (200°C.).

Rhubarb Fool good ½ pint (3 dl.) *very thick* sweetened rhubarb purée, ½ pint (3 dl.) thick custard, ¼ pint (1½ dl.) whipped cream.
Mix the rhubarb purée with the custard and half the whipped cream. Put into 4 glasses and top with the rest of the cream. Chill thoroughly before serving.
To vary: use all whipped cream in place of the custard.

SATURDAY

Ham and Chicken Patties cooked chicken breast, 4 oz. (100 g.) chopped ham, 2 oz. (50 g.) breadcrumbs, good pinch mixed herbs, 1 oz. (25 g.) chicken fat, 1 oz. (25 g.) flour, ¼ pint (1½ dl.) chicken stock, seasoning, 1 egg, breadcrumbs.
Dice cooked chicken breast, mix with ham, breadcrumbs, herbs and thick sauce made with chicken fat, flour, chicken stock. Season well, form into 4 large or 8 small patties. Coat in beaten egg and breadcrumbs. Fry until crisp and golden brown.

Carrot Potato Balls 1 lb. (½ kilo) cooked potatoes, 1 finely grated raw carrot.
Mash potatoes, add raw carrot, heat for 1 minute then serve in neat ball shapes, made with a soup spoon.

Coffee Sundaes top coffee ice cream with thin cream, grated chocolate and chopped nuts.

Foil baked steak, recipe on page 16

Week 7

Stewing veal makes a very delicious casserole on Wednesday. If veal is difficult to obtain buy lean pork instead.

For your shopping list the main meals need:
11 eggs, 3 pints (1¾ litres) milk, 8 oz. (200 g.) Cheddar or other cooking cheese.

Sunday, Monday and Tuesday need:
Stewing steak, ox kidney, lamb cutlets.
Potatoes, small marrows (or courgettes), onion, garlic, tomatoes, cauliflower, chives or spring onions, rosemary, mint, cooking apples, lemon, mixed fruit.

Wednesday and Thursday need:
Stewing veal, small piece fat bacon or bacon rashers, minced beef, sausagemeat (store carefully).
Thick cream.
Potatoes, tomatoes, carrots, onion, parsley, mixed herbs, lemon, cooking apples.

Friday and Saturday need:
Sausagemeat (store carefully).
Thick cream.
Potatoes, tomatoes (optional), large mushrooms, parsley, apricots.

Sunday

Steak and Kidney Pie 1–1¼ lb. (½–⅝ kilo) stewing steak, 4–6 oz. (100–150 g.) ox kidney, 1 oz. (25 g.) seasoned flour, 1 oz. (25 g.) fat, ¾ pint (4½ dl.) brown stock, 6 oz. (150 g.) shortcrust pastry, see page 10. Dice meats, roll in the flour, fry in the fat. Stir in stock, bring to the boil, cover pan and simmer *gently* for 1¼–1½ hours until meat is nearly cooked. Put into pie dish, cover with pastry. Bake for 20 minutes in a hot oven, Gas Mark 7, 425°F. (220°C.), lower the heat to moderate, Gas Mark 4, 350°F. (180°C.) for further 25 minutes, see picture, page 43.

Marrow Provençal wash, but do not peel, tiny marrows. Cut into neat slices. Fry a chopped onion and 1–2 chopped cloves of garlic in a little fat. Add 4 skinned tomatoes plus ¼ pint (1½ dl.) water *or* a medium can of tomatoes. Season, add sliced marrows, simmer for 25–30 minutes over low heat, stirring occasionally.

Eve's Sponge put a good layer of thinly sliced apples with very little water, sugar to taste, into a pie dish. Heat for 10 minutes, then cover with sponge mixture made by creaming 3 oz. (75 g.) margarine with 3 oz. (75 g.) sugar, then adding 2 beaten eggs and 4 oz. (100 g.) flour (with plain flour use 1 teaspoon baking powder). Put in coolest part of oven for 1 hour.

Wednesday

Veal and Tomato Casserole 1¼ lb. (⅝ kilo) stewing veal, 1 oz. (25 g.) fat or butter, 2 rashers fat bacon, 1 oz. (25 g.) seasoned flour, grated rind of 1 lemon, 4 large skinned, chopped tomatoes, ½ pint (3 dl.) white stock (or water and chicken stock cube), bouquet garni.
Dice veal, fry for 3 minutes in fat or butter with diced bacon. Place veal and bacon in a casserole. Stir seasoned flour and grated lemon rind into fat, then add tomatoes, white stock or water and stock cube, and bouquet garni. Bring to boil, pour over veal, cover casserole and cook for 1½ hours in very moderate oven, Gas Mark 3, 325°F. (170°C.).

Fruit Rice Cream 5 oz. (125 g.) pudding rice*, 3 oz. (75 g.) sugar, 1 pint (6 dl.) water, ½ pint (3 dl.) canned pineapple juice, ¼ pint (1½ dl.) lightly whipped cream, glacé cherries.
Cook rice with sugar and water in double saucepan. Remove half, cover with foil and save for Saturday's sweet. Blend the remaining rice with the pineapple juice. Simmer gently until rice is very soft and has absorbed the liquid. Cool slightly, then beat in cream and serve topped with glacé cherries.
Choosing rice: *pudding rice is also known as round or Carolina rice.
For savoury dishes choose a long grain or Patna rice.

Thursday

Thatched Beef Squares 8 oz. (¼ kilo) minced beef, 12 oz. (⅜ kilo) sausagemeat, 2 grated raw carrots, 1 grated raw onion, little chopped parsley, mixed herbs, beaten egg, seasoning, mashed potato, cornflakes.
Blend beef with sausagemeat, carrots, onion, parsley, herbs, egg and seasoning. Press into greased 7-inch (18-cm.) square tin, cover with mashed potato. Mark with a fork to form ridges, then sprinkle cornflakes over the top. Bake in the centre of a moderate oven, Gas Mark 4, 350°F. (180°C.) for approximately 45 minutes. Cut into squares to serve.

Apple Sultana Fingers 4 slices of bread, 2 oz. (50 g.) margarine, 1–2 oz. (25–50 g.) brown sugar, 2 large cooking apples, 2 oz. (50 g.) sultanas. To serve: custard sauce.
Remove crusts from bread and fry bread *very lightly* on either side in hot margarine. Sprinkle with brown sugar. Core cooking apples, halve (do not peel) and fill centre of each with sultanas. Turn flat side downwards on to crisp sweetened bread. Bake for 35–40 minutes. Serve with hot custard sauce.
To vary: the apples may be sprinkled with a little lemon juice before cooking, or brushed with melted butter.

Trout and almonds, recipe on page 79

MONDAY

Cheese Pudding 2 eggs, salt, pepper, $\frac{1}{2}$ teaspoon made-mustard, $\frac{3}{4}$ pint ($4\frac{1}{2}$ dl.) warm milk, 4 oz. (100 g.) grated cheese, 4 oz. (100 g.) breadcrumbs.
Beat eggs with salt, pepper, mustard, add warm milk and cheese. Pour over breadcrumbs, allow to stand for 30 minutes. Bake for 40 minutes in the centre of a moderately hot oven, Gas Mark 5, 375 °F. (190 °C.).

Stuffed Cauliflower cook a cauliflower whole until just tender but unbroken. Scoop out centre pulp, chop finely, then add to sauce made with 1 oz. (25 g.) margarine, 1 oz. (25 g.) flour, $\frac{1}{3}$ pint (2 dl.) tomato juice or milk. Season well, add 2 diced gherkins and 2 teaspoons chopped chives or green tops of spring onions. Put back into centre of cauliflower, heat in oven for 15 minutes.

Compote of Fruit $\frac{1}{3}$ pint (2 dl.) water, 2 oz. (50 g.) sugar, juice of 1 lemon, $1-1\frac{1}{4}$ lb. ($\frac{1}{2}-\frac{5}{8}$ kilo) mixed fruit.
Make a syrup with water, sugar and juice of the lemon. Add fruit and put in covered casserole in oven. Cook for 25 minutes until fruit is tender.

TUESDAY

Grilled Lamb Cutlets lamb cutlets, chopped rosemary, fresh mint.
Grill cutlets on both sides, then sprinkle with a very little finely chopped rosemary and finely chopped fresh mint.

Using the grill: make sure the grill is hot before cooking the meat rapidly on both sides (this seals in the flavour), lower the heat and cook the meat until tender. Lean meat must be brushed with fat or butter, or oil. Lamb cutlets take about 10 minutes; thicker chops a little longer; steaks *from* 2–3 minutes on either side for rare steak (except minute steaks which need 1 minute only on either side).

Apple Pancakes 2 apples, 4 oz. (100 g.) flour, grated rind of 1 orange, 1 egg, 2 tablespoons orange juice, $\frac{1}{4}$ pint ($1\frac{1}{2}$ dl.) milk, fat for frying, marmalade sauce.
Grate apples into flour, add orange rind, beaten egg, orange juice and milk. Fry spoonfuls in hot fat until crisp and brown on both sides. Serve with hot marmalade sauce.

FRIDAY

Salmon Mornay $1\frac{1}{2}$ oz. (40 g.) margarine, $1\frac{1}{2}$ oz. (40 g.) flour, $\frac{3}{4}$ pint ($4\frac{1}{2}$ dl.) milk, 4 oz. (100 g.) grated cheese, seasoning, $7\frac{1}{2}$ oz. (190 g.) can salmon, breadcrumbs.
Make cheese sauce with margarine, flour, milk and most of the grated cheese. Season and add flaked salmon. Put into dish, sprinkle top with crumbs and remainder of the grated cheese. Brown in moderately hot oven, Gas Mark 5, 375 °F. (190 °C.) for 15 minutes.

Flapjack Crumble can of cherry, blackcurrant or other pie filling, 2 oz. (50 g.) margarine, 1 oz. (25 g.) sugar, 1 oz. (25 g.) golden syrup, 4 oz. (100 g.) rolled oats.
Put pie filling in dish. Melt margarine with sugar and golden syrup, add rolled oats. Press over fruit and bake for approximately 35 minutes in the centre of oven.

SATURDAY

Scotch Eggs 4 hard-boiled eggs, 12 oz. ($\frac{3}{8}$ kilo) sausagemeat, 1 egg, breadcrumbs, deep fat for frying.
Wrap eggs in sausagemeat. Coat in beaten egg and breadcrumbs. Fry till crisp. Serve with bottled or home-made Tomato Sauce.
To test fat: put a cube of 24-hour bread into fat. If it turns golden brown within 1 minute, fat is sufficiently hot for Scotch eggs or other substantial food.

Stuffed Mushrooms 4 oz. (100 g.) mushrooms, 1 oz. (25 g.) breadcrumbs, 2 teaspoons chopped parsley, seasoning, 1 oz. (25 g.) butter, fat for frying.
Remove stalks from mushrooms; chop stalks finely. Add to breadcrumbs, parsley, seasoning and butter. Press into mushroom cups, fry carefully.

Apricot Condé $\frac{1}{4}$ pint ($1\frac{1}{2}$ dl.) lightly whipped cream, generous $\frac{1}{4}$ pint ($1\frac{1}{2}$ dl.) apricot syrup, cooked rice, halved apricots, 2 tablespoons apricot jam, 1 teaspoon cornflour or arrowroot.
Beat cream and 2 tablespoons of the apricot syrup into cooked rice (from Wednesday). Put into shallow dish, top with halved apricots and glaze made by simmering apricot jam and the rest of the apricot syrup blended with cornflour or arrowroot.

 WEEK 8

A Shepherd's Pie made with chicken is delicious. Cover the chicken with a good layer of sauce (either make extra on Sunday or prepare this on Monday from 1½ oz. (40 g.) margarine or chicken fat, 1½ oz. (40 g.) flour, ½ pint (3 dl.) milk, ¼ pint (1½ dl.) chicken stock and seasoning).

For your shopping list the main meals need:
11 eggs*, 3 pints (1¾ litres) milk, 3–4 oz. (75–100 g.) Cheddar or other cooking cheese (if making cheese sauce on Friday), cottage or soft cream cheese.
*more if making the sponge cake (Saturday).

Sunday, Monday and Tuesday need:
Kippers, smoked haddock, chicken or boiling fowl, bacon rashers.
Macaroon biscuits, cream (thick or thin), ice cream.
Potatoes, lettuce, red pepper, tomatoes, spring onions or chives, parsley, lemon, rhubarb.

Wednesday and Thursday need:
Steak, lamb's or pig's liver.
Swiss roll, thick cream.
Potatoes, garlic (optional), onion, carrots, fresh mixed herbs, fresh fruit.

Friday and Saturday need:
White fish (optional), veal chops, bacon rashers.
Cream (thick or thin) or ice cream, sponge (unless baking this), potatoes, onions, tomatoes, parsley (optional), cauliflower, bananas, orange juice, apples.

 SUNDAY

Mock Smoked Salmon remove flesh from 2 large uncooked kippers, moisten with little oil, vinegar, add little pepper. Leave overnight. Place on lettuce. Serve with lemon, red pepper, brown bread and butter.

Chicken Casserole chicken giblets, 1 oz. (25 g.) fat, 1 oz. (25 g.) flour, ¾ pint (4½ dl.) giblet stock, seasoning, small can corn, frozen peas, 2 rashers bacon, boiling fowl or chicken.
Simmer giblets for stock. Make sauce with fat, flour, stock and seasoning. Add small can corn, peas and diced bacon. Fry jointed chicken for a few minutes. Put into casserole, cover with the sauce and a lid. Cook boiling fowl for 2–2¼ hours in a slow oven, Gas Mark 2, 300°F. (150°C.); or chicken for 1½ hours.

Almond Mould 2 macaroon biscuits, 1–2 oz. (25–50 g.) blanched chopped almonds, 3 eggs, 2 oz. (50 g.) sugar, ¾ pint (4½ dl.) warm milk. To serve: cream.
Crumble biscuits and add almonds. Beat eggs with sugar and warm milk, strain over crumb mixture. Pour into greased mould or tin, stand in another tin of water and bake for 1¼ hours in coolest part of oven. Turn out, serve hot or cold with cream.

WEDNESDAY

Grilled Steak steak*, 3 tablespoons oil, crushed garlic clove or little garlic salt, pinch mixed herbs.
To give a new flavour to steak, marinate in oil for a short time before cooking. Add the crushed garlic clove, or a little garlic salt, to oil with a good pinch of mixed herbs. Put steaks in this, leave for 1 hour, turning until all the oil is absorbed. Grill in the usual way.
*Choosing steaks: select from fillet (the most tender meat), rump, point, sirloin, T-bone or Entrecôte steaks. A small steak means 4–6 oz. (100–150 g.) meat. Page 21 gives information on using the grill.

Sauté Potatoes slice cooked potatoes thickly. Fry in hot fat until golden brown, toss in parsley.

Cheese and Fresh Fruit try serving cottage or soft cream cheese with fresh fruit and crisp water biscuits.

THURSDAY

Casserole of Liver 1 lb. (½ kilo) lamb's or pig's liver, 2 oz. (50 g.) fat or oil, 1 large finely chopped onion, 2 large grated carrots, large can mushroom soup, ½ pint (3 dl.) water.
Cut liver into neat fingers. Fry in saucepan, in fat or oil, with onion and carrots for 5 minutes only. Add soup, water, bring to the boil. Put in the dumplings and simmer for 15 minutes.

Herb Dumplings 1 oz. (25 g.) shredded suet, 2 oz. (50 g.) self-raising flour, seasoning, 2 teaspoons chopped mixed fresh herbs, little water.
Add suet to flour, seasoning, fresh herbs and little water to bind. Make into small balls. Add to casserole for last 15 minutes.

Swiss Roll Pudding fruit-flavoured jelly, ½ pint (3 dl.) water, ½ pint (3 dl.) evaporated milk, about 5 slices of Swiss roll. To serve: little cream and chopped nuts.
Make up jelly with ½ pint (3 dl.) water only and allow to cool. Add evaporated milk. Arrange slices of Swiss roll at the bottom of a cake tin or soufflé dish, pour over the cream jelly and leave to set. Turn out, top with cream and nuts.

MONDAY

Chicken Shepherd's Pie chicken left over from casserole, sauce (see Introduction on page 22), 2 hard-boiled eggs, little extra milk or cream, mashed potato.
Dice the chicken and arrange at the bottom of a pie dish with a layer of sauce and sliced hard-boiled eggs. Add the milk or cream to the potatoes, spread over filling and bake for 25–30 minutes in the centre of a moderately hot oven, Gas Mark 6, 400°F. (200°C.).

Rhubarb Brown Betty about 6 oz. (150 g.) brown or wholemeal breadcrumbs, 1–1½ lb. (½–¾ kilo) rhubarb, sugar to taste, few sultanas, spice, little margarine, 2 tablespoons golden syrup, 2 tablespoons water.
Grease a plain ovenproof dish. Sprinkle thickly with breadcrumbs. Put a layer of diced rhubarb at the bottom of the dish with sugar and a few sultanas. Cover with a layer of breadcrumbs, sprinkling of sugar and spice, arrange another layer of rhubarb, sugar and sultanas, then a final layer of crumbs, sugar, spice and few small knobs of margarine. Heat the golden syrup with the water, pour slowly over pudding. Bake for 45 minutes in the coolest part of the oven.

TUESDAY

Haddock Kedgeree 1 oz. (25 g.) margarine, 12 oz. (300 g.) flaked cooked smoked haddock, 3 oz. (75 g.) boiled long grain rice, 2 tablespoons milk, 2 hard-boiled eggs. To serve: toast.
Heat margarine, add haddock, rice, milk and chopped egg whites. Heat slowly and pile on to hot dish. Garnish with chopped egg yolks and serve with toast.

Tomato Salad slice firm tomatoes and sprinkle with chopped spring onions or chives, parsley and seasoning. Leave for 1 hour before serving.

Pancakes cook pancakes and keep hot. Fill each with ice cream, roll and serve at once.
To make pancakes: 4 oz. flour, preferably plain, pinch salt, 1 egg, ½ pint (3 dl.) milk or milk and water, oil or fat for frying.
Sieve flour and salt together. Beat in the egg and enough milk or milk and water to give a stiff batter. Beat hard until smooth then gradually whisk in the rest of the liquid. Heat enough oil or fat to give a very thin coating in a small pan. Pour or spoon enough batter into the pan to give a paper-thin coating. Cook quickly for 2–3 minutes until golden brown on the under side then turn or toss and cook on second side. Always add more oil or fat before cooking any more pancakes.
To keep pancakes hot: stand on a large plate over boiling water or on a dish in a cool oven. Do not cover.

FRIDAY

Spicy Fish Ramekins 1 small chopped onion, 2 chopped tomatoes, 1½ oz. (40 g.) margarine, 8 oz. (200 g.) flaked white fish or canned tuna, seasoning, cheese or parsley sauce (page 5), breadcrumbs, grated nutmeg.
Fry onion and tomatoes in margarine, add fish and season well. Put into 4 individual dishes. Top with layer of cheese or parsley sauce, breadcrumbs and grated nutmeg. Crisp and brown under hot grill.

Cauliflower Fritters make a thick batter with 4 oz. (100 g.) flour, seasoning, 1 egg, good ¼ pint (1½ dl.) milk. Cook cauliflower sprigs very lightly, dip in batter and fry until crisp and brown.

Banana Orange Pie 6 oz. (150 g.) shortcrust pastry, page 10, 2 eggs, 2 oz. (50 g.) sugar, 2 teaspoons powdered gelatine, ¼ pint (1½ dl.) orange juice, 4 bananas.
Line a 7–8-inch (18–20-cm.) flan ring with the pastry and bake 'blind', see page 10, until crisp and golden brown, then cool. Meanwhile, separate the eggs and whisk the egg yolks and sugar until thick. Dissolve the powered gelatine in the hot orange juice (page 53 gives advice on dissolving gelatine), add to the yolks, allow to cool and begin to thicken. Add mashed bananas and finally the stiffly whisked egg whites. Pile into cooled pastry case.

SATURDAY

Stuffed Veal Chops 4 thick veal chops (or lamb could be used), 1 oz. (25 g.) raisins, 2 oz. (50 g.) breadcrumbs, 1 small grated apple, 1 small grated onion, seasoning, 2 chopped fried rashers bacon, little butter or fat for frying or grilling.
Cut the chops through centre to make a 'pocket'. Fill this with stuffing made by mixing the raisins, breadcrumbs, apple, onion, seasoning and bacon. Secure with skewers or thin string, then fry or grill the chops slowly for approximately 15–20 minutes, turning carefully. If frying, use about 2–3 oz. (50–75 g.) butter or fat; if grilling, brush with melted butter or fat several times during cooking. Fry or grill quickly on either side, then lower the heat to make sure the meat is cooked through to the centre. Remove skewers or string before serving.

Apple Walnut Gâteau 8 oz. (200 g.) peeled apples, little golden syrup, 2 oz. (50 g.) chopped dates or currants, 1–2 oz. (25–50 g.) chopped walnuts, 1 sponge cake. To serve: cream or ice cream.
Simmer apples with a little golden syrup, dates or currants until thick pulp, add walnuts. Split sponge cake and fill with this mixture, then serve with cream or ice cream.

WEEK 9

Small spring chickens can dry in cooking, so follow the suggestions in Sunday's menu.
If you bind the cheese pastry (Monday) with an egg yolk, save the white and add it to the Pineapple Cream (Wednesday) or use it in Meringues (Friday).

For your shopping list the main meals need:
8 or 9 eggs*, 3½ pints (2 litres) milk, 8–10 oz. (200–250 g.) Cheddar or other cooking cheese, cream cheese.
* more if making the sponge cake (Thursday) and meringues (Friday).

Sunday and Monday need:
Spring chickens (allow 1 small one for each person), bacon rashers, smoked cod or haddock.
Cream (thick or thin), potatoes, potato crisps, watercress, spring onions or chives, gooseberries.

Tuesday, Wednesday and Thursday need:
Sausages, lamb chops, stewing steak or topside, bacon rashers or bacon pieces, thick cream, sponge (unless baking this).
Potatoes (some large for baking), tomatoes, mushrooms, parsley, mixed herbs, carrots, turnips, broad and French beans, salad ingredients (optional), cooking apples, lemon, bananas, orange juice.

Friday and Saturday need:
Breast of lamb, ice cream, thick cream.
Meringues (unless baking these).
New potatoes, tomatoes, onion, carrot, mint, cucumber.

SUNDAY

Spring Chickens 2 spring chickens (poussins), 2–3 oz. (50–75 g.) margarine or butter, 2 oz. (50 g.) fat.
As chickens are not stuffed put a good knob of the margarine or butter inside each bird to keep them moist. Brush outside with plenty of melted fat. Roast for approximately 40 minutes in a moderately hot oven, Gas Mark 6, 400°F. (200°C.). Halve and serve with the bread sauce (page 5), brown gravy and savoury Bacon Rolls (below).

Savoury Bacon Rolls make whole or halved rashers of bacon into neat rolls and sprinkle lightly with paprika and celery salt; put in oven 15 minutes before the birds are cooked. Fry *coarse* breadcrumbs in hot butter or margarine. Arrange the spring chickens on a dish with the bacon rolls, heated potato crisps, watercress and fried crumbs.

Gooseberry Tart 1–1½ lb. (½–¾ kilo) gooseberries, very little water, sugar to taste, 2 oz. (50 g.) fine cake or biscuit crumbs, 8–10 oz. (200–250 g.) sweet shortcrust pastry (page 89). To serve: cream.
Simmer the fruit in the water and sugar. Sieve or mash and blend with the crumbs. Roll out half the pastry and line a 7–8-inch (18–20-cm.) pie plate. Cover with the filling, then the rest of the pastry. Bake for 30–35 minutes in the centre of the oven, reducing heat slightly after 15 minutes if the pastry is becoming too brown. Serve with cream.

WEDNESDAY

Beef Olives 4 thin large slices of stewing steak or topside. *Parsley stuffing:* 1 tablespoon chopped parsley, 1 teaspoon mixed herbs, grated rind and juice of ½ lemon, 1 oz. (25 g.) shredded suet or melted margarine, 3 oz. (75 g.) breadcrumbs, 1 egg, seasoning, 1 oz. (25 g.) fat, brown sauce (page 5).
Halve the slices of meat, spread with the stuffing made by blending parsley, herbs, lemon rind and juice, suet or margarine, crumbs, egg and seasoning. Roll and tie with cotton. Fry gently in the hot fat, lift into casserole, cover with sauce and a lid. Cook for 2 hours in centre of a very moderate oven, Gas Mark 3, 325°F. (170°C.).
Serve with *Macedoine of Vegetables*, i.e. diced young carrots, turnips, broad beans, French beans. Cook these in covered casserole with water and seasoning for 1¼ hours. Strain, toss in butter and chopped parsley.

Pineapple Cream medium can pineapple, juice and grated rind of ½ lemon, water, 1 level tablespoon (½ oz. – 15 g.) powdered gelatine, 2 eggs, 2 oz. (50 g.) sugar, ¼ pint (1½ dl.) whipped cream.
Strain syrup from pineapple, add lemon juice and water (if necessary) to give ½ pint (3 dl.) liquid. Dissolve gelatine in this. Beat egg yolks with sugar and lemon rind until thick, add cool jelly mixture, leave until beginning to stiffen, add chopped pineapple, whipped cream and stiffly beaten egg whites. Pile into 4 glasses

THURSDAY

Bacon and Egg Loaf 8 oz. (200 g.) bacon, 2 oz. (50 g.) margarine, 2 oz. (50 g.) flour, ½ pint (3 dl.) milk, 4 chopped hard-boiled eggs, 2 oz. (50 g.) breadcrumbs, seasoning, parsley and herbs (optional).
Chop bacon finely, make white sauce of margarine, flour and milk. Add bacon, eggs and breadcrumbs, season well. Add chopped parsley and herbs if wished. Put into greased loaf tin, cover top with greased foil or paper. Either steam for 45 minutes or bake in a moderately hot oven, Gas Mark 5, 375°F. (190°C.). This is excellent eaten hot with vegetables or cold with a salad.

Honey Banana Slices sponge cake, bananas, 2 oz. (50 g.) honey, 2 oz. (50 g.) raisins, 4 tablespoons orange juice.
Top slices of sponge cake with sliced banana and thick sauce made by simmering honey, raisins and orange juice for 3 minutes.

MONDAY

Spiced Fish Pie 1½ lb. (¾ kilo) smoked cod or haddock, 1½ oz. (40 g.) margarine, 1½ oz. (40 g.) flour, seasoning, 1 teaspoon curry powder, ½ pint (3 dl.) milk, ¼ pint (1½ dl.) fish stock, 1 teaspoon Worcestershire sauce, 1 tablespoon chopped spring onions or chives, mashed potato, cayenne pepper, little grated nutmeg.
Cook cod or haddock, flake coarsely and stir into a sauce made with margarine, flour, seasoning, curry powder, milk, fish stock, Worcestershire sauce and chopped spring onions or chives. Top with mashed potato seasoned with cayenne pepper and grated nutmeg. Brown in a moderately hot oven, Gas Mark 6, 400°F. (200°C.), for approximately 25 minutes.

Cheese and Fruit Fingers 1½ oz. (40 g.) margarine, 4 oz. (100 g.) seasoned flour, 1 oz. (25 g.) grated cheese, 1 egg yolk or water, cream cheese, canned pineapple.
Make a cheese-flavoured pastry by rubbing margarine into seasoned flour, add grated cheese and bind with egg yolk or water. Roll out thinly and cut into 8 fingers. Bake for 10 minutes near the top of the oven. Cool then top with cream cheese and well drained pineapple.

TUESDAY

Savoury Toad-in-the-Hole 4 small sausages, 4 lamb chops, halved tomatoes, 4 oz. (100 g.) seasoned flour, 1 egg, ½ pint (3 dl.) milk.
Heat sausages, chops and tomatoes for 10 minutes in a well greased Yorkshire pudding tin. Cover with batter made with seasoned flour, egg and milk. Bake for 35 minutes in centre of a hot oven, Gas Mark 7, 425°F. (220°C.), reducing heat after 20 minutes.

Mushroom Potatoes cook 4 potatoes in their jackets, remove centre pulp. Mash, mix with pulp of 3 skinned tomatoes, 2 oz. (50 g.) chopped fried mushrooms, seasoning. Return to potato cases and heat for a short time in the oven.

Apple Sultana Crumble 1 lb. (½ kilo) apples, 2 oz. (50 g.) sultanas, little water, sugar or honey, 2 oz. (50 g.) margarine, 4 oz. (100 g.) flour, 2–3 oz. (50–75 g.) sugar.
Peel and slice apples thinly, put into pie dish with sultanas, little water and sugar or honey to sweeten. Cover with crumble made by rubbing margarine into flour, then adding sugar. Press firmly over fruit, bake in coolest part of oven for 30–40 minutes then reduce heat to moderate, Gas Mark 4, 350°F. (180°C.), after taking the Savoury Toad-in-the-Hole out of the oven.

FRIDAY

New Potato Mould 1 lb. (½ kilo) new potatoes, seasoning, tomatoes, grated cheese, margarine.
Cook the potatoes carefully (cook some extra for Saturday's salad). Slice, fill greased tin with layers of potato, seasoned skinned sliced tomatoes, grated cheese, ending with potatoes. Brush top with melted margarine, cook for 30 minutes in a hot oven, Gas Mark 7, 425°F. (220°C.). Turn out and serve with a cheese sauce made with 1 oz. (25 g.) margarine 1 oz. (25 g.) flour, ½ pint (3 dl.) milk, seasoning, 3 oz. (75 g.) grated cheese.

Meringue Glacé sandwich halves of meringue together with ice cream.
To make meringues: 2 egg whites, 4 oz. castor sugar.
Whisk the egg whites until very stiff. Gradually beat in half the sugar and then fold in the remainder. Pipe or spoon into 8 large or 12–14 smaller rounds on a lightly oiled baking tray. Dry out for about 2–2½ hours in a very cool oven, Gas Mark 0–½, 200–275°F. (90–140°C.). Ovens vary a great deal at this low temperature, so check during cooking to make sure the meringues do not brown too quickly. Lift off the tray with a warm palette knife. Store in an airtight tin until ready to fill.

SATURDAY

Lamb Pies breast of lamb, seasoning, flour, 1 onion, 1 grated carrot, ½ teaspoon chopped mint, 3 tablespoons cooked peas, 2 tablespoons stock, 8–10 oz. (200–250 g.) shortcrust pastry (page 10).
Dice meat from breast of lamb, coat with seasoned flour. Slice or chop the onion. Fry the meat and onion together for 10 minutes, add the carrot, mint, peas and stock. Line 4 large or 8 small deep patty tins with pastry, fill with lamb mixture, cover with pastry, bake in centre of moderately hot oven, Gas Mark 6, 400°F. (200°C.), for 45 minutes, reducing heat after 20 minutes.

New Potato and Cucumber Salad mix diced potatoes and cucumber with chopped chives, parsley, mayonnaise.

Vanilla Creams vanilla-flavoured blancmange, 1 pint (6 dl.) milk, 1–2 oz. (25–50 g.) sugar, 4 tablespoons thin cream, whipped cream, few chopped nuts.
Make up blancmange with the milk and sugar as directed on the packet. When the mixture has thickened add thin cream for a softer texture. Spoon into glasses and cool. Top with whipped cream and a few chopped nuts.

Cheese scones, recipe on page 29

WEEK 10

Veal fillets are made into a rather special dish (Tuesday). The topping gives flavour and keeps the meat moist. The method of coating lamb cutlets (Saturday) is an unusual one and enables this main dish to be prepared well in advance.

For your shopping list the main meals need:
11 eggs, 1 pint (generous ½ litre) milk, 9–12 oz. (225–300 g.) Cheddar or other cooking cheese, cream cheese.

Sunday and Monday need:
Topside.
Plain chocolate, thin cream.
Potatoes, onions, green pepper, mushrooms, mixed herbs, selection vegetables, tomatoes, cucumber, fresh fruit.

Tuesday and Wednesday need:
Veal fillets, white fish.
Potatoes, tomatoes, garlic, parsley, marrow, bananas (optional), lemon, gooseberries.

Thursday, Friday and Saturday need:
Sausagemeat, lamb cutlets.
Thin cream or yoghourt (optional), thick cream.
Potatoes, tomatoes, onions, chives, mint, parsley, spring onions, salad ingredients, apricots, cherries, fruit for dessert on Friday, lemon, strawberries.

SUNDAY

Beef Masquerade 2 lb. (1 kilo) joint topside beef, 2 onions, 1 green pepper, 2 oz. (50 g.) mushrooms, 2 oz. (50 g.) fat, 3 oz. (75 g.) cooked rice, 1 teaspoon mixed herbs, seasoning. To serve: cooked vegetables. Make a cut halfway through meat. Chop the vegetables, fry in the fat. Mix with the cooked rice, herbs and seasoning. Put half the mixture in centre of meat, pile the rest on top. Roast in covered roaster or greased foil for 1¼–1½ hours in the centre of a moderately hot oven, Gas Mark 6, 400°F. (200°C.). Serve with a selection of vegetables.

Chocolate Nut Tart 5–6 oz. (125–150 g.) shortcrust pastry (page 10), 1 tablespoon cornflour, ½ pint (3 dl.) milk, 1 oz. (25 g.) sugar, 4 oz. (100 g.) plain chocolate, 2 oz. (50 g.) chopped nuts, 3 tablespoons thin cream. Make and bake a flan case (page 10). Blend cornflour with milk, cook until thickened, add sugar and chocolate, allow to melt then add most of the nuts and the cream. Put into pastry case and top with remaining nuts.
To melt chocolate: the chocolate is melted in the cornflour mixture in the recipe above. Normally chocolate is melted in a basin over hot but not boiling water.

WEDNESDAY

Baked Fish Croquettes 12 oz. (300 g.) cooked white fish, 1 oz. (25 g.) margarine, 1 oz. (25 g.) flour, ¼ pint (1½ dl.) milk, seasoning, few drops anchovy essence, 2 oz. (50 g.) soft breadcrumbs, little chopped parsley, few capers, 1 egg, 2 oz. (50 g.) crisp breadcrumbs, little oil.
Flake fish, mix with sauce made with margarine, flour, milk, seasoning and anchovy essence. Stir in soft crumbs, parsley and capers. Cool, form into fingers, coat with beaten egg and crisp crumbs. Put on oiled baking sheet, bake for 20 minutes in a moderately hot oven, Gas Mark 5, 375°F. (190°C.). Serve with *Roast Marrow:* wash and slice marrow; peel and de-seed (unless very young). Heat little fat in roasting tin, turn marrow in this, cook for 50 minutes.

Fruit Bars 2 oz. (50 g.) butter, 3 oz. (75 g.) sugar, 1 tablespoon golden syrup, 1 egg, 6 oz. (150 g.) flour (with plain flour use 1½ teaspoons baking powder), 6 oz. (150 g.) dates, 2 oz. (50 g.) nuts, 4 oz. (100 g.) sultanas, 2 oz. (50 g.) mixed peel.
Cream butter, sugar and golden syrup, add egg, flour, chopped dates, chopped nuts, sultanas and mixed peel. Press into shallow greased 8-inch (20-cm.) tin. Bake for 35 minutes in centre of oven, mark into fingers while hot, cool in tin.

THURSDAY

Chilled Tomato Soup 1 lb. (½ kilo) tomatoes, 1 onion, 1 tablespoon chopped chives, 1 teaspoon chopped mint, seasoning, ¼ pint (1½ dl.) stock or water, ¼ pint (1½ dl.) thin cream or yoghourt, cream cheese.
Skin tomatoes, simmer with chopped onion, chives, mint, seasoning and stock or water. Sieve, blend with the cream or yoghourt. Chill, serve in cold soup cups topped with cream cheese.

Sausage Galantine 1 lb. (½ kilo) sausagemeat, 2 teaspoons chopped parsley, 1 teaspoon mixed herbs, 2 tablespoons chopped spring onions, 1 egg, crisp breadcrumbs.
Blend sausagemeat with parsley, herbs, spring onions, and egg. Put into greased tin coated with crisp breadcrumbs, cover with greased foil, bake for 45 minutes (in a tin of water to prevent drying) in a hot oven, Gas Mark 6, 400°F. (200°C.).

Apricot and Cherry Pie this is an excellent mixture of fruits for a pie. Add a few kernels from the apricot stones to the fruit. Sweeten with honey instead of sugar. Page 46 gives details on making a fruit pie.

MONDAY

Spaghetti Favourite cooked meat from Sunday's joint, large can of mixed vegetable soup or packet soup, cooked spaghetti. To serve: grated cheese.
Mince or chop meat left from joint. Heat the canned soup or make up the packet soup. Add meat and any pieces of stuffing left over from Sunday; pour over cooked spaghetti. Serve with grated cheese.
To cook spaghetti: always use sufficient water so the pasta does not stick together.
To 4 oz. (100 g.) spaghetti use at least 2 pints (generous 1 litre) water. Bring the water to the boil, add salt to taste, put the ends of the spaghetti into the boiling water; wait until these are softened then twist so the rest of the long pieces of spaghetti drop into the water. Cook until just tender, do not over-cook, then strain.

Tomato and Cucumber Salad slice tomatoes and cucumber thinly, skinned if preferred, arrange in layers in a dish, add seasoning, little oil, chopped parsley, vinegar.

Follow this meal with fresh fruit.

TUESDAY

Veal Caribbean 4 slices veal (cut from leg), 1 egg, breadcrumbs, little oil, 3–4 chopped skinned tomatoes, crushed garlic clove, few drops Worcestershire or Tabasco sauce, seasoning, 2 bananas (optional), slices of Cheddar or Gruyère cheese.
Coat veal with egg and breadcrumbs, fry in oil for 3 minutes on either side. Put in a shallow casserole. Fry tomatoes and garlic until a thick purée, add sauce and seasoning. For an original touch, slice bananas over meat (these can be omitted if you wish), cover with tomato purée and slices of cheese, then cook for 20 minutes in a moderately hot oven, Gas Mark 6, 400°F. (200°C.).

Gooseberry Flan $\frac{1}{3}$ pint (2 dl.) water, 2–3 oz. (50–75 g.) sugar, squeeze of lemon juice, 1 lb. ($\frac{1}{2}$ kilo) gooseberries, baked pastry or sponge flan case, pages 10 and 46, 1 teaspoon arrowroot or cornflour.
Make syrup of water, sugar and lemon juice. Poach gooseberries in this until tender but unbroken. Drain fruit, arrange in flan case. Blend syrup with arrowroot or cornflour. Boil until thickened and clear, stirring all the time; cool, then carefully coat fruit with this glaze.

FRIDAY

Egg and Vegetable Medley few tomatoes, 1 onion, 1 oz. (25 g.) fat, seasoning, 6 eggs, little made-mustard, 1 oz. (25 g.) butter. Topping: few tablespoons cream, 2–3 tablespoons breadcrumbs, little butter.
Slice the tomatoes and onions and fry in the fat until tender. Season and put at the bottom of a shallow dish. Hard boil the eggs, shell, remove the yolks without breaking the white cases, blend the mashed yolks with a little mustard, seasoning and the 1 oz. (25 g.) butter. Put back into the white cases, put cut side of eggs on the vegetables, cover with the few tablespoons cream, a sprinkling of breadcrumbs and knob of butter and heat for a few minutes in a hot oven, Gas Mark 7, 425°F. (220°C.).

Cheese Scones 1 oz. (25 g.) margarine, 6 oz. (150 g.) seasoned flour, 2 oz. (50 g.) grated cheese, 1 egg yolk, milk.
Rub margarine into flour, add grated cheese. Bind with egg yolk and milk, roll out to $\frac{1}{2}$ inch (1 cm.) in thickness, cut into rounds, bake for good 10 minutes in oven, see picture page 26.

Jelly Cream Whip 1 lemon jelly, $\frac{1}{2}$ pint (3 dl.) hot water, $\frac{1}{4}$ pint ($1\frac{1}{2}$ dl.) thick fruit purée, $\frac{1}{4}$ pint ($1\frac{1}{2}$ dl.) whipped cream, 1 stiffly beaten egg white.
Dissolve jelly in hot water, cool, add fruit purée, whipped cream and egg white. Pile into glasses.

SATURDAY

Minted Lamb Cutlets 2 level teaspoons aspic jelly, 12 tablespoons water, 1 tablespoon lemon juice, 1 tablespoon chopped mint, 1 teaspoon sugar, lamb cutlets, green salad, mint-flavoured mayonnaise.
Dissolve aspic jelly in water, add lemon juice, chopped mint and sugar. Cool slightly, brush over cooled cooked lamb cutlets, serve on green salad with mint-flavoured mayonnaise.

French Peas peas, little water, outer lettuce leaves, chopped spring onions, little butter, seasoning.
Cook peas in saucepan in a little water between layers of outer lettuce leaves with spring onions, little butter and seasoning.

Strawberries and Cream chill strawberries slightly before serving with cream.

WEEK 11

Remember to prick the skin of duckling (Sunday) so this crisps and allows the surplus fat to run out of the bird into the tin.

A small duckling serves two people only, but if you buy a good sized bird you could have 4 small portions. The two stuffings make this more substantial and more interesting.

Kebab cooking is extremely popular at the moment and the vegetable kebabs (Wednesday) look as good as they taste.

For your shopping list the main meals need:
19 eggs, 2 pints (generous 1 litre) milk, 8 oz. (200 g.) Cheddar or other cooking cheese.

Sunday and Monday need:
Duckling.
Thick cream.
Potatoes, onions, sage, green pepper, parsley, oranges, lemons, fruit (for shortcake), cherries.

Tuesday, Wednesday and Thursday need:
Minced beef, cooked ham, steaks (store carefully).
Ice cream, thick cream.
Potatoes, onions (some small), tomatoes (some small), mixed root vegetables, red and green pepper, spring onions, green salad ingredients, mushrooms, cucumber, chives, fresh fruit.

Friday and Saturday need:
Lamb cutlets.
Salad ingredients, small carrots, peas.

SUNDAY

Roast Duckling sage and onion stuffing, page 10. *Orange stuffing*: finely grated rind 2 oranges, 2 oz. (50 g.) crisp breadcrumbs, cooked duck liver, seasoning, 1 oz. (25 g.) melted margarine, little chopped green pepper. 1 large or 2 smaller duckling (ducks if you cannot get duckling).

Make the two stuffings. For the orange stuffing, mix rind with crumbs, add chopped liver, seasoning, margarine and green pepper. Weigh duckling after stuffing and allow good 15 minutes per lb. (½ kilo) and 15 minutes over in moderately hot to hot oven, Gas Mark 6–7, 400–425°F. (200–220°C.), lower heat slightly after 30 minutes. Prick skin after 30 minutes cooking for surplus fat to run out and to crisp outside. Garnish with sliced oranges, cherries, picture, page 138.

Orange Sauce cut peel from 1 orange in thin matchsticks. Simmer in ½ pint (3 dl.) giblet stock until tender. Add 1 oz. (25 g.) butter, juice of 3 oranges and 1 lemon blended with 1 tablespoon cornflour, seasoning and pinch sugar. Cook until smooth and thickened.

Fruit Shortcake cream 5 oz. (125 g.) margarine with 5 oz. (125 g.) sugar, add 2 eggs and 8 oz. (200 g.) flour (with plain flour use 2 teaspoons baking powder). Take out one-third of mixture for Monday's sweet (wrap in foil). Divide rest between two 6–7-inch (15–18-cm.) greased tins. Flatten on top, bake for 10–15 minutes. Cool, then fill and top with fruit and cream.

WEDNESDAY

Vegetable Kebabs with Ham Rice small firm tomatoes, parboiled tiny onions, mushrooms, thick slices cucumber, green pepper, seasoning, melted butter, 3 oz. (75 g.) boiled rice, 1 oz. (25 g.) margarine, 4 oz. (100 g.) diced ham, 2 egg yolks.

Put tomatoes, onions, mushrooms, cucumber (especially good cooked) and pieces of green pepper on metal skewers. Season, brush with butter and grill for 5–10 minutes. Toss boiled rice in margarine, add ham, egg yolks and seasoning. Heat gently. Serve round kebabs.

Coffee Mousse ½ oz. (15 g.) powdered gelatine, ½ pint (3 dl.) strong coffee, 2 oz. (50 g.) sugar, ¼ pint (1½ dl.) milk, ¼ pint (1½ dl.) lightly whipped cream, 2 egg whites.

Dissolve gelatine in coffee, add sugar and milk. Allow mixture to cool. Fold whipped cream and stiffly beaten egg whites into the coffee mixture. Pile in glasses.

THURSDAY

Pocket Steaks 4 thick steaks (fillet or see choice on page 22), 3 oz. (75 g.) butter, seasoning, 2–4 oz. (50–100 g.) mushrooms (fried in a little extra butter), 1 tablespoon chopped chives.

Split the steaks to make 'pockets', fill with half the butter, seasoning, thinly sliced mushrooms and chives. Grill in the usual way, basting with the rest of the butter as the steaks cook. Allow 3 minutes on either side for underdone steaks, but if you require medium or well done steaks lower the heat after this time and cook for a further 6–8 minutes. This makes sure the filling is heated.

Green Salad lettuce, watercress, cucumber, well seasoned oil and vinegar.
Shred the lettuce, sprig the watercress, slice the cucumber. Toss in well seasoned oil and vinegar.

Serve cheese or fruit to follow.

MONDAY

Fish Scramble 12 oz. ($\frac{3}{8}$ kilo) cooked potatoes, grated cheese, medium can salmon, 2 beaten eggs, seasoning, 2 tablespoons milk, 1 oz. (25 g.) butter. To garnish: lemon and parsley.
Slice potatoes. Put into dish, top with grated cheese and heat while preparing fish mixture. Open can of salmon. Flake fish, then add to beaten eggs, seasoning and milk. Scramble in butter. Arrange on potatoes, garnish with lemon and parsley.

Cherry Macaroon Fingers shortcake mixture (left from Sunday), 1$\frac{1}{2}$ oz. (40 g.) margarine, 2 oz. (50 g.) sugar, 1 egg, 3 oz. (75 g.) cake crumbs, 1 oz. (25 g.) ground almonds, ripe cherries.
Press out shortcake mixture into 6–7-inch (15–18-cm.) square greased tin. Bake mixture for 10 minutes in hot oven, Gas Mark 6, 400°F. (200°C.). Cream margarine, sugar, add egg, cake crumbs and ground almonds. Spread over shortcake and cover with cherries. Lower heat to moderately hot, Gas Mark 5, 375°F. (190°C.), and continue cooking in centre of oven for 25 minutes.

TUESDAY

Hamburger Loaf 1 lb. ($\frac{1}{2}$ kilo) minced steak, 1 tablespoon tomato ketchup, $\frac{1}{2}$ teaspoon mixed herbs, 1 grated small onion, 2 oz. (50 g.) breadcrumbs, seasoning, 1 egg. Filling: 2 thinly sliced onions, 2 skinned tomatoes, 1$\frac{1}{2}$ oz. (40 g.) fat, grated raw potato, seasoning.
Mix minced steak, tomato ketchup, mixed herbs, grated onions, breadcrumbs, seasoning and egg. Spread half in greased loaf tin, cover with filling made by frying sliced onions and tomatoes in fat, add grated raw potato, seasoning, cover with rest of steak mixture and greased foil. Bake for 50–60 minutes in moderately hot oven, Gas Mark 5, 375°F. (190°C.). Excellent for a picnic, with salad carried in screw-top jars.

Mixed Salads try a Russian salad made by tossing diced cooked vegetables in mayonnaise; diced red and green pepper and spring onion mixed with oil, vinegar and seasoning. Serve with green salad.

Fruit Sundaes fresh fruit, ice cream, cream.
Serve layers of fresh fruit and ice cream topped with cream. Remember ice cream can be carried in a vacuum flask for a picnic.

FRIDAY

Egg and Sardine Mayonnaise 4 hard-boiled eggs, salad, sardines, mayonnaise, paprika.
Halve hard-boiled eggs, arrange on salad with sardines, coat with mayonnaise and garnish with paprika.

Cheese Soufflés 3 eggs, 4 oz. (100 g.) grated cheese, $\frac{1}{4}$ pint (1$\frac{1}{2}$ dl.) thick white sauce*, seasoning.
Separate eggs. Add yolks and grated cheese to white sauce, season well. Fold in stiffly beaten egg whites, bake in individual soufflé dishes for 20–25 minutes in moderately hot oven, Gas Mark 5, 375°F. (190°C.).
* To make a *Thick White Sauce* (often called a *Panada*): heat 1 oz. (25 g.) butter or margarine in a pan, stir in 1 oz. (25 g.) flour and cook over a gentle heat for 2–3 minutes. Gradually blend in $\frac{1}{4}$ pint (1$\frac{1}{2}$ dl.) milk and stir as the mixture comes to the boil, season and cook, stirring all the time, for several minutes.

If you prefer to have a sweet dessert you can serve a selection of fresh fruit or a fruit salad.

SATURDAY

Summer Lamb Casserole 8 best end neck of lamb cutlets, 1 oz. (25 g.) margarine, 1 oz. (25 g.) flour, $\frac{1}{2}$ pint (3 dl.) milk, $\frac{1}{2}$ pint (3 dl.) stock, seasoning, 12 oz. ($\frac{3}{8}$ kilo) tiny carrots and peas.
Fry lamb cutlets for few minutes, put into casserole, cover with sauce made with margarine, flour, milk, stock, seasoning. Add carrots and peas. Cover casserole, cook for 1$\frac{1}{2}$ hours in a slow oven, Gas Mark 2, 300°F. (150°C.).

Caramel Custard 3 oz. (75 g.) sugar, 3 tablespoons water, 4 eggs, 1 oz. (25 g.) sugar, 1 pint (6 dl.) milk.
Make caramel by cooking sugar and water until golden brown. Put into mould. Cover with custard made by beating eggs, sugar and milk. Stand in tin of water and cook for 1$\frac{1}{2}$–2 hours in oven until the mixture has set.

Week 12

The leg of lamb (Sunday) is easier to stuff and serve if the bone is removed. The butcher will probably do this for you, but it is not a particularly difficult job. Use a sharp firm knife, make a deep straight cut down the joint; insert the knife into the meat and cut the flesh carefully and slowly away from the bone. Put in the stuffing and shape the meat back into its original shape.

For your shopping list the main meals need:
20–22 eggs, 2 pints (generous 1 litre) milk, about 2 oz. (50 g.) Cheddar or other cooking cheese, 4 oz. (100 g.) processed cheese.
Sunday, Monday and Tuesday need:
Lamb, chicken.
Sponge cake, thick cream.
Potatoes, onions, thyme, French beans, spring onions, carrots, garlic, tomatoes, green salad ingredients, lemon, prunes, raspberries (optional), gooseberries, strawberries (you may need to buy these on Tuesday).
Wednesday, Thursday, Friday and Saturday need:
Cooked ham or luncheon roll, calf's or lamb's liver, bacon rashers.
Thick cream.
New potatoes, peas, tomatoes (some large), chives or spring onions, onions, green pepper, parsley, mint, mixed berry fruits – cherries, etc., oranges, lemons (store any berry fruit left carefully for Friday), apricots.

Sunday

Asparagus Eggs small can or bundle cooked asparagus, 4 egg yolks, 4 tablespoons thick cream, seasoning, 1 oz. (25 g.) butter, toast.
Chop the asparagus, mix with the beaten egg yolks and cream and season well. Heat the butter in a saucepan and scramble the mixture lightly. Put on to hot toast.

Prune Stuffed Lamb *for the stuffing*: pour boiling water over 6 oz. (150 g.) prunes, leave for 10 minutes, drain, chop and mix with 3 oz. (75 g.) soft breadcrumbs, 1 chopped onion, grated rind and juice of 1 lemon, 1 oz. (25 g.) melted butter or margarine and 1 teaspoon chopped fresh thyme.
Remove the bone from a small leg of lamb (or half large leg), put in the stuffing, skewer or tie and roast as page 54. Serve with French beans, tossed in margarine and chopped spring onions and herbs and boiled potatoes. Cook extra potatoes for Layer Pie on Monday and beans for one of the salads on Tuesday.

Raspberry Alaska cover a sponge cake with crushed sweetened fresh, drained frozen or canned raspberries, then with a block of ice cream. Coat with a meringue made from 4 egg whites and 4 oz. (100 g.) castor sugar. Brown for 3–4 minutes in a very hot oven, top with fruit, see picture, page 50.

Wednesday

Luncheon Rolls with Jiffy Cheese Sauce 4 hard-boiled eggs, 2 gherkins, 1 oz. (25 g.) butter, seasoning, 8 slices of ham or luncheon roll.
For sauce: $\frac{1}{4}$ pint ($1\frac{1}{2}$ dl.) evaporated milk, 1 teaspoon made-mustard, 4 oz. (100 g.) diced processed cheese.
To serve: new potatoes, peas.
Chop hard-boiled eggs, mix with chopped gherkins, butter and seasoning. Put on slices of ham, roll and warm for about 5 minutes. If using luncheon roll, cut into 8 slices, sandwich egg mixture between 2 slices and warm. Meanwhile, prepare sauce: put evaporated milk, mustard and processed cheese into basin over hot water, heat until cheese is melted. Pour over ham mixture, serve with new potatoes and peas.

Summer Fruit Salad berry fruits, ripe cherries, ripe summer fruits, 1 sliced orange, sugar, little orange juice or Kirsch (optional).
Mix berry fruits, cherries and any ripe summer fruits with orange. Sweeten. Moisten mixture with orange juice or, for special occasions, you can use a little Kirsch.

Thursday

Liver Soufflé 2 oz. (50 g.) margarine, 2 oz. (50 g.) flour, $\frac{1}{2}$ pint (3 dl.) milk, 8 oz. (200 g.) finely chopped calf's or lamb's liver, seasoning, 4 eggs (separated).
Make thick sauce of margarine, flour and milk. Add liver, seasoning, egg yolks. Finally fold in stiffly beaten egg whites. Put in greased soufflé dish, bake in centre of moderately hot oven, Gas Mark 5, 375°F. (190°C.) for approximately 35 minutes.

Baked Stuffed Tomatoes large tomatoes, few breadcrumbs, chopped chives or spring onions, chopped mixed herbs, seasoning.
Take tops from tomatoes. Scoop out pulp, chop and mix with breadcrumbs, chives or spring onions and herbs, season well. Return to tomato cases, bake in greased dish for 10–15 minutes.

Coconut Cherry Crumble cherries, sugar, little water, few drops almond essence (optional), 1 oz. (25 g.) margarine, 2 oz. (50 g.) flour, 2 oz. (50 g.) desiccated coconut, 2–3 oz. (50–75 g.) sugar.
Put cherries into dish with sugar and water; a few drops almond essence can be added. Rub margarine into flour, add coconut and sugar. Press over cherries. Bake for 35–40 minutes.

MONDAY

Layer Pie meat left over from joint, about 10 spring onions and little fat for frying, 1 large carrot, any stuffing left or 2 tablespoons chutney, 3 tablespoons stock, seasoning, sliced cooked potatoes, little margarine.
Dice or mince meat left from joint; fry chopped white part of spring onions, mix with meat, grated carrot, any stuffing left or chutney and stock, season well. Put half into pie dish, cover with layer of sliced potatoes, little finely chopped green stem of spring onions, then rest of meat mixture. Top with sliced potatoes and little margarine; bake the pie for approximately 35 minutes in centre of hot oven, Gas Mark 6, 400°F. (200°C.).

Gooseberry Fool 1 lb. ($\frac{1}{2}$ kilo) gooseberries, 2–4 tablespoons water, 3 oz. (75 g.) sugar, $\frac{1}{2}$ pint (3 dl.) thick sweetened custard, green colouring.
Cook gooseberries with water and sugar in double saucepan until thick pulp. Sieve and mix with custard, tint pale green. Pile into glasses and serve the fool as cold as possible.

TUESDAY

Barbecued Chicken 2 tablespoons oil, crushed garlic clove, $\frac{1}{4}$ pint ($1\frac{1}{2}$ dl.) tomato purée, $\frac{1}{2}$ tablespoon Worcestershire sauce, seasoning, few drops Tabasco sauce, pinch curry or chilli powder, 1 chicken. To serve: fresh bread rolls.
Make barbecue sauce by blending oil, garlic, tomato purée, Worcestershire sauce, seasoning, Tabasco sauce, curry or chilli powder. Brush chicken with sauce. Either roast chicken in usual way, basting with sauce as it cooks, or put on spit, or cook over outside barbecue fire. When cooked, joint and serve with fresh rolls.

Mixed Salads green salad, seasoning, oil and vinegar, French beans, mayonnaise, tomato purée, tomatoes, cooked or canned corn.
Toss green salad in seasoned oil and vinegar. Mix the French beans with mayonnaise flavoured with tomato purée. Cut wedges of tomato and blend with corn and mayonnaise or oil and vinegar.

Strawberry Boats 6 oz. (150 g.) sweet shortcrust pastry (page 89), vanilla essence, sugar, whipped cream, strawberries.
Line boat-shaped tins with pastry, bake until crisp, fill with a little vanilla-flavoured sweetened whipped cream and top each boat with strawberries.

FRIDAY

Tuna Croquettes 2 oz. (50 g.) margarine, 2 oz. (50 g.) flour, $\frac{1}{2}$ pint (3 dl.) milk, seasoning, 1 teaspoon grated lemon rind, 1 tablespoon chopped parsley, 8–12 oz. (200–300 g.) flaked tuna fish, 2 oz. (50 g.) breadcrumbs. To coat: egg and crumbs.
Make sauce with margarine, flour and milk. Remove half and save for Devilled Sauce. Add seasoning to rest of sauce with lemon rind, parsley, tuna fish and breadcrumbs. Form mixture into croquettes, coat with egg and crumbs and fry until golden brown, or bake on greased tin for 10–15 minutes in hot oven, Gas Mark 7, 425°F. (220°C.).

Devilled Sauce fry 2 chopped onions in little fat, add $\frac{1}{2}$ teaspoon curry powder, 1 teaspoon Worcestershire sauce, shake cayenne pepper. Add the thick sauce, heat and gradually add another $\frac{1}{4}$ pint ($1\frac{1}{2}$ dl.) milk.

Feather Sponge Pudding berry fruit, sugar, 2 eggs, 3 oz. (75 g.) sugar, 3 oz. (75 g.) self-raising flour, 1 oz. (25 g.) melted butter.
Put layer of fruit at bottom of basin with sugar but no water. Whisk eggs and sugar until thick, fold in flour and butter. Put over fruit, cover with greased foil or paper. Steam for 1 hour.

SATURDAY

Bacon Piperade 6 oz. (150 g.) bacon, little fat, 1 onion, 1 green pepper, 2–3 tomatoes, 4–6 eggs, seasoning.
Dice bacon. Fry in a little fat in a saucepan with the chopped onion, diced green pepper and skinned chopped tomatoes. Beat the eggs with seasoning in a basin, add to the bacon mixture and scramble lightly.

Cheese Potatoes small new potatoes, butter, finely grated cheese.
Cook potatoes, strain, toss in butter and grated cheese.

Minted Apricot Whip few mint leaves, egg white, castor sugar, 1–$1\frac{1}{4}$ lb. ($\frac{1}{2}$–$\frac{5}{8}$ kilo) apricots, juice of 1 lemon, $\frac{1}{4}$ pint ($1\frac{1}{2}$ dl.) water, small bunch fresh mint tied in muslin, sugar to taste, lightly whipped cream.
Prepare mint leaves: wash, dry and brush with egg white, then sprinkle with castor sugar and allow to dry. Cook apricots with lemon juice, water, mint, arrange fruit in dish, top with whipped cream and crystallised mint leaves.
Note. The egg yolk left over can be used in the Bacon Piperade, above.

Tomato and onion salad, recipe on page 9

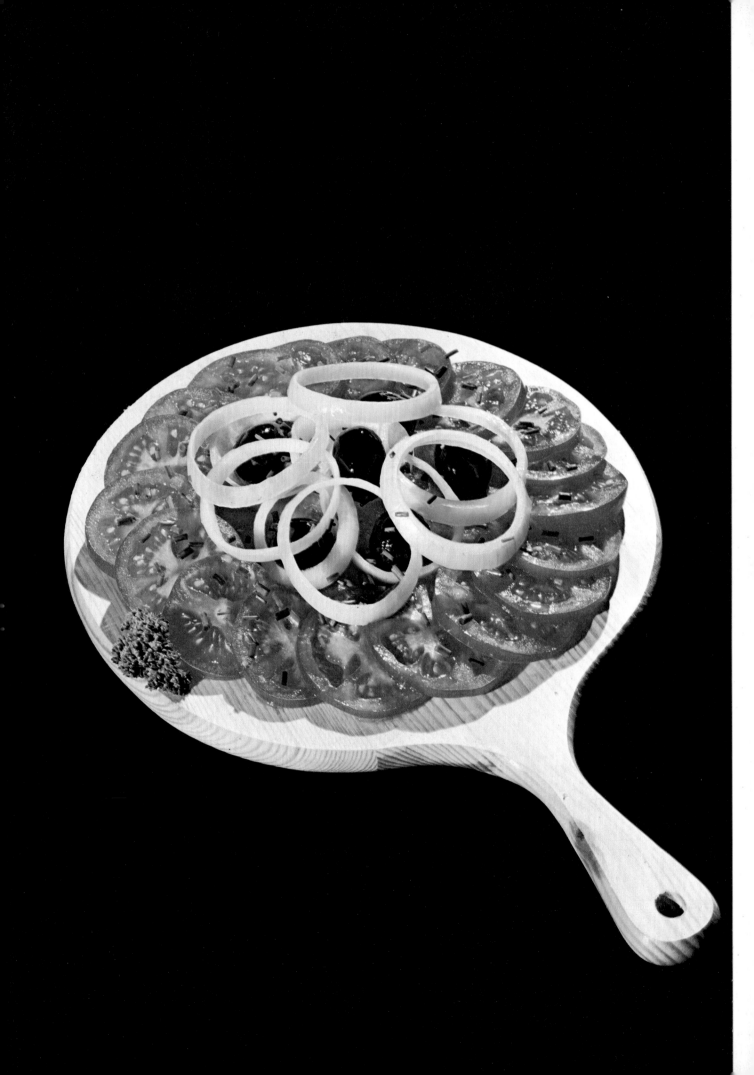

WEEK 13

Pot Roasting is an excellent way of cooking a roasting joint without using the oven. It enables you to buy a less expensive joint, i.e. topside of good quality, fresh brisket.

For your shopping list the main meals need:
13 eggs, 6 pints (3½ litres) milk, 3 oz. (75 g.) Cheddar or other cooking cheese.
Sunday and Monday need:
Beef.
Sponge cakes, cream (thick or thin).
White wine.
Potatoes, carrots, broad beans, onions, tomatoes, peas, cucumber, parsley, strawberries, oranges.
Tuesday and Wednesday need:
White fish, frankfurters.
Potatoes, broccoli, lettuce, cucumber (unless left from Monday), green salad ingredients, lemon, fresh fruit.
Thursday, Friday and Saturday need:
Steak, cooked tongue (keep well wrapped to prevent drying).
Chocolate, thin cream (optional).
Potatoes, onions, mixed salad ingredients (including tomatoes), parsley, beetroot, chives (optional), spring onions, watercress, root vegetables.

SUNDAY

Pot Roasted Beef fat, joint roasting beef, seasoning, potatoes, large carrots, stock.
Heat knob of fat in large pan. Brown joint in this on either side — topside fits into pan well. Lift meat on to a bed of whole, lightly-seasoned potatoes, large carrots, if meat is about 3 lb. (1½ kilos) in weight. If more than 3 lb. (1½ kilos), the vegetables must be very large or meat should first be put on a trivet and vegetables added during cooking. Add enough stock to give 1 inch (2½ cm.) liquid. Put very tightly-fitting lid on pan, cook over moderate heat for 25–30 minutes for each 1 lb. (½ kilo) of meat, i.e. 3 lb. (1½ kilos) would take 1¼ hours for medium cooked beef, 1½ hours for well done. Use stock for gravy. This is an ideal way of cooking meat to save using an oven.

Creamed Broad Beans broad beans, white sauce, recipe page 5, chopped onion or chives.
Cook beans, stir into white sauce flavoured with a little chopped onion or chives.

Strawberry Trifle sponge cakes, strawberries, sugar, white wine, custard.
Split sponge cakes, fill with crushed sweetened strawberries, put into a dish or sundae glasses, see picture page 51, moisten with wine. Top with strawberries, custard, etc.

WEDNESDAY

Frankfurter Flan 6–8 oz. (150–200 g.) shortcrust pastry, see page 10, 2 eggs, seasoning, ½ pint (3 dl.) milk, 3 oz. (75 g.) grated Cheddar cheese, 8 small frankfurter sausages. To serve: green salad.
Line 8–9-inch (20–23-cm.) tin or flan ring with pastry. Beat eggs with seasoning, add milk and grated cheese. Arrange sausages in pastry case, add cheese custard mixture, cook for 40–50 minutes in centre of a hot oven, Gas Mark 6, 400°F. (200°C.), reducing heat to moderate after first 20 minutes. Serve hot or cold with green salad.

Potatoes Anna 1–1¼ lb. (½–⅝ kilo) potatoes, seasoning, melted margarine or butter.
Peel or scrape potatoes, wash and dry, cut into wafer-thin slices. Pack in layers in well greased 5–6-inch (13–15-cm.) cake tin, seasoning each layer and brushing with little margarine or butter. Cook for 1¼ hours in centre of oven. Turn out carefully.

Junket 1 pint (6 dl.) milk, 1 tablespoon sugar, ½ teaspoon vanilla essence, 2 teaspoons rennet, grated nutmeg.
Bring milk to blood heat only with sugar and vanilla essence, stir in rennet. Pour into 4 dishes, leave undisturbed in room temperature to clot. Top each junket with grated nutmeg.

THURSDAY

Steak Patties 1 lb. (½ kilo) rump steak, 1 medium onion, 1 small potato, ½ teaspoon herbs, 1 egg, seasoning, fat for frying. To serve: buttered rolls, mixed salad.
Mince steak, mix with grated onion, grated potato, herbs and egg. Season well. Form into 4 rounds, fry steadily on both sides. Serve on halved, buttered rolls with mixed salad.

Floating Islands 1 pint (6 dl.) milk, 3 oz. (75 g.) sugar, ½ teaspoon vanilla essence, 2 eggs.
Heat milk in frying pan with 1 oz. (25 g.) sugar and vanilla essence (or use vanilla-flavoured sugar). Whisk egg whites until very stiff, gradually beat in remaining sugar. Drop spoonfuls of this meringue mixture on to hot milk, cook for 3 minutes; turn over and cook meringue balls for 2 minutes on second side, then lift on to wire sieve and drain. Strain milk over beaten egg yolks, cook in double saucepan until custard coats back of wooden spoon. Pour into dish and top with meringue balls.

Baked apples, recipe on page 11   Fruit jelly, recipe on page 39
Lattice tart, recipe on page 41

MONDAY

Durham Cutlets 2 oz. (50 g.) fat, 1 onion, 2 tomatoes, 1 oz. (25 g.) flour, ¼ pint (1½ dl.) well seasoned brown stock, pinch herbs, 12 oz. (300 g.) minced cooked beef from Sunday (raw meat can be used), 2 oz. (50 g.) breadcrumbs. To coat: egg, crisp crumbs.
Heat fat in pan, fry chopped onion, skinned tomatoes, stir in flour, cook for 2–3 minutes. Add stock and herbs. Bring to the boil, cook until thickened then add cooked beef (or raw meat) and breadcrumbs. Form mixture into cutlet shapes, coat in egg and crumbs, fry until brown. Drain and serve cold.

Rice Salad cooked long grain rice, mayonnaise, cooked peas, grated raw carrot, cucumber, parsley.
Toss rice in mayonnaise, add peas, carrot, diced cucumber and chopped parsley.

Chocolate Mould chocolate blancmange powder, milk, sugar, 2 teaspoons finely grated orange rind, 4 tablespoons orange juice. To serve: cream.
Make blancmange as directed on packet, using 4 tablespoons less milk. Cool slightly, whisk in orange rind and juice. Put into mould to set, turn out and serve with cream.

TUESDAY

Fish Mould 1 lb. (½ kilo) cooked white fish, 1 oz. (25 g.) flour, 1 oz. (25 g.) fat, ½ pint (3 dl.) milk, ½ tablespoon powdered gelatine, 2 tablespoons hot water, seasoning, few drops anchovy essence, 1 hard-boiled egg, 1 teaspoon grated lemon rind, 1 tablespoon lemon juice, 2 egg whites. To serve: lettuce, sliced cucumber.
Stir flaked fish into white sauce made with flour, fat, milk, then add gelatine dissolved in hot water. Season, flavour with anchovy essence, add chopped hard-boiled egg, lemon rind, lemon juice and stiffly beaten egg whites. Put into basin or mould; when set turn out on bed of lettuce and sliced cucumber.

Broccoli and Hollandaise Sauce fresh or frozen broccoli, 2 left-over egg yolks, ½ level teaspoon made-mustard, pinch salt and pepper, 1 tablespoon lemon juice, 2 oz. (50 g.) butter.
Cook broccoli and serve with *Hollandaise Sauce*. To made this, put egg yolks in basin with mustard, salt and pepper. Add lemon juice, whisk over hot water until thick. Slowly whisk in butter, adding small knob at a time, until blended into sauce.

Follow this meal with fresh fruit.

FRIDAY

Golden Crusted Loaf small sandwich loaf, melted margarine, 1 oz. (25 g.) margarine, 1 oz. (25 g.) flour, ½ pint (3 dl.) milk, seasoning, can sweetcorn, 2 teaspoons chopped parsley, 2 hard-boiled eggs, medium can tuna or salmon.
Cut crust from long side of loaf, scoop out crumb, make into breadcrumbs; save few for Saturday, crisp rest in oven for coating. Brush inside of loaf case with melted margarine, crisp for 15 minutes in a hot oven, Gas Mark 6, 400°F. (200°C.). Make white sauce with margarine, flour, milk, add seasoning, corn, parsley, chopped egg whites, flaked fish. Put into bread case, top with chopped egg yolks.

Hot Beetroot dice cooked beetroot, heat in a little melted margarine with chopped parsley or chives.

Choco Fingers 3 oz. (75 g.) butter, 2 oz. (50 g.) brown sugar, 1 egg, 4 oz. (100 g.) flour, 2 oz. (50 g.) chocolate powder, 2 oz. (50 g.) castor sugar, 3 oz. (75 g.) desiccated coconut, ½ tablespoon water, 2–4 oz. (50–100 g.) melted chocolate.
Cream butter with brown sugar, add egg yolk, flour and chocolate powder. Press into oblong; chill. Mix egg white, castor sugar, coconut and water. Spread over base, bake in moderate oven for 20–25 minutes. Top with melted chocolate.

SATURDAY

Stuffed Tongue Rolls 2 tablespoons fine breadcrumbs, 2 large tomatoes, 1 tablespoon chopped spring onions, seasoning, 8 thin slices cooked tongue. To serve: watercress.
Blend breadcrumbs with skinned chopped tomatoes, spring onion and seasoning. Spread over tongue and roll; serve on a bed of watercress.

Egg and Russian Salad cook mixture of diced root vegetables, strain, toss in mayonnaise, garnish with sliced hard-boiled egg.

Bavarian Cream 1 lemon jelly, ½ pint (3 dl.) plus ¼ pint (1½ dl.) water, 1 level teaspoon powdered gelatine, ½ pint (3 dl.) evaporated milk or thin cream.
Dissolve jelly in ½ pint water only. Add further ¼ pint water to half of jelly only and pour into bottom of plain mould. Allow to set. Blend gelatine with rest of jelly — which should be kept warm. Allow to cool then add to evaporated milk or thin cream. Pour over set jelly. When set, turn out of mould.
To whip evaporated milk: boil can in water for 15 minutes, chill well then whip. 1 teaspoon powdered gelatine softened in 1 tablespoon cold water can be dissolved in the hot evaporated milk.

Week 14

Sunday

Gammon steaks can be cooked in the oven instead of under the grill (see Sunday's menu). This is a method needing less attention than cooking under the grill. Take care the gammon steaks are not over-cooked and keep them moist with butter.

For your shopping list the main meals need:
10 or 12 eggs (if making sponge), generous 1 pint (generous ½ litre) milk, 9–10 oz. (225–250 g.) Cheddar or other cooking cheese.

Sunday, Monday and Tuesday need:
Gammon, chickens.
Thick cream.
New potatoes, peas, tomatoes (some large), spring onions, radishes, lettuce, parsley, mushrooms (store carefully), dessert apple, fruit for jelly.

Wednesday and Thursday need:
Mackerel, lamb chops.
Fudge, ice cream.
Potatoes, rosemary or garlic, green peppers, tomatoes, onions, gooseberries, pears (optional).

Friday and Saturday need:
Minced beef.
Soft rolls, sponge cake (if not baking this), wafer biscuits, thick cream.
Onions, garlic, tomatoes, lettuce, cucumber, carrots, marrow, raspberries and strawberries, blackcurrants.

Oven Baked Gammon and Pineapple butter, 4 1-inch (2½-cm.) thick gammon slices*, 4 pineapple rings. To serve: new potatoes, peas.
*plus extra slice gammon for Monday's salad or use cheaper boiled bacon.
Butter a sheet of aluminium foil, arrange gammon slices on this, brush with melted butter. Cook for 20 minutes towards top of hot oven, Gas Mark 7, 425°F. (220°C.), then put pineapple rings over gammon slices, brushing with a little melted butter; heat for a further 10 minutes. Serve with new potatoes and peas. Cook extra potatoes and peas for Monday.

Coffee Chiffon Pie 6 oz. (150 g.) shortcrust pastry (page 10), ½ level tablespoon powdered gelatine, 4 tablespoons water, ½ pint (3 dl.) hot strong coffee, 3 oz. (75 g.) sugar, 2 eggs, ¼ pint (1½ dl.) thick cream. To decorate: halved walnuts, thick cream.
Line 1-pint (6-dl.) pie dish with pastry, bake 'blind' (page 10) in a hot oven until brown and crisp. Soften gelatine in cold water, add to coffee and sugar, stir until dissolved then whisk on to beaten egg yolks. Leave until cool and beginning to thicken, fold in whipped cream and stiffly beaten egg whites. Spoon into cool pastry case and decorate with walnuts and cream.

Wednesday

Baked Mackerel 4 large or 8 small mackerel, seasoning, margarine or butter.
Remove heads from mackerel, split, clean and remove backbones. Season the fish, put into a greased dish. Put margarine or butter on top of fish; put on lid. Bake for approximately 30–35 minutes towards top of moderate oven, Gas Mark 4, 350°F. (180°C.).

Gooseberry Sauce good 8–12 oz. (200–300 g.) green gooseberries, ¼ pint (1½ dl.) water, 1–2 oz. (25–50 g.) sugar, ½ oz. (15 g.) butter.
Simmer gooseberries with water until soft. Sieve, then reheat with sugar and butter.

Cheese Shortbreads 2½ oz. (65 g.) margarine, seasoning, 1½ oz. (40 g.) finely grated cheese, 4 oz. (100 g.) self-raising flour.
Cream margarine with seasoning and cheese; work in flour. Roll into 12 balls, flatten slightly, put on to greased baking tins, allowing plenty of space for mixture to spread. Bake for 15 minutes in centre of moderate oven, cool on tin for 5 minutes. Serve with cheese.

Thursday

Lamb Noisettes 4 large or 8 small lamb chops, seasoning, little chopped fresh rosemary or crushed garlic.
Ask butcher to bone chops. Roll meat to form neat rounds, secure with small skewers or tie with fine string. Season lightly, flavour with rosemary or crushed garlic. Bake for 25–30 minutes towards top of a hot oven, Gas Mark 6, 400°F. (200°C.).

Green Pepper and Tomato Bake 2 medium green peppers, 1 lb. (½ kilo) tomatoes, 2 large onions, seasoning, 1 oz. (25 g.) margarine.
Slice peppers, removing cores and seeds. Skin and thinly slice tomatoes and onions. Grease shallow casserole, arrange vegetables in layers, beginning and ending with tomatoes; season each layer well. Top with margarine, cover casserole, bake in coolest part of oven for 1¼ hours.

Fudge Ice Cream Sundae 4 oz. (100 g.) vanilla fudge, 2 tablespoons milk, vanilla ice cream, slices canned or fresh pears.
Put fudge into basin with milk. Heat slowly over pan of boiling water. Allow sauce to cool. Arrange ice cream with slices of pear, top with sauce.

MONDAY

Stuffed Tomato Cups left-over gammon steak or cold boiled bacon, 1 dessert apple, 1 tablespoon chopped spring onion, 1 tablespoon sliced radishes, 8 tomatoes, seasoning. To serve: lettuce, green peas.
Dice gammon steak or boiled bacon, mix with peeled, diced apple, spring onion and radishes. Halve tomatoes, scoop out pulp, chop, mix with gammon mixture, season well and pile into seasoned tomato cases. Serve on bed of lettuce and garnish with peas.

Potato Salad dice potatoes left from Sunday and mix with mayonnaise, chopped spring onion and chopped parsley.

Fresh Fruit Jelly 1 jelly, just under 1 pint (6 dl.) water, 8 oz. (¼ kilo) fresh fruits.
Dissolve jelly in the water, cool slightly, then add fresh fruits in season, such as raw red or blackcurrants, strawberries, etc.
Segments of cooked apple and raw ripe blackberries are used in the blackcurrant jelly shown on page 35.
If the fruit is rather soft and juicy make sure you use under the 1 pint (6 dl.) water.
Raw pineapple is the only fruit that cannot be used in a jelly; it prevents the jelly setting.

TUESDAY

Grilled Chicken 2 small chickens, melted butter or oil, seasoning, tomatoes, mushrooms, little fat. To serve: spinach or other green vegetable.
Halve chickens, brush with melted butter or oil, season lightly. Put on grid of grill pan. Place seasoned halved tomatoes, mushrooms and little fat in grill pan. Grill chicken quickly until brown, lower heat, continue cooking for approximately 10–15 minutes. Serve with spinach or other vegetable.

Caramel Meringue 4 oz. (100 g.) granulated sugar, 4 tablespoons water, 1 pint (6 dl.) milk, 2 eggs, 3 oz. (75 g.) sugar, 2 oz. (50 g.) fine breadcrumbs.
Stir granulated sugar and water in strong pan until sugar is dissolved, boil rapidly until golden brown caramel. Cool slightly, add milk and heat slowly, stirring well, until caramel is dissolved. Pour milk over egg yolks beaten with 1 oz. (25 g.) sugar and bread-crumbs. Pour into 7-inch (18-cm.) soufflé dish, cover with greased foil; steam gently for 1 hour, or set for just over 1 hour in very moderate oven, Gas Mark 3, 325°F., (170°C.). Whip egg whites until stiff, fold in remaining sugar, pile over sweet, then brown either for a few minutes under a low grill while serving chicken, or for 15 minutes in the oven.

FRIDAY

Hasty Pizza 4 large soft rolls, little oil, 1 onion, 1 garlic clove, 1 tablespoon oil, 1 lb. (½ kilo) tomatoes, season-ing, ½ teaspoon marjoram, anchovy fillets, grated cheese.
Cut rolls in half; brush cut tops with little oil. Fry finely chopped onion and crushed garlic in oil, add skinned chopped tomatoes, seasoning, marjoram. Cover rolls with this, arrange anchovy fillets over, and thick layer grated cheese, heat for few minutes in hot oven. Serve with mixed salads (as below).

Stuffed Hard-Boiled Egg Salad halve hard-boiled eggs, mash yolks, blend with little mayonnaise, anchovy essence, pile back into white cases, serve on lettuce, with sliced cucumber.

Carrot and Cheese Salad blend equal amounts of grated carrot and cheese and bind with mayonnaise.

Raspberry and Strawberry Mousse 4 oz. (100 g.) raspberries, 4 oz. (100 g.) strawberries, 1 raspberry jelly, ½ pint (3 dl.) hot water, 1 oz. (25 g.) sugar, 2 egg whites.
Rub fruit through a sieve. Dissolve jelly in hot water, add sugar, then fruit purée. Allow to stiffen slightly, fold in stiffly beaten egg whites. Pile into shallow dish.

SATURDAY

Stuffed Marrow Rings 1 onion, 2 tomatoes, little fat, 12 oz. (300 g.) minced beef, seasoning, 2 egg yolks (left from Friday), pinch herbs, rings of marrow.
Fry chopped onion and skinned tomatoes in the fat, add minced beef, seasoning, egg yolks and herbs. Steam de-seeded and peeled marrow rings for 5 minutes. Arrange in greased dish, top with meat mixture, cover with greased foil, bake for 45 minutes in moderately hot oven, Gas Mark 5, 375°F. (190°C.).

Fruit Gâteau home-made or bought sponge cake, fruit, whipped cream.
Fill and top the sponge cake with fruit and cream.

Wafer Blackcurrant Gâteau the picture on page 58 shows a particularly interesting gâteau. Prepare a sponge mixture. Cream 4 oz. (100 g.) margarine, 4 oz. (100 g.) castor sugar, gradually beat in 2 large eggs, then fold in 4 oz. (100 g.) self-raising flour (or plain flour and 1 teaspoon baking powder). Put into one greased and floured 8–9-inch (20–23-cm.) shallow cake tin. Bake for approximately 20 minutes in a moderate oven. When cool, split and fill with fruit and cream. Coat sides and top with whipped cream. Decorate sides with halved wafer biscuits and the top with fruit and cream.

WEEK 15

Vichyssoise is one of the most appetising of cold soups. If you wish to make this as a hot dish, increase the amount of onion so it has a more definite flavour. A Summer Pudding needs plenty of bread, so check your supply on Tuesday.

For your shopping list the main meals need:
18–19 eggs, 2 pints (generous 1 litre) milk (more if making custard on Wednesday), 8 oz. (200 g.) Cheddar or other cooking cheese or cream cheese.
Sunday and Monday need:
Stewing veal, ham or piece bacon.
Ice cream (optional), cream (thick or thin).
New potatoes, leeks, onions, chives, green salad ingredients, lemon, strawberries, red and blackcurrants.
Tuesday, Wednesday and Thursday need:
Lambs' kidneys, cooked ham, frying chicken.
Cream (thick *and* thin).
Potatoes, mushrooms, parsley or rosemary, tomatoes (some large), lettuce, fruit for Cream Ring, raspberries and loganberries, fruit for omelette (optional).
Friday and Saturday need:
White fish, mussels (optional), shrimps, minced beef.
Cream (thick or thin).
Potatoes, mint, lettuce, onion, fresh herbs, mixed salad ingredients, oranges and grapefruit (optional), raspberries.

SUNDAY

Vichyssoise 2 or 3 leeks, 1 small onion, 2 medium potatoes, 1 pint (6 dl.) well seasoned chicken stock (or water and stock cubes), ½ pint (3 dl.) milk, little cream or white wine. To garnish: chopped chives.
Simmer chopped leeks, onion and potatoes in chicken stock for 35 minutes. Sieve, cool, add milk and cream, or use part milk and part white wine. Pour into cold soup cups, garnish with chopped chives.

Veal and Ham Pie 1½ lb. (¾ kilo) stewing veal, 8 oz. (200 g.) ham or boiled bacon, seasoning, little finely grated lemon rind, 3–4 hard-boiled eggs, 8 tablespoons stock, 6–8 oz. (150–200 g.) shortcrust or flaky pastry, pages 10 and 137. To glaze: 1 egg yolk.
Dice meats. Roll veal in seasoning and lemon rind. Put meats into pie dish with eggs and stock; cover with pastry. Glaze with beaten egg yolk. Bake in centre of hot oven, Gas Mark 7, 425°F. (220°C.), for 30 minutes. Lower heat to very moderate, cook for 1 hour.

Strawberry Almond Shortbread cream 6 oz. (150 g.) margarine and 6 oz. (150 g.) castor sugar. Add 4 egg whites (save 3 yolks for Monday), 2 oz. (50 g.) ground almonds and 10 oz. (250 g.) plain flour.
Press nearly two-thirds mixture into greased 8–9-inch (20–23-cm.) tin. Bake for 35–40 minutes in very moderate oven. Press rest into second tin and bake for 20–25 minutes. Mark into sections while warm; cool, dust with icing sugar. Top as picture page 51.

WEDNESDAY

Toadstool Eggs and Salad 4 hard-boiled eggs, 2 large tomatoes, mayonnaise, small lettuce leaves, tomatoes.
Cut a thin slice from ends of hard-boiled eggs so they stand easily. Cut a slice from each side of tomatoes. Balance these on eggs. Dot with mayonnaise to look like toadstools. Garnish with lettuce leaves, pieces of egg and thinly sliced tomatoes.

Ham Boats 4–6 oz. (100–150 g.) cooked ham, ¼ pint (1½ dl.) white sauce, see page 5, boat-shaped cases (make Tuesday) *or* bridge rolls.
Chop ham finely, blend with white sauce. Put into boat-shaped cases. Serve cold or heat gently. If liked, split bridge rolls, scoop out little of the crumb. Heat in oven for few minutes then fill.

*Summer Pudding line bottom and sides of basin with thin slices crustless bread. Mix few raspberries and loganberries with cooked currants from Monday, sweeten well. Pour into basin, cover with bread. Put saucer and weight on top; leave overnight. Turn out, serve with custard or cream. See picture page 98. Any fruit can be used for this pudding but fruit with red or dark juice gives a more attractive result.

THURSDAY

Stuffed Chicken Joints 4 joints frying chicken, packet sage and onion stuffing, butter or fat.
Make a 'pocket' in each chicken joint. Make stuffing as instructions. Insert into chicken, fry or grill for approximately 15–20 minutes.

Speedy Mushroom Sauce make sauce by using packet sauce mix or small can mushroom soup.

Sweet Omelette 4 eggs, ½–1 oz. (15–25 g.) sugar, 2 tablespoons milk, 1 oz. (25 g.) melted butter. Filling: fruit purée or jam, icing sugar.
Separate eggs; beat yolks with sugar and milk. Fold in stiffly beaten whites. Cook in frying pan in melted butter until bottom is set, then cook on top under low grill. Fill with fruit purée or jam, fold, then dust with icing sugar.

MONDAY

Cheese and Tomato Shape $\frac{3}{4}$ oz. (20 g.) powdered gelatine, 1 pint (6 dl.) tomato juice, seasoning, 3 egg yolks, 8 oz. (200 g.) cream cheese or finely grated Cheddar cheese, 3 tablespoons hot water, $\frac{1}{4}$ pint (1$\frac{1}{2}$ dl.) milk or evaporated milk, $\frac{1}{2}$ tablespoon chopped chives. To serve: green salad.
Dissolve $\frac{1}{2}$ oz. (15 g.) gelatine in tomato juice. Season well. Pour half into mould, basin or loaf tin. Allow to set. Keep other half in warm place so it remains a liquid. Beat egg yolks into cheese (add 1 tablespoon cream if using Cheddar). Dissolve remaining gelatine in hot water, add milk. Gradually beat liquid into cheese mixture until a smooth cream; taste, add seasoning and chives. Pour over tomato layer, leave until firm, cover with remaining tomato and gelatine mixture. When set, turn out on to green salad.

Potato and Olive Salad dice cooked, warm new potatoes, mix with sliced olives and mayonnaise.

Compote of Red and Blackcurrants make syrup of $\frac{1}{2}$ pint (3 dl.) water and 4 oz. (100 g.) sugar; add 2 lb. (1 kilo) mixed red and blackcurrants. Cook for 2–3 minutes until fruit is soft. Reserve half juice and good one-third of fruit for Summer Pudding. Serve rest in glasses topped with ice cream or cream.

TUESDAY

Kidney and Mushroom Flan 6–8 oz. (150–200 g.) shortcrust pastry, page 10, 4 lambs' kidneys, 1 oz. (25 g.) butter, 2–4 oz. (50–100 g.) sliced mushrooms, 2 egg yolks, $\frac{1}{4}$ pint (1$\frac{1}{2}$ dl.) milk, seasoning, little chopped parsley or rosemary, tomato.
Line 8-inch (20-cm.) flan ring with pastry. Also make pastry boats for Wednesday. Bake 'blind' in hot oven, Gas Mark 7, 425°F. (220°C.), for 15 minutes only until pastry is set but still pale. Skin kidneys, slice thinly, toss in butter with sliced mushrooms. Beat egg yolks with milk, seasoning and parsley or rosemary, mix with kidneys and mushrooms. Spoon into flan case, return to centre of moderately hot oven, Gas Mark 6, 400°F. (200°C.), for about 25 minutes until filling is just set. Garnish with tomato.

Bavarian Cream Ring 1 raspberry jelly, $\frac{1}{2}$ pint (3 dl.) water, $\frac{1}{4}$ pint (1$\frac{1}{2}$ dl.) thin cream or top of milk, $\frac{1}{4}$ pint (1$\frac{1}{2}$ dl.) whipped cream or evaporated milk, 2 egg whites, fruit.
Dissolve jelly in water, cool, add to cream or top of milk; allow to thicken very slightly. Fold in whipped cream or evaporated milk and stiffly beaten egg whites. Put into ring mould. When set, turn out; fill centre with fruit.

*Make Summer Pudding today for Wednesday.

FRIDAY

Minted Orange Juice Cocktail mix equal quantities of fresh or canned orange juice and grapefruit juice, top with mint. Serve very cold.

Fish Rolls 8 small fillets whiting, plaice or sole, little melted butter, 16 cooked mussels *or* anchovy paste, little butter, milk.
Wash and dry fish. Brush with melted butter. Put either mussels or a spoonful anchovy paste on buttered side; roll firmly. Secure with cocktail sticks. Bake in covered dish with little butter and milk for 20 minutes in moderate to moderately hot oven, Gas Mark 5–6, 375–400°F. (190–200°C.). Serve with anchovy sauce, below.

Anchovy Sauce 1 oz. (25 g.) margarine, 1 oz. (25 g.) flour, $\frac{1}{2}$ pint (3 dl.) milk, few drops anchovy essence, seasoning.
Heat the margarine, stir in the flour and cook for 2–3 minutes. Gradually blend in the milk, bring to the boil and stir until thickened. Add the anchovy essence and seasoning.

Lattice Tart use your chosen pastry, line a pie plate with this. Prick, bake 'blind' until just set. Top with fruit and sugar, thin strips of pastry; return to the oven and continue cooking, see picture page 35.

SATURDAY

Shrimp Cocktail 1 lettuce, shrimps, mayonnaise, tomato purée or ketchup, few drops Worcestershire or Tabasco sauce.
Put finely shredded lettuce in glasses. Top with shrimps in mayonnaise, flavoured with tomato purée or ketchup and Worcestershire or Tabasco sauce.

Savoury Galantine and Salad 4 oz. (100 g.) long grain rice, seasoning, 1 lb. ($\frac{1}{2}$ kilo) minced beef, 1 onion, 1 oz. (25 g.) fat, 1 teaspoon chopped fresh herbs, 1 egg. To serve: mixed salad.
Cook rice in boiling salted water. Save half for Sunday. Mix rest with minced beef, chopped onion fried in fat, seasoning, herbs and egg. Press into greased loaf tin. Bake for 1 hour in very moderate oven, Gas Mark 3, 325°F. (170°C.). Cool, turn out on to bed of mixed salad.

Raspberries and Cream sprinkle fruit lightly with sugar some time before serving to bring out the flavour.

Steak and onion pie, recipe on page 71   Roast sirloin of beef with horseradish puddings, recipe on page 118

WEEK 16

Scotch eggs are an old-established favourite with most families. The recipe for Wednesday gives a cheese instead of a sausagemeat coating to the eggs. It is an excellent way of using a piece of Cheddar cheese that has become stale.

For your shopping list the main meals need:
14–15 eggs, 2 pints (generous 1 litre) milk, 13 oz. (325 g.) Cheddar or other cooking cheese, also some cream cheese or cream cheese spread.

Sunday, Monday and Tuesday need:
Veal, bacon rashers, sausagemeat, lamb cutlets.
Potatoes, parsley, onion or chives, fresh herbs, turnips, swedes, carrots, beans, peas, tomatoes, spring onions, beetroot, cucumber, lemons, summer fruits or soft fruits, oranges.

Wednesday and Thursday need:
Chicken.
Cream (thick *and* thin – both optional).
Potatoes, cucumber, parsley, chives, onions, bay leaves, rosemary, dessert apples, oranges, bananas, fresh fruit or strawberries.

Friday and Saturday need:
Herrings.
Chocolate, cream (thick or thin).
New potatoes, onion, beetroot, mixed salad, dessert apple, blackcurrants.

SUNDAY

Rice Stuffed Veal and Forcemeat Balls 2 large rashers bacon, 1 tablespoon chopped parsley, 1 tablespoon chopped onion or chives, seasoning, 1 egg, cooked rice, boned breast of veal *or* meat cut from fillet, fat, 2 teaspoons chopped fresh herbs, 8 oz. (200 g.) pork sausagemeat.
Add chopped bacon, parsley, onion or chives, seasoning and egg to the rice. Spread over meat, roll firmly. Weigh; put in roasting tin with generous amount fat, cover with foil, cook for 25–30 minutes per lb. (½ kilo) and 25 minutes over in hot oven, Gas Mark 7, 425°F. (220°C.). Lift off foil for last 25 minutes. Blend herbs with sausagemeat, roll in balls, put round meat for last 25 minutes. Serve with as large a selection of young diced vegetables as possible.

Lemon Meringue Pie 6 oz. (150 g.) shortcrust pastry, page 10, ½ oz. (15 g.) cornflour, 2 lemons, 1 oz. (25 g.) butter, 6 oz. (150 g.) castor sugar, 2 eggs.
Line deep flan ring with pastry, bake 'blind' for 25 minutes, see page 10. Blend cornflour with grated lemon rind and juice made up to ½ pint (3 dl.) with water. Put in pan, bring to boil, stir and cook for 1–2 minutes with butter and 2 oz. (50 g.) sugar. Cool, stir in egg yolks. Put into pastry case. Add rest of sugar gradually to stiffly whisked egg whites. Pile on filling, put into oven, Gas Mark ½–1, 250–275°F. (130–140°C.), for 1 hour.

WEDNESDAY

Cheese Scotch Eggs 4 hard-boiled eggs, little butter, 1 oz. (25 g.) grated cheese, seasoning, 12 oz. (300 g.) finely grated Cheddar cheese, 3 oz. (75 g.) flour, 1 egg, Worcestershire sauce. To coat: 1 egg, crisp crumbs, fat for frying.
Shell eggs, halve, blend yolks with butter, 1 oz. (25 g.) grated cheese, seasoning, return to white cases, press halves together. Mix the 12 oz. (300 g.) cheese with flour, egg, seasoning and few drops Worcestershire sauce. Divide in 4, wrap around eggs, using damp hands. Coat with beaten egg and crumbs, fry 2–3 minutes only in hot fat; drain.

Stuffed Cucumber 2 egg yolks from Tuesday, 2 tablespoons milk, seasoning, chopped parsley, chopped chives, cucumber.
Pour water off egg yolks, mix with milk, season, scramble lightly, adding parsley, chives. Cut rings of cucumber, remove little of centre, chop, add to egg mixture, pile into cucumber rings.

Fruit Cocktail Whip grate 2 peeled dessert apples. Dice pulp from 2 oranges, slice 2 bananas thinly. Mix into ¼ pint (1½ dl.) sweetened whipped cream or evaporated milk.

THURSDAY

Chicken Supreme 1 boiling chicken, salt, water, 2 onions, bay leaf or sprig rosemary.
Simmer chicken slowly in salted water, adding onions, bay leaf or rosemary to flavour. Allow a good 30 minutes per lb. (½ kilo) and 30 minutes over for older bird. Serve slices from breast and wings (save legs) and coat with:

Hard-Boiled Egg and Chive Sauce 1 oz. (25 g.) butter, 1 oz. (25 g.) flour, ¼ pint (1½ dl.) milk, ¼ pint (1½ dl.) chicken stock, 2 tablespoons cream or top of milk, 1–2 hard-boiled eggs, 1 tablespoon chopped chives.
Make a white sauce using butter, flour, milk and chicken stock, add cream or top of milk, chopped eggs and chives.

Cheese and Fresh Fruit serve fresh strawberries and cream cheese or cream cheese spread.

Steak and kidney pie, recipe on page 20

MONDAY

Tomato Meat Mould meat left from Sunday, equal amount cooked potatoes, 6 large tomatoes, seasoning, chopped chives or spring onion, little mayonnaise.
Make on Sunday or early Monday. Dice meat and potatoes; skin and slice tomatoes. Put layer of tomatoes into basin, season, add chives or spring onion, add layer meat and potato tossed in very little mayonnaise; repeat layers, ending with tomato layer. Put plate and light weight over; leave for few hours, then turn out on to a large platter.

Mixed Salad surround mould with neat piles diced beetroot mixed with chopped chives or onion; any cooked vegetables tossed in mayonnaise and mixed with diced cucumber.

Summer Fruit Sponge good 8 oz. (200 g.) any summer fruits, sugar, ½ pint (3 dl.) water, ½ oz. (15 g.) gelatine, 2 eggs, ¼ pint (1½ dl.) lightly whipped evaporated milk.
Cook fruits with sugar to taste and water. Sieve to give thin purée. Soften gelatine in little of this, heat rest, pour over gelatine, stir until dissolved; pour on to whisked egg yolks, mix well, cool. When beginning to thicken, fold in evaporated milk and stiffly beaten egg whites. Pile into glasses.

TUESDAY

Lamb Cutlets in Orange Sauce 1–2 lamb cutlets per person, ¼ pint (1½ dl.) orange juice, 1 dessertspoon grated orange rind, pinch salt, pepper, sugar, nutmeg, 1 teaspoon vinegar.
Put cutlets into greased ovenproof dish. Blend orange juice with orange rind, salt, pepper, sugar, nutmeg and vinegar. Pour over cutlets, cover dish, bake for 1 hour in very moderate oven, Gas Mark 3, 325°F. (170°C.).

Nut Fingers 2 oz. (50 g.) margarine, 4 oz. (100 g.) sugar, 4 oz. (100 g.) crushed cornflakes, little jam, 2 egg whites, 1 oz. (25 g.) chocolate powder, ½ oz. (15 g.) cornflour, 2 oz. (50 g.) chopped nuts.
Cream margarine with 2 oz. (50 g.) sugar, add crushed cornflakes. Press over base and sides of a pie plate to form a flan shape. Spread bottom with little jam. Whisk egg whites, add 2 oz. (50 g.) sugar, chocolate powder, cornflour and nuts. Spread over jam. Cook for 25–30 minutes in coolest part of oven.

Cover yolks with cold water for Wednesday.

FRIDAY

Soused Herrings 4 large or 8 small herrings, 1 sliced onion, ½–1 tablespoon pickling spice, 1 bay leaf, seasoning, 1 teaspoon sugar, ¼ pint (1½ dl.) vinegar, ¼ pint (1½ dl.) water.
Remove heads, backbones and intestines from fish, wash and dry, then roll towards tail. Put into dish with onion, pickling spice, bay leaf, seasoning and sugar. Add vinegar and water. Cover dish and bake in oven Gas Mark 1, 275°F. (140°C.) for about 1 hour; cool. Serve with:

Piquant Cucumber Salad mix diced cucumber with 1 diced dessert apple, small diced beetroot, several chopped spring onions, oil, vinegar, seasoning.

Blackcurrant Pudding 3–4 oz. (75–100 g.) shredded suet, pinch salt, 8 oz. (200 g.) self-raising flour, water to bind, 1 lb. (½ kilo) blackcurrants, 2 tablespoons water, 2–3 oz. (50–75 g.) sugar. To serve: custard.
Add suet and salt to flour; bind with water. Roll out until very thin, use just over half to line a pudding basin; fill with blackcurrants, water and sugar.
Cover with suet pastry 'lid', then greased foil or paper. Steam for 1½–2 hours. Serve with custard.
Note. Plain flour, without raising agent, could be used in this recipe for a thin crust which does not rise.

SATURDAY

Chaudfroid Chicken leg joints chicken from Thursday, ½ tablespoon aspic jelly crystals, barely ¼ pint (1½ dl.) hot water, ¼ pint (1½ dl.) mayonnaise. To serve: salad.
Skin and bone chicken joints. Dissolve aspic jelly crystals in the hot water, cool, add to mayonnaise. When on the point of setting, coat the chicken and arrange on a bed of salad.

Curried Potatoes new potatoes, 2 tablespoons breadcrumbs, ½–1 teaspoon curry powder, knob of butter.
Cook potatoes, strain. Toss breadcrumbs and curry powder in the butter in pan. Stir in potatoes.

Mocha Creams chocolate blancmange powder, sugar, ½ pint (3 dl.) milk, ½ pint (3 dl.) strong coffee, little cream, grated chocolate.
Make blancmange as directed on packet, using milk and coffee. Put into glasses, top with cream and grated chocolate.

Week 17

The Timbales for Sunday's menu are a very good way to use topside of beef in an economical way. Do not over-cook the mixture otherwise the eggs and milk could separate (curdle).
If you cannot buy veal fillets for Tuesday use thin slices of lean pork instead.

For your shopping list the main meals need:
15 eggs*, ¾ pint (generous ⅜ litre) milk†, 3 oz. (75 g.) Cheddar or other cooking cheese.
*more if making sponge on Tuesday.
†less if using mayonnaise for sauce on Wednesday.
Sunday and Monday need:
Topside beef, cooked ham, thin cream or ice cream (optional), little port wine, thick cream.
Potatoes, green peppers, onions, tomatoes, mixed root vegetables, orange, lemon, fruit for filling choux.
Tuesday, Wednesday and Thursday need:
Fillets veal, white fish, prawns (store carefully), minute steaks.
Sponge cake and flan case (unless making your own), cream (thick and thin).
Potatoes, parsley, peas, carrots, mushrooms, tomatoes, green salad ingredients, chives, raspberries, fruit for pie, blackcurrants (store carefully).
Friday and Saturday need:
Fresh salmon (optional), thick cream.
Potatoes, salad ingredients, strawberries, grapefruit, fresh fruit.

Sunday

Beef Timbales 1 lb. (½ kilo) topside beef, 2 tablespoons fine breadcrumbs, ½ tablespoon horseradish cream *or* 1 teaspoon made-mustard, 2 eggs, 4 tablespoons milk, seasoning.
Mince beef; blend 12 oz. (⅜ kilo) with breadcrumbs, horseradish cream or mustard, eggs, milk. Season, put into greased dariole tins or 4 small basins. Bake for 35–40 minutes in dish of water, in centre of moderately hot oven, Gas Mark 6, 400°F. (200°C.).

Stuffed Peppers 2 green peppers, seasoning, remaining 4 oz. (100 g.) minced meat, 2 onions, 2 tomatoes, 2 oz. (50 g.) fat, 2 tablespoons fine breadcrumbs, pinch mixed herbs.
Halve peppers, remove seeds and cores, simmer in boiling salted water for 10 minutes. Drain, put into greased dish, fill with meat blended with chopped onions, skinned chopped tomatoes, both fried lightly in fat, breadcrumbs, seasoning, herbs. Cover with greased foil, bake for 40 minutes towards top of oven.

Orange Mould blend 1 pint (6 dl.) sweetened canned orange juice with 1¼ oz. (35 g.) cornflour (or packet vanilla blancmange powder). Put into pan, heat and allow to thicken slowly, stirring all the time. Taste, add extra sugar if wished. Put into mould rinsed in cold water. Turn out when set. Serve with thin cream or ice cream.

Wednesday

Savoury Fish Cakes 12 oz. – 1 lb. (300 g. – ½ kilo) white fish, seasoning, 8 oz. (200 g.) mashed potato, 2 teaspoons chopped parsley, 2 teaspoons diced gherkin, 1 teaspoon capers, 2 eggs, flour, crisp crumbs, fat.
Cook fish in minimum of water with salt to taste. Flake, add to mashed potato (if new potatoes do not mash easily, use packet potato), add parsley, gherkin, capers. Bind with 1 egg and form into 8 flat cakes. Coat in seasoned flour, beaten egg and crumbs. Either fry until crisp, or bake on greased tin for approximately 20 minutes towards top of a hot oven, Gas Mark 7, 425°F. (220°C.).

Prawn Sauce add 2 oz. (50 g.) chopped defrosted prawns to ½ pint (3 dl.) white sauce or, to save time, heat mayonnaise, diluted with little milk, in basin over hot water.

Mixed Fruit Pie 1–1½ lb. (½–¾ kilo) mixed summer fruits, sugar, shortcrust pastry, as recipe page 10.
Put fruits in pie dish with sugar and very little water if using soft fruits. Top with shortcrust pastry. Bake in centre of hot oven for about 30 minutes.

Thursday

Minute Steaks Garni 4 thin rump or sirloin steaks, mushrooms, tomatoes, little fat, green salad.
Buy really thin steaks. Fry or grill for 1–2 minutes on each side. Cook the mushrooms and tomatoes at the same time in a little fat. Serve with new potatoes tossed in butter or margarine and chopped chives.

Blackcurrant Flan *for sponge flan:* 2 eggs, 3 oz. (75 g.) sugar, 2 oz. (50 g.) self-raising flour, ½ tablespoon water. For filling: ½ pint (3 dl.) water, 3 oz. (75 g.) sugar, 8–12 oz. (200–300 g.) blackcurrants, 2 level teaspoons arrowroot or cornflour. To serve: cream.
Whisk eggs with sugar until thick. Fold in flour and warm water. Put into greased and floured 8-inch (20-cm.) sponge flan tin. Bake for approximately 12 minutes in hot oven, Gas Mark 7, 425°F. (220°C.). Turn out carefully. Make syrup of water and sugar; simmer fruit in this gently for few minutes. Strain fruit from syrup, cool, put into flan. Blend syrup with arrowroot or cornflour. Boil, stirring well until thickened and clear. Brush or spread over fruit. Serve with cream. A bought sponge flan can be used.
Note. You could make both the sponge cake (Tuesday) and sponge flan together. Store flan in airtight tin.

MONDAY

Ham and Cumberland Sauce finely grated rind and juice of 1 orange and 1 lemon, ½ pint (3 dl.) water, ½ oz. (15 g.) cornflour, 2 tablespoons apple jelly, seasoning, little made-mustard, pinch sugar, 1 tablespoon port wine. Slices of cooked ham.

Simmer grated rinds in water in frying pan or large saucepan for 10 minutes; strain if wished. Blend cornflour with juice of 1 orange and ½ lemon (save rest for Tuesday), return to pan with liquid, apple jelly, seasoning including mustard, pinch sugar, port wine. Cook gently, stirring well, until sauce is clear. Put slices of ham in this, heat for a few minutes only. Serve with macedoine of vegetables. For a cold dish serve cooked ham with cold sauce and Russian salad.

Fruit Choux make choux pastry by melting 1 oz. (25 g.) margarine in ¼ pint (1½ dl.) water. Stir in 3 oz. (75 g.) flour and heat gently until dry mixture. Gradually blend in 2 eggs plus enough yolk to make a sticky mixture. Put spoonfuls on to greased baking tray. Bake for 30–35 minutes in moderate to moderately hot oven, Gas Mark 5–6, 375–400°F. (190–200°C.), lower heat slightly after 15–20 minutes. When cooked, slit the buns, remove any uncooked mixture and dry out for a short time in the oven. Cool away from a draught, fill with whipped cream and fruit, top with icing sugar, see picture page 51.

TUESDAY

Veal Escalopes seasoning, 4 thin fillets of veal, 2 oz. (50 g.) butter, ¼ pint (1½ dl.) thin cream, 1 dessertspoon chopped parsley, juice of ½ lemon. To serve: green peas, carrots.

Season fillets of veal well, fry in butter; when tender put on to hot dish. Stir cream, parsley, lemon juice into pan, heat without boiling; pour cream sauce over veal. Serve in a border of green peas and young carrots.

Savoury Potato Straws fry thin matchstick shapes of potato, or heat ready prepared potato sticks (or crisps). Toss in a mixture of celery salt, cayenne pepper and chilli powder (remember this is very hot).

Raspberry Pyramids bought or home-made plain sponge, good 8 oz. (¼ kilo) raspberries, sugar. Topping: few whole raspberries.

Split sponge through centre to give really thin layers. Cut four 2½–3-inch (6–8-cm.) rounds and four 1½-inch (4-cm.) rounds. Crush raspberries with sugar. Put the large rounds on serving plate, cover with some of fruit purée, then smaller rounds and rest of purée. Leave in a cool place so sponge absorbs the raspberry flavour. Top each one with whole fruit before serving.

Note. Sponge recipe (Thursday) could be used.

FRIDAY

Cheese and Salmon Boats bread, 2 egg yolks, 3 tablespoons milk, grated cheese, cooked or canned salmon, mayonnaise.

Cut fingers of bread, shape ends to look like boats. Save pieces cut away for Sunday. Beat egg yolks with milk. Dip bread in this, then coat with grated cheese. Crisp in oven, cool. Pile flaked salmon blended with a little mayonnaise on top.

Strawberry Soufflé 8 oz. (¼ kilo) strawberries, 1 strawberry jelly, ¼ pint (1½ dl.) hot water, 2 egg whites. Topping: whole strawberries, whipped cream.

Rub strawberries through a sieve. Dissolve jelly in hot water, add to strawberry purée. If necessary, add extra water to give ¾ pint (4½ dl.). Cool. Fold in stiffly beaten egg whites. Put into a soufflé dish. Top with whole strawberries and cream.

SATURDAY

Stuffed Eggs with Meat Roll canned meat roll, salad, 4 hard-boiled eggs, 1 oz. (25 g.) butter, 1 teaspoon curry powder, 1 tablespoon chutney.

Cut meat roll into 8 slices, arrange on dish of salad. Halve eggs, remove yolks, mash and mix with butter, curry powder and chutney. Return mixture to white cases, arrange cut side down on the meat roll.

Cheese and Fresh Fruit arrange cubes of various cheeses on cocktail sticks stuck in a grapefruit, with biscuits and fruit round the dish.

Note. As soft fruit has been used generously during this week choose apples, oranges, or bananas to serve with the cheese. Try some of the stronger flavoured cheeses, Danish Blue, Stilton, Gruyère, etc., with the fruit.

Week 18

When melons are readily available and inexpensive they make delicious desserts (see Friday's menu), as well as a refreshing start to a meal.

The stuffing suggested for pork (Sunday) makes a pleasant change from the more familiar sage and onion.

For your shopping list the main meals need:
12 eggs, 3 pints (1¾ litres) milk, 6–9 oz. (150–225 g.) Cheddar or other cooking cheese.

Sunday, Monday and Tuesday need:
Loin pork.
Thick cream, ice cream.
Potatoes, onions (some small), sage, tomatoes, mint, lettuce, parsley, chives, dessert apples, berry fruits, peaches, lemon.

Wednesday, Thursday and Friday need:
Stewing veal, sausagemeat (store carefully), bacon rashers.
Macaroon biscuits.
Potatoes, parsley, onions, carrots, cauliflower, tomatoes, lettuce, lemon, melon, fruit to fill melon.

Saturday needs:
Chickens' or calves' liver.
Thick cream.
Potatoes, onions, tomatoes, mushrooms, marrow, strawberries.

Sunday

Stuffed Loin of Pork 3 oz. (75 g.) breadcrumbs, 2 oz. (50 g.) raisins, 1 medium onion, 1 teaspoon chopped sage, 1 oz. (25 g.) suet or melted margarine, 2 egg yolks, seasoning, piece loin of pork, little oil.
Mix breadcrumbs (from stale bread) with raisins, chopped onion, sage, suet or melted margarine and egg yolks; season well. Slit down fat of pork to make a 'pocket', put in stuffing, brush with little oil, weigh. Roast for 25 minutes per lb. (½ kilo) and 25 minutes over in hot oven, Gas Mark 7, 425°F. (220°C.). Lower heat slightly after 30–40 minutes.

Glazed Baby Onions and Apple Rings put small onions, thick slices of cored but not peeled dessert apples round meat 40 minutes before end of cooking time. Baste with fat in the pan and sprinkle the onions and apples lightly with sugar.

Berry Fruit Mousse 1 oz. (25 g.) cornflour, ¾ pint (4½ dl.) fruit purée, 2–3 oz. (50–75 g.) sugar, ¼ pint (1½ dl.) lightly whipped cream, 2 egg whites.
Blend cornflour with fruit purée. Cook slowly, stirring all the time as it thickens, adding sugar. Cool, stirring from time to time, then add whipped cream and stiffly beaten egg whites.

Wednesday

Veal Birds in Tomato Sauce 2 rashers streaky bacon, 2 oz. (50 g.) breadcrumbs, grated rind and juice of ½ lemon, ½ teaspoon mixed herbs, 2 teaspoons chopped parsley, seasoning, 1 oz. (25 g.) margarine, 1 egg, 4 large thin slices stewing veal, 2 oz. (50 g.) fat, 1 large onion, 1 small carrot, ½ pint (3 dl.) tomato juice, ½ pint (3 dl.) stock, 1½ oz. (40 g.) flour.
Chop bacon finely. Mix with breadcrumbs, lemon rind and juice, herbs, parsley, seasoning, margarine and egg. Divide mixture into 4, put on to slices of veal, roll firmly; tie or skewer. Fry for 2 minutes in fat. Put in casserole. Add sliced onion, grated carrot to fat remaining in pan, fry for few minutes; add tomato juice, stock blended with flour. Bring to boil, cook until smooth and thick, pour over veal. Cover, bake in centre of very moderate oven, Gas Mark 3, 325°F. (170°C.) for 1¾ hours.

Oven Pancakes 2 oz. (50 g.) butter, 2 oz. (50 g.) sugar, 2 eggs, 2 oz. (20 g.) flour or rice flour, ¼ pint (1½ dl.) plus 4 tablespoons milk.
Cream butter with sugar, add egg yolks, flour or rice flour and milk. Grease 8–12 ovenproof plates and warm. Fold stiffly beaten egg whites into mixture, pour on to plates, bake in hot oven, Gas Mark 7, 425°F. (220°C.) for approximately 20 minutes. Lower heat slightly after 12 minutes. Serve with jam.

Thursday

Sausage Puffs ½ tablespoon chopped parsley, 1 lb. (½ kilo) sausagemeat, 2 oz. (50 g.) flour, 6 tablespoons milk, seasoning, 2 egg whites, fat for frying.
Blend parsley with sausagemeat; form into balls or cakes. Dip in batter made with flour, milk, seasoning and stiffly beaten egg whites. Fry in shallow or deep fat.

Paprika Cauliflower 1 cauliflower, 1 oz. (25 g.) margarine, 1 oz. (25 g.) flour, ½ pint (3 dl.) milk, seasoning, 1 teaspoon paprika, 1 tablespoon milk.
Cook cauliflower. Make white sauce with margarine, flour, milk, seasoning, add paprika blended with 1 tablespoon milk. Stir well into thickened sauce. Pour over cauliflower.

Macaroon Pudding 2 eggs, 2 egg yolks, 2 oz. (50 g.) sugar, ¼ teaspoon almond or ratafia essence, 1 pint (6 dl.) milk, 2 macaroon biscuits.
Beat eggs and egg yolks with sugar, essence and milk. Strain on to crumbled macaroon biscuits then pour into greased basin. Cover with greased foil. Steam over simmering water for 2 hours. Cool, turn out.

MONDAY

Cheese Tomato Bake 4 oz. (100 g.) flour, pinch salt, 1 egg, ½ pint (3 dl.) milk, 4–6 oz. (100–150 g.) grated Cheddar cheese, seasoning, tomatoes, parsley, chives. Make a batter with flour, salt, egg and milk. Beat in cheese. Arrange halved, seasoned tomatoes in well greased, shallow baking dish. Sprinkle lightly with chopped parsley and chives. Heat for 5 minutes in hot oven, Gas Mark 7, 425°F. (220°C.). Add cheese batter, cook for 30–35 minutes in centre of the oven.

Minted Potatoes toss cooked potatoes in butter and very finely chopped fresh mint.

Peach Melba 4 oz. (100 g.) raspberries, good 1 tablespoon redcurrant jelly, 1 oz. (25 g.) sugar, 1 level teaspoon arrowroot or cornflour, 4 tablespoons water, peaches, ice cream.
Crush raspberries, put into a saucepan with redcurrant jelly, sugar, and arrowroot or cornflour blended with water. Simmer, stirring well until clear. Arrange halved peaches in glasses with ice cream. Coat with sauce.
Note. The Melba Sauce may be made in larger quantities and stored in the freezer.

TUESDAY

Tomato Juice Cocktails little celery salt, few drops Worcestershire sauce, ½ pint (3 dl.) canned tomato juice, squeeze of lemon juice, mint.
Blend celery salt and Worcestershire sauce with tomato juice and lemon juice. Serve cold in small cocktail glasses topped with mint.

Pork and Apple Salad Ring cold pork, 1 lettuce, dessert apples, mayonnaise, chopped chives.
Arrange neat slices of cold pork in a ring on a bed of lettuce, then a ring of sliced dessert apple coated with mayonnaise, topped with chopped chives. Follow with a further ring of pork.

Crispy Jam Tarts shortcrust pastry, jam, crushed cornflakes or sweet biscuit crumbs.
Line 9 patty tins with pastry; fill with jam. Sprinkle a layer of crushed cornflakes or sweet biscuit crumbs over jam. Bake for 12–15 minutes towards top of a hot oven, Gas Mark 7, 425°F. (220°C.).
Note. 4 oz. (100 g.) shortcrust pastry, i.e. pastry made with 4 oz. (100 g.) flour, pinch salt, 2 oz. (50 g.) fat and water to mix, will fill 9 shallow patty tins. For an economical sweet shortcrust pastry add 1 tablespoon sugar to the flour.

FRIDAY

Tuna and Anchovy Salad 8 oz. (200 g.) cooked potatoes, medium sized can tuna, 2 hard-boiled eggs, 2 tomatoes, few anchovy fillets, little oil and vinegar, lettuce. To garnish: anchovy fillets. Dice potatoes, mix with flaked tuna, chopped hard-boiled eggs, chopped tomatoes, chopped anchovy fillets. Toss in little oil and vinegar. Serve on lettuce, garnished with anchovy fillets. Serve with:

Cheese Bread 2 oz. (50 g.) margarine, 8 oz. (200 g.) self-raising flour, good pinch salt, pepper and mustard, 2–3 oz. (50–75 g.) finely grated Cheddar cheese, milk.
Rub margarine into flour sieved with salt, pepper and mustard. Add grated cheese and enough milk to make a sticky dough. Put into a 1-lb. (½-kilo) greased and floured loaf tin, bake in centre of a moderately hot oven, Gas Mark 6, 400°F. (200°C.) for 35 minutes.
Note. Using plain flour: in the Cheese Bread recipe above you can substitute plain flour with 2 teaspoons baking powder. This is the usual proportion of baking powder to 8 oz. (200 g.) plain flour to make the equivalent of self-raising flour.

Melon Basket cut top off a small melon, remove seeds. Remove fruit pulp, dice and add to a mixture of fruits, sweetening to taste. Pile back into melon case.

SATURDAY

Risotto 2 onions, 4 tomatoes, 2 tablespoons oil or 2 oz. (50 g.) margarine, 2 oz. (50 g.) mushrooms, 4 oz. (100 g.) long grain rice, 1½ pints (9 dl.) stock, 1–2 oz. (25–50 g.) sultanas, 4–6 oz. (100–150 g.) diced chickens' liver or calves' liver.
Fry sliced skinned onions and tomatoes in oil or margarine. Add chopped mushrooms, rice, toss in oil until rice is golden. Add stock. Bring to boil, lower heat, simmer steadily for 20 minutes. Add sultanas and liver. Continue cooking for a further 15 minutes.

Fried Marrow Rings peel marrow, cut into slices, remove seeds. Fry in a little fat until tender.

Strawberry Shortcakes 4 oz. (100 g.) margarine, 4 oz. (100 g.) sugar, 1 egg, 6 oz. (150 g.) self-raising flour, milk, strawberries, cream.
Cream margarine and sugar, add egg and flour. Knead well. Work in just enough milk to give a scone-like consistency. Roll out to a good ½ inch (1 cm.) thick, cut into 8 small or 4 large rounds. Put on to lightly greased and floured baking tray. Bake for a good 10 minutes towards the top of a hot oven, Gas Mark 8, 450°F. (230°C.). Cool slightly, turn out. When cold, sandwich the rounds together with strawberries and cream.

Raspberry alaska, recipe on page 32

Week 19

Unless you are cooking for a large number an ox tongue is too big for the average family, so buy the smaller calves' tongues for Thursday's and Saturday's meals. These are rarely salted so soaking is unnecessary. If calves' tongues are not available use lambs' tongues, but increase the number, since these are very small.

For your shopping list the main meals need:
8–9 eggs, 1¾ pints (1 litre) milk, 10–12 oz. (250–300 g.) Cheddar or other cooking cheese.

Sunday, Monday and Tuesday need:
Chicken (you need the giblets), bacon rashers, thin fillet steaks (unless using frozen meat cakes).
Thick cream.
Potatoes, onions, fresh herbs including parsley, sage and chives, tomatoes, lemon, peaches, loganberries, prunes.

Wednesday and Thursday need:
Calves' tongues.
Potatoes, mushrooms, large tomatoes, parsley, cabbage, spring onions, cherries, bananas.

Friday and Saturday need:
Cod steaks.
Cider, individual bricks ice cream.
Potatoes, onions, tomatoes, lettuce, mixed salad ingredients, dessert apples, orange.

Sunday

Devilled Chicken with Creamed Savoury Rice
rice stuffing: 2–3 oz. (50–75 g.) long grain rice, 1 pint (6 dl.) milk, 1–2 onions, seasoning, raw chicken liver, 1–2 oz. (25–50 g.) butter, 2 teaspoons chopped herbs. 2½ lb. (1¼ kilo) chicken, little fat, 1 teaspoon curry powder, 1 teaspoon Worcestershire sauce, 2 oz. (50 g.) breadcrumbs, seasoning, chopped parsley.
Cook rice in milk, add chopped onions, seasoning, chopped liver, butter, herbs. Put into chicken, cover breast with a little fat, roast for 40 minutes in hot oven, Gas Mark 7, 425–450°F. (220–230°C.). Remove chicken from oven, pour fat into a basin, blend with curry powder, sauce, breadcrumbs, seasoning. Spread over chicken, cook uncovered for 25–30 minutes. Cut into 4 joints to serve. Arrange rice stuffing in centre of dish, top with parsley, put jointed chicken round.

Peach Flan cream 5 oz. (125 g.) butter with 2 oz. (50 g.) sugar. Work in 10 oz. (250 g.) flour, 2 egg yolks (use whites on Monday) and a little water. Roll just over half pastry (wrap rest, keep cool for Wednesday) into round, put into 8-inch (20-cm.) flan ring, bake 'blind' (see page 10) in moderately hot oven, Gas Mark 6, 400°F. (200°C.) until crisp and golden, cool. Make glaze: blend 1 teaspoon cornflour or arrowroot with ¼ pint (1½ dl.) water, 1 tablespoon lemon juice, 3 tablespoons apricot jam and ½ tablespoon sugar. Boil until clear then cool. Skin and slice peaches, arrange in flan, coat with glaze. Serve topped with cream.

Wednesday

Cheese and Mushroom Charlotte 6 slices bread, 3 oz. (75 g.) margarine, 4 oz. (100 g.) mushrooms, 6 oz. (150 g.) grated cheese.
Cut bread into neat fingers. Fry in margarine until crisp and golden brown. Fry sliced mushrooms. Put one-third of the fingers into an ovenproof dish, cover with half the cheese and mushrooms, then more bread, remainder of the cheese and mushrooms and finally a top layer of bread. Bake for 25 minutes in centre of moderately hot oven, Gas Mark 6, 400°F. (200°C.).

Corn Stuffed Tomatoes 4 large tomatoes, small can corn, seasoning, about ½ oz. (15 g.) melted margarine.
Slice tops off tomatoes, scoop out centre pulp, chop, mix with corn, seasoning, melted margarine. Return to seasoned tomato cases and bake for 10–15 minutes.

Fresh Cherry Fingers flan pastry left from Sunday, jam, 1 oz. (25 g.) butter, 1 oz. (25 g.) sugar, 1 egg, 3 oz. (75 g.) fine stale cake or biscuit crumbs, approximately 8 oz. (¼ kilo) cherries, little sugar.
Roll out pastry, line 6–7-inch (15–18-cm.) square tin, bake for 10 minutes. Spread with jam. Cream butter and sugar, add egg and crumbs. Spread over jam, top with cherries and dusting of sugar. Bake for further 20–25 minutes. Cut into fingers.

Thursday

Calves' Tongues in Parsley Sauce 4 fresh calves' tongues, salt. For sauce: 1 oz. (25 g.) margarine, 1 oz. (25 g.) flour, ¼ pint (1½ dl.) milk, ¼ pint (1½ dl.) tongue stock, seasoning, 1 tablespoon chopped parsley.
Simmer tongues in salted water until tender, about 1 hour. Skin and remove tiny bones, then slice 3 of the tongues neatly (use remainder on Saturday) and serve with parsley sauce made with margarine, flour, milk and stock. Season and add parsley.

Spiced Cabbage 1 cabbage, knob of margarine, pinch mixed spice, 1 tablespoon chopped spring onions.
Shred cabbage, cook lightly, strain. Toss in margarine, adding spice and chopped spring onions.

Jellied Bananas 1 pint jelly, bananas.
Make up jelly, cool slightly, then pour over sliced bananas.

Strawberry trifle, recipe on page 36   Strawberry choux, recipe on page 47   Strawberry almond shortbread, recipe on page 40

MONDAY

Bacon Olives 8 rashers back bacon, sage and onion stuffing, page 10.
Wrap bacon rashers round a little sage and onion stuffing. Cook covered in centre of a moderately hot oven, Gas Mark 6, 400°F. (200°C.), for 15 minutes. Uncover and cook for further 10 minutes, or until bacon is lightly crisped.

Golden Onion Rings 2 onions, egg whites, seasoning, flour, little fat.
Peel and slice onions, dip in egg white and seasoned flour, fry until golden in a little fat, or put on a warmed greased tin and bake at top of oven.

Loganberry Crunch 1 lb. ($\frac{1}{2}$ kilo) loganberries, 2 tablespoons sugar, 2 tablespoons water. For topping: 2 oz. (50 g.) margarine or butter, 2 oz. (50 g.) sugar, 4 oz. (100 g.) crushed cornflakes.
Put loganberries into pie dish with sugar and water. Cream margarine or butter with sugar, add crushed cornflakes. Press over fruit, bake in coolest part of oven for 25 minutes.

TUESDAY

Steaklets with Savoury Scrambled Egg thin fillets steak or frozen meat cakes, little fat, 2–3 eggs, seasoning, little chopped chives, parsley, 1 oz. (25 g.) butter, 2 tomatoes.
Fry steak or meat cakes. Beat eggs with seasoning, little chopped chives and parsley. Heat butter, add skinned chopped tomatoes, then eggs, cook lightly. Top meat with the savoury egg mixture.

Almond Prune Mould 8 oz. (200 g.) prunes, 1 pint (6 dl.) water, $\frac{1}{2}$–1 teaspoon almond essence, 2 oz. (50 g.) brown sugar, $\frac{1}{2}$ oz. (15 g.) powdered gelatine. To decorate: blanched almonds, cream.
Soak and simmer prunes in water with almond essence and sugar. Sieve, measure pulp and juice; it should be 1$\frac{1}{4}$ pints (7$\frac{1}{2}$ dl.) (if less, add little water; if more, use extra for a sauce). Dissolve gelatine in hot pulp. Put into mould, allow to set, turn out; decorate with blanched almonds and cream.
To dissolve gelatine: gelatine dissolves more readily if it is first softened in a little cold liquid (in the recipe above use some of the prune liquid from the 1$\frac{1}{4}$ pints (7$\frac{1}{2}$ dl.)), then added to very hot mixture.

FRIDAY

Cod Bake 4 cod steaks, 1 teacup cider, seasoning, 2 onions, 4 tomatoes, little margarine.
Arrange cod in a casserole, add cider, seasoning, very thinly sliced onions; top with thickly sliced skinned tomatoes and little margarine. Cook, uncovered, towards top of a moderately hot oven, Gas Mark 6, 400°F. (200°C.) for 30 minutes.

Hot Chocolate Soufflé 1 oz. (25 g.) butter, $\frac{1}{2}$ oz. (15 g.) cornflour, $\frac{1}{2}$ oz. (15 g.) cocoa, $\frac{1}{4}$ pint (1$\frac{1}{2}$ dl.) milk, $\frac{1}{2}$ teaspoon vanilla essence, 2 oz. (50 g.) sugar, 3 eggs.
Make a thick sauce with butter, cornflour, cocoa, milk. Add vanilla essence, sugar and egg yolks. Fold in stiffly beaten egg whites, put into 6-inch (15-cm.) soufflé dish. Bake in centre of oven for approximately 25–30 minutes. Serve with:

Hot Coffee Sauce $\frac{1}{2}$ oz. (15 g.) cornflour, $\frac{1}{4}$ pint (1$\frac{1}{2}$ dl.) strong coffee, $\frac{1}{4}$ pint (1$\frac{1}{2}$ dl.) milk, 1 oz. (25 g.) sugar.
Blend cornflour with coffee, milk and sugar. Boil, stirring well, until thickened. Transfer to a jug and keep warm in pan of hot water until required.

SATURDAY

Tongue and Cheese Salad cooked tongue left from Thursday, cheese, mustard, mayonnaise. To serve: lettuce, mixed salad.
Dice tongue, mix with diced cheese, toss in a little mustard-flavoured mayonnaise, serve on bed of lettuce with mixed salad.

Apple Nut Slices individual bricks ice cream, dessert apples, chopped nuts, juice of 1 fresh orange, 1 tablespoon orange marmalade.
Arrange ice cream bricks on small serving plates. Cut apples into neat slices, arrange on top of ice cream with a layer of chopped nuts. Blend orange juice with marmalade, heating if necessary to give a smoother sauce. Spread over top of apples and nuts.

Week 20

Breast of lamb is one of the most economical cuts, with an excellent flavour. The main drawback though is that it has an excess of fat, so remove this before cooking.

Since raw minced beef is highly perishable it would be a good idea to prepare the Hotpots (Tuesday) as soon as possible after buying the meat.

As the vegetables used in the pie on Wednesday would be mostly root vegetables, shopping for these can be done well ahead.

For your shopping list the main meals need:
7 eggs, 2 pints (nearly 1¼ litres) milk, 6–8 oz. (150–200 g.) Cheddar or other cooking cheese.
Sunday, Monday, Tuesday and Wednesday need:
Breast of lamb, minced beef.
Thick cream.
Potatoes, rosemary, lettuce or endive, peas, spring onions, mint, onions, tomatoes, parsley, mixed root vegetables, strawberries, prunes, fresh fruit (peaches), cooking apples, orange.
Thursday, Friday and Saturday need:
Pork (optional), plaice fillets.
Thick cream, chocolate.
Potatoes, spring onions, parsley, onions, cooked beetroot, lemon, peaches, loganberries (store carefully).

Sunday

Rosemary-flavoured Breasts of Lamb fresh rosemary, 4–5 small breasts of lamb. To serve: peas.
Chop rosemary finely and sprinkle lightly over lamb before roasting, removing excess fat. Roast for 20 minutes per lb. (½ kilo) then 20 minutes more in a hot oven, Gas Mark 7, 425°F. (220°C.). Serve with peas.

Golden Potato Cake crisp breadcrumbs, raw potatoes, seasoning, melted margarine.
Grease a small cake tin well, coat sides and base with crisp breadcrumbs. Fill with layers of thinly sliced potato, seasoning each layer and brushing with margarine. Bake for 1½ hours. Turn out carefully.

Strawberry Baskets 3 oz. (75 g.) margarine, 3 oz. (75 g.) sugar, 1 egg, 4 oz. (100 g.) self-raising flour, milk, jam or redcurrant jelly, strawberries, whipped cream.
Cream margarine with sugar, add egg, flour and enough milk to make a soft consistency. Bake in greased patty tins for 12 minutes near top of hot oven. When cold, brush tops with little jam or jelly. Arrange small strawberries and whipped cream over this. Make 'handles' of angelica strips if desired.
Use any other fresh, drained canned or frozen fruit.

Wednesday

Cheese and Vegetable Pie fresh vegetables, 1½ oz. (40 g.) margarine, 1½ oz. (40 g.) flour, ¾ pint (4½ dl.) milk, seasoning, 4–6 oz. (100–150 g.) grated cheese. For topping: grated cheese, few breadcrumbs.
Cook a selection of fresh vegetables. Arrange in pie dish and cover with cheese sauce made with margarine, flour, milk, seasoning, grated cheese. Sprinkle top of sauce with grated cheese and a few breadcrumbs, heat for approximately 25 minutes in centre of a hot oven, Gas Mark 7, 425°F. (220°C.).

Norfolk Pudding knob of lard, 8–12 oz. (200–300 g.) apples, 1–2 oz. (25–50 g.) raisins, 4 oz. (100 g.) flour, pinch salt, 1 egg, ½ pint (3 dl.) milk.
Heat lard in ovenproof dish. Cover bottom of dish with thinly sliced apples and raisins. Warm for about 10 minutes in the oven, then top with a batter made from flour, salt, egg and milk. Bake towards top of oven for 30 minutes.

Raisin Sauce 3 oz. (75 g.) raisins, finely grated rind and juice 1 orange, 1 oz. (25 g.) sugar (preferably brown), ¼ pint (1½ dl.) water.
Put all ingredients into a pan, heat until sugar has melted. Stand for a while to 'plump' raisins. Reheat at the last minute.

Thursday

Sweet and Sour Pork 2 level teaspoons cornflour, ½ pint (3 dl.) water, 2 tablespoons vinegar, 2 tablespoons sugar or honey, good 1 teaspoon tomato ketchup, 1–2 teaspoons soy sauce, seasoning, 1 tablespoon finely chopped spring onions, ½ tablespoon chopped mustard pickle, 12 oz. (⅜ kilo) diced fresh pork or canned chopped pork.
Blend cornflour with water, put into saucepan with vinegar, sugar or honey, tomato ketchup, soy sauce and little seasoning. Stir over heat until clear and slightly thickened then add spring onions and mustard pickle. Either fry seasoned fresh pork or use canned pork, put into sauce, heat gently. Serve in border of:

Noodles put at least 4 oz. (100 g.) noodles into 2 pints (1¼ litres) water, adding 1 level teaspoon salt. Boil steadily until just tender, then strain.

Lemon Frosted Peaches 1 lemon jelly, ¾ pint (4½ dl.) hot water, juice of 1 lemon, 2 egg whites, 2–3 fresh peaches.
Make jelly with hot water; cool. Add lemon juice and stiffly beaten egg whites. Save yolks for Friday. Pile over skinned, sliced peaches.

MONDAY

Cold Breast of Lamb meat left from Sunday, lettuce or endive, peas, spring onions, mint sauce.
Cut meat into neat pieces, put on a bed of lettuce or endive with peas and chopped spring onions tossed in mint sauce.

Stuffed Prune Salad prunes, redcurrant jelly, tomatoes.
Soak prunes overnight but do not cook unless tough. Stone, fill centres with redcurrant jelly. Serve on a bed of sliced tomato.

Sardine Fingers sardines, seasoning, toast, grated cheese.
Mash sardines and season; spread on toast. Sprinkle with grated cheese and grill for a few minutes.

Or serve fresh fruit as dessert.

TUESDAY

Individual Hotpots of Steak 2 onions, 2 oz. (50 g.) fat, 1 oz. (25 g.) flour, pinch cayenne pepper or chilli powder, seasoning, ½ pint (3 dl.) brown stock, 1 lb. (½ kilo) minced beef, raw potatoes, little fat.
Fry grated or chopped onions in fat for 2–3 minutes, add flour with cayenne pepper or chilli powder, salt, pepper. Cook for several minutes then gradually blend in stock. Bring to boil, cook until smooth and thickened. Add minced beef and stir this well, breaking up any lumps. Divide between 4 individual dishes, top each one with sliced raw potatoes, season, brush with a little fat, cook for 1¼–1½ hours in very moderate oven, Gas Mark 3, 325°F. (170°C.).

Piquant Tomatoes halve tomatoes, sprinkle with a little seasoning, chopped parsley, sprinkling Worcestershire sauce, bake for about 15 minutes.

Cheese, Fresh Fruit serve a strong cheese (Danish Blue, Gorgonzola, Stilton) with wholemeal biscuits, fresh peaches.

FRIDAY

Plaice Ribbons with Tartare Sauce 4 large or 8 small fillets plaice, seasoning, flour, 2 egg yolks, water, crisp breadcrumbs, fat for frying. Sauce: 2 teaspoons chopped gherkins, 2 teaspoons chopped parsley, 1–2 teaspoons capers, mayonnaise.
Cut plaice into thin strips. Coat in seasoned flour then brush with beaten egg yolks blended with water. Give final coating of crisp breadcrumbs. Fry in hot fat until crisp and golden brown; drain. Serve with sauce made by mixing gherkins, parsley and capers with mayonnaise.

Chocolate Flan 4 oz. (100 g.) shortcrust pastry (page 10) *or biscuit crumb crust:* 2 oz. (50 g.) margarine or butter, 1–2 oz. (25–50 g.) sugar, 4 oz. (100 g.) crushed biscuit crumbs. For filling: ½ pint (3 dl.) chocolate blancmange, 1 egg yolk, 3 tablespoons cream, 1 egg white. For topping: whipped cream, grated chocolate.
Line a 7-inch (18-cm.) flan ring with pastry, bake 'blind' until crisp and golden brown *or* make biscuit crust: cream margarine or butter with sugar, add crushed biscuit crumbs. Form into flan shape; leave to set. Make up blancmange; allow to cool slightly. Beat in egg yolk mixed with cream, then stiffly beaten egg white. Put into flan case, top with whipped cream and grated chocolate.

SATURDAY

Swedish Hash 1–2 onions, 2 oz. (50 g.) fat, 12 oz. (300 g.) cooked potatoes, 1 can corned beef, seasoning. To serve: gherkin or parsley.
Fry finely chopped onions in fat, dice potatoes, toss in the fat. Add diced corned beef. Mix well, season, then arrange on a hot dish topped with gherkin or parsley.

Spiced Beetroot 1 large cooked beetroot, 1 tablespoon redcurrant jelly, 2 tablespoons vinegar, ½ teaspoon mixed spice.
Dice beetroot. Heat jelly, vinegar, spice. Pour over beetroot and allow to cool.

Fluffy Loganberry Pudding 12 oz. (⅜ kilo) loganberries, 2–3 oz. (50–75 g.) sugar, 2 eggs.
Crush loganberries, mix with sugar and egg yolks. Fold in the stiffly beaten egg whites. Put into a pie dish or soufflé dish and bake for just 25 minutes in centre of a moderately hot oven, Gas Mark 6, 400°F. (200°C.).

Week 21

Sunday

A home-made brawn is not only delicious but relatively inexpensive compared to other meat dishes. Since a calf's head will produce a large sized brawn (see Thursday) this will serve a family of 4 for several meals. Your butcher may be willing for you to buy half the head or you may prefer to purchase a much smaller sheep's head.

For your shopping list the main meals need:
6 eggs*, nearly 2 pints (nearly 1¼ litres) milk, no cheese in cooking.
*more if making sponge on Thursday, for recipe see page 39.
Sunday, Monday, Tuesday and Wednesday need:
Silverside of beef, boiling fowl.
Cream (thick or thin), ice cream.
Potatoes, onions (some small), tomatoes, celery, parsley, thyme, green salad ingredients, spring onions, cucumber, beetroot, garlic, peas, plums, greengages, fresh fruit.
Thursday needs:
Calf's head, sponge (if not making this), thick cream.
Potatoes, mixed herbs, tomatoes, cucumber, radishes, carrot, chives, endive or lettuce, apples, blackberries.
Friday and Saturday need:
White fish, prawns, sausages, macaroon biscuits, potato crisps, potatoes, parsley, tomatoes, lemon, pear, fruit for Popovers.

Boiled Salted Silverside soak meat in cold water overnight. Put into large pan, cover with fresh water, bring to boil, remove any scum on top of liquid. Cover, then simmer very gently, allowing 40 minutes per lb. (½ kilo) and 40 minutes over.

Glazed Onions and Potatoes about an hour before meat is ready, add small onions and good sized potatoes to the stock; as stock contains a certain amount of fat, vegetables becomes slightly glazed. Dish up vegetables, arrange round meat, sprinkle with chopped parsley.

Plum Charlotte 1–1¼ lb. (½–⅝ kilo) early plums, little water, sugar, 6 slices bread, 3 oz. (75 g.) margarine, brown sugar.
Simmer plums with a little water and sugar to taste. Remove crusts from bread, cut bread into fingers. Fry in margarine until golden brown. Put a third of the bread at bottom of a dish with sprinkling of brown sugar, spread with half plum pulp, layer of bread and sugar, remainder of fruit, final layer of bread and sugar. Bake for approximately 45 minutes in centre of very moderate oven, Gas Mark 3, 325°F. (170°C.).

Wednesday

Rice and Chicken Savoury 1 large onion, 1 garlic clove, 2 oz. (50 g.) fat or oil, 6 oz. (150 g.) long or medium grain rice, 1 pint (6 dl.) stock or water and stock cube, seasoning, about 1 teacup fresh or frozen peas, 1–2 oz. (25–50 g.) sultanas, diced chicken meat (from Monday), little chopped parsley.
Fry finely diced onion and garlic in fat or oil, add rice, cook for 2–3 minutes. Pour in stock from Monday or water and stock cube, season well, bring to boil; lower heat, cook for 10 minutes. Add peas, sultanas, chicken, parsley. Taste and re-season if needed. Continue cooking until peas are cooked.

Fried Cucumber Slices peel and slice cucumber. Dip in seasoned flour, fry until crisp and golden brown.

Ice Cream and Chocolate Sauce 3 tablespoons water, 1½ tablespoons sugar, 1 tablespoon golden syrup, 1 tablespoon cocoa, few drops vanilla essence, ice cream.
Put water, sugar, golden syrup into a pan, add cocoa, vanilla essence. Stir well to blend, heat gently for 1–2 minutes. Put ice cream in glasses; top with sauce.

Thursday

Veal Brawn 1 calf's head, salt, bay leaf, bunch mixed herbs tied with cotton or bag of dried herbs.
Wash calf's head in plenty of cold water. Put into large pan, cover with cold water, add salt, bay leaf and herbs. Simmer gently for 1½ hours. Allow meat to cool, remove bones of head, dicing meat neatly. The tongue should be skinned. Put meat into a basin. Boil stock vigorously for 20 minutes in an open pan until much more concentrated, strain enough over meat to cover. Put a plate and light weight over top of meat, leave until firm. For a stiffer jelly, dissolve 1 teaspoon powdered gelatine in just under ½ pint (3 dl.) stock.

Pinwheel Salad tomatoes, cucumber, radishes, carrot, little mayonnaise, chopped chives, endive or lettuce.
Slice tomatoes, cucumber, radishes, grate carrot, mix with a little mayonnaise and chopped chives. Arrange in wheel effect on a bed of endive or lettuce.

Blackberry and Apple Sponge fill a bought or home-made sponge cake with a thick apple and blackberry purée. Top with cream, sliced apples and blackberries.

MONDAY

Chicken and Vegetable Pie boiling fowl, seasoning, ½ pint (3 dl.) chicken stock, 2 onions, 2 tomatoes, 2 oz. (50 g.) fat, 1 oz. (25 g.) flour, ½ teaspoon chopped thyme, 6 oz. (150 g.) shortcrust pastry, see page 10.
Simmer chicken in salted water for 1¼ hours. Measure out ½ pint (3 dl.) stock for this recipe, save rest for Wednesday in refrigerator. Cut chicken into joints; keep breasts for Wednesday. Fry sliced vegetables in fat, put into pie dish with chicken joints. Stir flour into fat remaining in pan. Cook for several minutes, stir in stock. Boil until smooth, season, add thyme. Pour over chicken, etc.; cool. Cover with pastry, bake for 20 minutes in hot oven, Gas Mark 7, 425°F. (220°C.); lower heat to very moderate, Gas Mark 3, 325°F. (170°C.) for further 20 minutes.

Creamed Celery dice outer sticks of celery. Simmer in salted water until tender, strain, toss in butter and a little cream.

Greengage Meringue cook 1 lb. (½ kilo) greengages with a little water and sugar to taste. Remove stones, sieve or beat until smooth purée. Add 2 egg yolks, pour into pie dish. Whisk 2 egg whites until very stiff, fold in 2–3 oz. (50–75 g.) sugar. Pile over fruit, set in very moderate oven, Gas Mark 3, 325°F. (170°C.) for approximately 30 minutes. Serve hot.

TUESDAY

Cold Silverside, Mustard Relish cooked silverside, green salad, 1 oz. (25 g.) spring onions, 1 oz. (25 g.) diced cucumber, 1 oz. (25 g.) diced beetroot, 2 teaspoons French or made-mustard, 2 tablespoons vinegar.
Slice silverside thinly, arrange in a border of green salad. Chop spring onions, mix with cucumber and beetroot. Blend mustard with vinegar, add to vegetables.

Potato Griddle Cakes 12 oz. (300 g.) cooked potatoes, 1 oz. (25 g.) flour, 1 oz. (25 g.) margarine, seasoning, 1 egg. To coat: seasoned flour.
Mash potatoes, add flour, margarine and seasoning while warm, but no milk. Lastly add the egg. Form into round, flat cakes, coat in seasoned flour and cook on a greased, heated griddle or in a thick frying pan until golden brown.

Cheese and Fruit plums are delicious when served with soft cream cheese.

FRIDAY

Prawn Roll 1 lb. (½ kilo) white fish, 2–4 oz. (50–100 g.) shelled, chopped prawns, 8 oz. (¼ kilo) mashed potatoes, seasoning, 2 eggs, breadcrumbs, parsley.
Cook and flake fish, mix with prawns, mashed potatoes, seasoning and 1 egg. Form into a roll shape, brush with beaten egg, roll in crumbs, put on to a hot greased baking tin, cook for 30 minutes in a moderately hot oven, Gas Mark 6, 400°F. (200°C.). Garnish with parsley.

Lemon Sauce 1 oz. (25 g.) butter, 1 oz. (25 g.) flour, ½ pint (3 dl.) milk, seasoning, grated rind and juice of 1 lemon.
Make a white sauce with butter, flour, milk and seasoning. Add finely grated lemon rind to the milk so it becomes soft as sauce thickens. Remove sauce from heat, whisk in lemon juice.

Almond Custard Pudding 1 pint (6 dl.) thick custard, small macaroon biscuits, chopped almonds, 1 ripe dessert pear. To decorate: almonds.
Make rather thick custard from packet of custard powder. Arrange a small macaroon biscuit, few chopped almonds and a little sliced pear in each glass. Top with custard, decorate with almonds.

SATURDAY

Sausage Bean Casserole sausages, can beans in tomato sauce. To garnish: potato crisps, tomatoes.
Put pricked sausages into a casserole, cook in the oven until golden brown. Pour beans over sausages; heat through in the oven. Garnish with potato crisps and wedges of tomato.

Fruit Popovers 4 oz. (100 g.) flour, pinch salt, 1 egg, ⅓ pint (2 dl.) milk, thick fruit purée.
Make fairly thick batter with flour, salt, egg and milk. Grease and heat fairly deep patty tins towards top of a hot oven, Gas Mark 7, 425°F. (220°C.). Spoon in batter, bake for 12–15 minutes until crisp and golden brown. Fill popovers with thick fruit purée.

Wafer blackcurrant gâteau, recipe on page 39
Fruit savarin, recipe on page 61

Week 22

Sunday

When you braise vegetables you give them a new flavour and also give a sauce to serve with meat, etc., so avoiding the necessity of making gravy.

In the menu for Sunday mixed vegetables are braised; leeks and celery are suitable for braising, see pages 110 and 95.

For your shopping list the main meals need:
14 eggs, nearly 3½ pints (nearly 2 litres) milk, 4 oz. (100 g.) cream cheese.

Sunday, Monday and Tuesday need:
Best end mutton, sausagemeat, cooked ham (store very carefully).
Thick cream.
Potatoes, tomatoes, mixed vegetables (for braising), parsley, onions, marrow, chives, carrots, cabbage, cooking and dessert apples, dates, damsons, peaches.

Wednesday, Thursday and Friday need:
Smoked haddock, shrimps, ingredients for mixed grill (store carefully).
Thick cream.
Potatoes, parsley, lemon, spinach (store carefully), large tomatoes, cucumber, peas.

Saturday needs:
Steaks.
Rum.
Potatoes, lettuce, onions, fruit for Savarin.

Braised Vegetables and Neck of Mutton 1 oz. (25 g.) fat, 1 oz. (25 g.) flour, ¾ pint (4½ dl.) brown stock, 2–3 tomatoes, seasoning, 1–1½ lb. (½–¾ kilo) mixed vegetables, chopped parsley, best end neck of mutton. Make a sauce with fat, flour, stock, skinned chopped tomatoes, season well. Put in prepared vegetables, simmer steadily in covered pan for 1 hour. Top with chopped parsley. Roast the mutton in centre of a moderately hot oven, Gas Mark 6, 400°F. (200°C.), allowing 25 minutes per lb. (½ kilo) and 25 minutes over. Serve with:

Onion Sauce 3 large onions, ¾ pint (4½ dl.) salted water, ½ oz. (15 g.) cornflour, ¼ pint (1½ dl.) milk, ¼ pint (1½ dl.) onion stock, 1 oz. (25 g.) margarine.
Simmer chopped onions in salted water until tender. Save half for Monday. Blend cornflour with milk, put into a pan with onion stock and margarine and cook, stirring well until a smooth sauce. Add the cooked onion and heat thoroughly.

Apple and Date Pie fill pie dish with sliced apple, few dates, sugar and a small amount of water. Cover with foil. Bake towards top of oven for 20 minutes, remove foil. Sprinkle with a thick layer of desiccated coconut. Lower the heat to very moderate, move the pie to the centre of the oven when dishing up the meat, and heat for another 20 minutes.

Wednesday

Haddock Cutlets 2 oz. (50 g.) margarine, 2 oz. (50 g.) flour, ½ pint (3 dl.) milk, 12 oz. (300 g.) cooked smoked haddock, 2 egg yolks from Tuesday, 2 oz. (50 g.) breadcrumbs, 2 teaspoons chopped parsley, seasoning; crisp crumbs for coating, little fat for frying (optional).
Make a thick sauce with margarine, flour, milk. Pour half into a basin. Add flaked haddock, 1 egg yolk, breadcrumbs and parsley; season lightly. Form into 4 cutlet shapes. Brush with second egg yolk, roll in crumbs, bake or fry until crisp and golden brown. Garnish with:

Shrimp Sauce reheat remaining ¼ pint (1½ dl.) thick sauce, add another ¼ pint (1½ dl.) milk, stirring hard until smooth, add 2 oz. (50 g.) shelled shrimps.

Lemon Castle Puddings 3 oz. (75 g.) margarine, 3 oz. (75 g.) sugar, grated rind of 1 lemon, 1 egg, 3 oz. (75 g.) self-raising flour, 1 tablespoon lemon juice. To serve: lemon curd or lemon marmalade.
Cream margarine and sugar with lemon rind, add egg, flour and lemon juice. Put into 8 well greased, floured castle pudding tins. Cover with greased paper. Steam for 15–20 minutes. Turn out, serve with hot lemon curd or lemon marmalade.

Thursday

Mixed Grill allow a small cutlet and/or 2–3 oz. (50–75 g.) liver, a sausage, rasher of bacon, ½–1 lamb's kidney, 2 mushrooms per person. Cook under a hot grill, keeping the food well brushed with melted fat. Serve with:

Spinach in Tomato Cups 1 lb. (½ kilo) fresh spinach, 1 oz. (25 g.) butter, 4 large tomatoes, seasoning, good 1 tablespoon cream.
Cook spinach, strain, chop or sieve, return to pan with butter and the chopped centre pulp of the tomatoes, season and heat well. Lastly add cream. Put into tomato cases, which should be heated under the grill.

Raisin Fritters 4 oz. (100 g.) raisins, ¼ pint (1½ dl.) milk, 4 oz. (100 g.) self-raising flour, 1 egg, 1 tablespoon honey or golden syrup, fat for frying, honey or syrup for topping.
Bring raisins and milk to the boil; cool. Add to flour with egg and honey or syrup. Drop spoonfuls into hot fat, fry until brown on both sides. Top with hot honey or syrup.
Using plain flour: in the puddings for Wednesday you can use plain flour and ¾ teaspoon baking powder. In the fritters above you can use plain flour and 1 teaspoon baking powder.

Roast Stuffed Marrow onions from Sunday, 12 oz.–1 lb. ($\frac{3}{8}$–$\frac{1}{2}$ kilo) sausagemeat, little chopped parsley, 1 marrow, little fat.
Mix the onions from Sunday with sausagemeat and parsley. Peel marrow, halve lengthways, remove seeds. Put in the stuffing, tie halves together. Grease a sheet of foil liberally or put knob of fat in roasting tin and heat. Either wrap marrow in foil or turn in hot fat. Roast for 1$\frac{1}{4}$ hours in tin or 1$\frac{1}{2}$ hours in foil in a moderately hot oven, Gas Mark 6, 400°F. (200°C.), opening foil for last 20 minutes.

Damson Fool 1 lb. ($\frac{1}{2}$ kilo) damsons, sugar, little water. For custard: 2 level tablespoons custard powder, 1 oz. (25 g.) sugar, $\frac{3}{4}$ pint (4$\frac{1}{2}$ dl.) milk.
Cook damsons with sugar and very little water until a thick pulp. Sieve or beat well, removing stones. Make a thick custard with custard powder, sugar, milk; cool slightly, whisk into damson pulp. Put in glasses. Serve very cold.

Cheese and Ham Rolls with Salad 1 teaspoon chopped gherkins, few capers, $\frac{1}{2}$ teaspoon made-mustard, 4 oz. (100 g.) cream cheese, 8 slices lean ham. Beat gherkins, capers, mustard into cream cheese. Spread over ham, roll firmly, serve with:
(a) *Tomato and Chive Salad:* mix sliced tomatoes, chopped chives, grated carrots and chopped walnuts with mayonnaise.
(b) *Coleslaw:* mix 2 grated dessert apples, a few sultanas, shredded cabbage and mayonnaise.

Fresh Peach Pavlovas 2 eggs, 4 oz. (100 g.) castor sugar, 1 level teaspoon cornflour, little oil, $\frac{1}{4}$ pint (1$\frac{1}{2}$ dl.) thick cream, little sugar, 2 fresh peaches, 2 tablespoons redcurrant jelly, 1 tablespoon water.
Separate egg whites from yolks; cover yolks with water for Wednesday. Whisk whites until very stiff; gradually beat in half the castor sugar blended with cornflour, fold in remainder of sugar. Brush a sheet of greaseproof paper with oil. Form meringue into 4 rounds. Bake for 1$\frac{1}{2}$–2 hours in very slow oven, Gas Mark $\frac{1}{2}$, 250°F. (130°C.) until crisp. Lift from paper with warmed knife, cool. Whip cream lightly, sweeten, put on meringue with halved skinned peaches. Coat with redcurrant jelly melted with water. Leave to set.

Piquant Salmon and Rice 3–4 oz. (75–100 g.) long grain rice, salt, 1 pint (6 dl.) water, 1 oz. (25 g.) butter, medium can salmon, 3 tablespoons milk, 2 hard-boiled eggs, diced cucumber, chopped parsley.
Boil rice in salted water. Strain, mix rice, butter, flaked salmon, milk, chopped egg yolks, diced cucumber (see below). Heat for a few minutes. Pile on to hot dish, top with chopped egg white and parsley. Serve with:
Cucumber Boats: cook about 8 oz. (200 g.) peas. Drain, toss in mayonnaise and chopped chives or parsley. Cool. Cut 2-inch (5-cm.) fingers of cucumber, peel, halve lengthways. Scoop out centre pulp, chop finely, add to rice mixture above. Season 'boats' of cucumber, squeeze lemon juice over them, fill with peas.

Vanilla Pudding 1 tablespoon cornflour, $\frac{3}{4}$ pint (4$\frac{1}{2}$ dl.) milk, 2 oz. (50 g.) sugar, $\frac{1}{2}$ teaspoon vanilla essence, 2 eggs, 4 tablespoons thick cream, $\frac{1}{2}$ tablespoon powdered gelatine, 2 tablespoons water.
Blend cornflour with milk. Bring to the boil, cook until thickened slightly, stir well, add sugar, essence, egg yolks beaten with cream, and the gelatine softened in the cold water. Cook without boiling for 2–3 minutes. Allow mixture to cool and begin to stiffen, fold in whisked egg whites. Spoon into prepared mould, allow to set.

Anchovy Eggs 4 hard-boiled eggs, little butter, anchovy essence. To serve: lettuce.
Halve eggs, remove yolks, mash with butter and essence. Put back into white cases. Serve on lettuce.

Fried Steaks and Onion Rings cut 3–4 onions into slices, divide into rings, dip in a little milk and seasoned flour. Fry in hot fat until golden brown. Keep hot. Fry 4 rump, fillet or other steaks to personal taste.

Fruit Savarin cream *generous* $\frac{1}{4}$ oz. (10 g.) yeast with a teaspoon sugar. Add 3 tablespoons warm water, $\frac{1}{4}$ pint (1$\frac{1}{2}$ dl.) warm milk and a sprinkling flour. Leave for 15 minutes. Melt and cool 2 oz. (50 g.) butter, add to 5 oz. (125 g.) plain flour, $\frac{1}{2}$ oz. (15 g.) sugar, the yeast liquid and 2 large eggs. Beat well, put into warm ring tin and 'prove' for 45 minutes. Bake for 25 minutes in centre of hot oven, Gas Mark 6–7, 425–450°F. (220–230°C.). Turn out, prick and soak with a rum syrup made by heating 3 oz. (75 g.) sugar, 12 tablespoons water, 3–4 tablespoons rum and 1 tablespoon golden syrup. Cool and fill with fruit, as picture page 58.

Week 23

Sunday

If using a frozen chicken for Sunday's menu allow this to *thaw out completely* before cooking. This will take about 18–24 hours.

For your shopping list the main meals need:
10–12 eggs*, generous 2 pints (1¼ litres) milk, approximately 7 oz. (175 g.) Cheddar or other cooking cheese, little cream cheese.
*more if making sponge cake for Sunday.

Sunday, Monday and Tuesday need:
Roasting chicken, bacon rashers.
Sherry, sponge cake (if not making this), plain chocolate, vanilla ice cream, thick cream (optional).
Potatoes, onions, celery, parsley, green vegetable, corn on the cob (optional), tomatoes, watercress, cabbage, carrots, large oranges.

Wednesday, Thursday and Friday need:
Sausagemeat, veal cutlets (store carefully).
Coffee ice cream, little thick cream (optional).
Potatoes, mushrooms, parsley, cooking apples, blackberries (optional), dessert pears, lemon, plums.

Saturday needs:
Minced steak.
Potatoes, mint, chives, green salad ingredients, mushrooms, grapefruit (optional), oranges.

Roast Chicken with Celery Stuffing 1 onion, 2 teacups finely chopped celery, 1 teacup breadcrumbs, 1 tablespoon chopped parsley, 2 oz. (50 g.) suet or melted margarine, seasoning, chicken liver, 1 egg, 1 roasting chicken, little fat.
Chop onion finely, add to celery (use outer sticks – save heart for Tuesday), breadcrumbs, parsley, suet or melted margarine, seasoning, chopped chicken liver and egg. Put into chicken, cover bird with fat. Weigh; roast for 15 minutes per lb. (½ kilo) and 15 minutes over in centre of a hot oven. Allow 15 minutes more if wrapping in foil; open this for last 20 minutes to brown bird. Lower oven temperature to moderately hot after 30 minutes cooking. Serve with potatoes and green vegetable, cook extra for Monday's Bubble and Squeak.

Sherry Sauce make a brown gravy using chicken giblets (except liver) for stock. Flavour with sherry.

Mocha Mousse 4 oz. (100 g.) plain chocolate, 1–2 tablespoons concentrated coffee essence, 1 oz. (25 g.) sugar, 2 eggs. To serve: sponge cake (recipe page 39). Put chocolate, coffee essence and sugar in basin over hot water. When melted, add egg yolks, beat until fluffy; cool slightly, fold in beaten egg whites. Put into 4 glasses, serve with fingers of sponge.

Wednesday

Sausagemeat Nests with Mushroom Filling little chopped parsley, 1 egg, 1 lb. (½ kilo) sausagemeat, 4 oz. (100 g.) mushrooms, ½ pint (3 dl.) milk, 1 level tablespoon cornflour, seasoning, 1 oz. (25 g.) butter.
Add parsley and beaten egg to sausagemeat. Form into 4 nest shapes on well greased ovenproof dish. Bake for 25–30 minutes towards top of a moderate oven, Gas Mark 5, 375°F. (190°C.). Simmer mushrooms in ¼ pint (1½ dl.) milk for 5 minutes. Blend cornflour with remaining milk, add to mushrooms with seasoning and butter. Cook until a creamy mixture. Pile in centre of sausagemeat nests.

Bird's Nest Pudding 4 cooking apples, blackberries and sugar *or* bramble jelly, 1 pint (6 dl.) milk, 2 oz. (50 g.) rice or tapioca, 2 oz. (50 g.) sugar.
Peel and core apples. Put into a dish, fill centres with crushed blackberries and sugar or with bramble jelly. Heat milk, add rice or tapioca and sugar. Cook for about 10 minutes, pour over apples, bake in centre of a moderate oven, Gas Mark 5, 375°F. (190°C.) for about 45 minutes.

Thursday

Veal Cutlets au Gratin veal cutlets, fat or melted butter, grated cheese, breadcrumbs.
Brush veal with fat or melted butter, grill steadily until tender, then press grated cheese and breadcrumbs on to one side of the meat and return to the grill to crisp and brown. Serve with sauce below.

Creamy Cheese Sauce 4 oz. (100 g.) finely grated Cheddar cheese, ½ teaspoon made-mustard, ¼ pint (1½ dl.) evaporated milk, pinch salt and pepper.
Put cheese, mustard, evaporated milk, salt and pepper into a basin. Heat over boiling water until cheese has melted, stirring well.

Coffee Sundae put a layer of peeled, sliced, ripe dessert pears and a large spoonful coffee ice cream into glasses. Top with chopped nuts and little whipped cream, and glacé cherries, if liked.

MONDAY

Bacon, Egg and Onion Pie seasoning, 10 oz. (250 g.) flour, 5 oz. (125 g.) fat, water to mix, 2 onions, 4–5 rashers streaky bacon, little fat, 2–4 eggs.
Make shortcrust pastry with seasoned flour, fat and water to mix. Line 8-inch (20-cm.) deep pie plate or tin with half the pastry. Fry chopped onions and bacon for a few minutes in a little fat. Put over pastry, then break eggs over this mixture. Season lightly, cover with pastry. Seal edges, make slit in top for steam to escape. Brush pastry with milk or any egg white left in shells. Bake in centre of hot oven, Gas Mark 7, 425°F. (220°C.), for 20 minutes, then lower heat to moderate, Gas Mark 5, 375°F. (190°C.). The Lady Fingers for Tuesday could be baked at the same time.

Bubble and Squeak mash left-over potatoes and greens together, season. Heat little fat in frying pan, cook mixture until golden brown. Fold like an omelette and serve.

Orange Creams 4 large oranges, vanilla ice cream.
Cut a slice from each orange. Scoop out centre pulp, remove pips and skin. Beat into ice cream, pile back into the orange cases.

TUESDAY

Chicken and Corn Moulds chicken left from Sunday, canned or cooked corn, salad dressing, tomatoes, watercress.
Dice chicken meat, mix with well drained canned or cooked corn and salad dressing. Form into neat shapes on a bed of sliced tomatoes. Garnish with watercress.

Crispy Coleslaw chop inner sticks and few of the celery leaves finely. Mix with shredded cabbage, grated raw carrot and salad dressing.

Lady Fingers 2 eggs, 2 oz. (50 g.) sugar, 2 oz. (50 g.) self-raising flour, ¼ pint (1½ dl.) thick cream *or* creamy powder topping, chopped nuts, chopped glacé cherries.
Beat eggs and sugar until thick and creamy, fold in sieved flour. Pipe into finger shapes on well greased baking tin, using plain ½-inch (1-cm.) pipe. Bake for 8–10 minutes near top of a moderate oven, Gas Mark 5, 375°F. (190°C.). Cool; store in airtight tin until ready to serve. For a quick dessert, whip cream or powder topping, add few chopped nuts and cherries, spread a little between two fingers.

FRIDAY

Tuna Scallops about 12 oz. (300 g.) cooked potato, 1 oz. (25 g.) butter, 1 oz. (25 g.) flour, ⅓ pint (2 dl.) milk, seasoning, medium can tuna. To garnish: parsley, lemon.
Mash potato, put or pipe round the edge of scallop shells, brown in the oven or under the grill. Meanwhile, make sauce with butter, flour, milk, seasoning, add flaked tuna, put into scallop shells and garnish with parsley and lemon.

Plum Amber 1 lb. (½ kilo) plums, little water, 2 oz. (50 g.) sugar, 2 tablespoons fine stale biscuit or cake crumbs, 2 eggs, 3 tablespoons milk, 2–4 oz. (50–100 g.) sugar.
Cook plums with water and sugar. Sieve, then add to the purée the biscuit or cake crumbs and egg yolks beaten with milk. Put into a pie dish and bake for 30 minutes in a very moderate oven, Gas Mark 3, 325°F. (170°C.). Whisk egg whites until stiff, fold in sugar, pile over the plum mixture and return to oven for a further 20 minutes.

SATURDAY

Grapefruit Cocktail arrange segments of sweetened fresh or canned grapefruit and orange in glasses. Top with sprigs of mint.

Steak and Tomato Balls on Spaghetti 2 oz. (50 g.) margarine, 2 oz. (50 g.) flour, ½ pint (3 dl.) tomato juice, 8 oz. (¼ kilo) minced steak, 1 tablespoon finely chopped chives, 1 tablespoon rolled oats, seasoning, little fat, can spaghetti, green salad.
Make a sauce with margarine, flour and tomato juice. Add minced steak, chives, rolled oats, seasoning. Form into acorn-sized balls and fry for about 10 minutes. Heat spaghetti and serve balls on this, with a green salad.

Stuffed Mushrooms mushrooms, cream cheese, fried bread or toast.
Grill mushrooms for a few minutes, fill with cream cheese then put under the grill or in the oven for a very short time to heat mushrooms and cheese. Serve on slices of fried bread or toast.
To prepare mushrooms. Cultivated mushrooms do not need peeling. Wash, dry and trim stalks. Brush with plenty of melted dripping or butter when grilling, be generous with fat when frying.

Week 24

If you buy good quality beef, such as prime sirloin or rib, then roast in a hot oven (Sunday's menu). Beef is a meat that is traditionally served underdone, as the picture page 42, which shows sirloin roasted to give 'rare' meat. Allow only 15 minutes per lb. and 15 minutes over to give this result. Page 86 gives details of slower roasting of beef.

If you like very mild-flavoured gammon (Monday's menu), soak the bacon in cold water for 24 hours or buy green gammon or sweet-cure bacon.

For your shopping list the main meals need:
13–15 eggs (if making omelettes for 4 people), 3 or 4 pints (1¾ or 2¼ litres) milk, 3–4 oz. (75–100 g.) Cheddar or other cooking cheese.

Sunday, Monday and Tuesday need:
Sirloin beef, piece gammon, cream (thick or thin).
Potatoes (some large), parsnips, onion, mushrooms, parsley, cooking apples, plums, blackberries, orange.

Wednesday, Thursday and Friday need:
Fresh haddock, middle or scrag end lamb.
Individual ice cream bricks.
Potatoes, onions (some large), tomatoes, carrots, parsley, lemon thyme, sage, marrow, lemon, greengages, oranges.

Saturday needs:
Minced beef.
Red wine (optional), cream (thick or thin).
Potatoes, onion, chives, pears.

Sunday

Sirloin of Beef allow 15–20 minutes per lb. (½ kilo) and 15–20 minutes over in a hot oven, Gas Mark 6–7, 400–425°F. (200–220°C.). Do not use too much fat on outside, since this hardens the meat.

Roast Parsnips boil peeled parsnips for 15–20 minutes in salted water. Strain, put into hot fat, roast for approximately 45 minutes.

Potato Pyramids cooked potatoes, margarine, 1 egg, seasoning.
Mash potatoes, add good knob margarine, egg and seasoning. Form into pyramid shapes on greased ovenproof serving dish. Brown in oven for 15–20 minutes.

Autumn Pudding* 1½ lb. (¾ kilo) apples and plums, sugar, water, thin slices bread. To serve: custard or cream. Stew fruit with sugar and enough water to give just over ¼ pint (1½ dl.) juice. Line side and base of basin with bread, removing crusts. Pour in fruit and juice, cover with bread, put a saucer and weight on top. Leave for some hours, preferably overnight, turn out. Serve with custard or cream.
*make Saturday or early Sunday.

Wednesday

Foil-Baked Haddock with Onion Stuffing 1 whole haddock 2½–3 lb. (1¼–1½ kilo), 4 medium onions, 2 oz. (50 g.) margarine, 2 tablespoons breadcrumbs, 4 tomatoes, seasoning, chopped parsley, chopped thyme, grated rind of 1 lemon.
Cut off head of fish, split and clean fish. Slice onions, fry in margarine. Add breadcrumbs, skinned, chopped tomatoes, seasoning, parsley, thyme and lemon rind. Put into haddock, wrap in well greased foil. Bake for 45 minutes in centre of a moderate oven, Gas Mark 4–5, 350–375°F. (180–190°C.). Make a white sauce using half milk and half fish stock, obtained by simmering fish head. Whisk in juice of 1 lemon, chopped parsley, see recipe page 5.

Greengage Slices greengages, little water, sugar, small bricks ice cream, 1 teaspoon cornflour, chopped nuts.
Poach greengages in water and sugar until tender but unbroken. Top individual ice cream bricks with drained fruit. Cover with a sauce made from blending cornflour with greengage syrup and boiling until thick and clear. Top with chopped nuts.

Thursday

Lamb Hotpot seasoning, raw potatoes, tomatoes, carrots, middle or scrag end of neck of lamb, melted margarine.
Arrange layers of seasoned, thinly sliced potatoes, tomatoes, carrots and lamb in a casserole, ending with potatoes and a little melted margarine. Cover casserole, cook for approximately 2 hours in centre of a very moderate oven, Gas Mark 3, 325°F. (170°C.). Remove lid for last 30 minutes.

Stuffed Onions boil 4 medium onions until just soft; remove centres. Chop finely, mix with 1 oz. (25 g.) margarine, 1 teaspoon chopped fresh sage, 2 tablespoons breadcrumbs, 1 egg. Pile back into cases, bake in greased covered casserole for approximately 1 hour.

Rice Meringue 2 oz. (50 g.) rice, 1 oz. (25 g.) chopped walnuts, 2 oz. (50 g.) raisins, 1 oz. (25 g.) sugar, ½–1 oz. (15–25 g.) butter, 1 pint (6 dl.) milk, 3 egg whites (from Tuesday), 3 oz. (75 g.) castor sugar.
Put rice, walnuts, raisins into pie dish. Add 1 oz. (25 g.) sugar, butter and milk. Bake in coolest part of oven for 1 hour. Whip egg whites until very stiff. Fold in castor sugar, pile over rice, bake for 20 minutes. Serve hot.

MONDAY

Baked Gammon 1–1¼-lb. (½–⅝-kilo) piece gammon, melted butter, brown sugar.
Brush gammon liberally with melted butter. Bake for 30–35 minutes towards top of a moderately hot oven, Gas Mark 6, 400°F. (200°C.). Sprinkle lightly with brown sugar for last 5–10 minutes and snip the fat to encourage it to crisp.

Cheese Baked Potatoes bake potatoes in jackets for 45 minutes to 1 hour in coolest part of oven. Cut slice from each, scoop out pulp, mash with margarine, seasoning, grated cheese. Pile back into cases, top with grated cheese, reheat.

Apple Blackberry Dumplings 12 oz. (300 g.) short-crust pastry, see page 10, 4 cooking apples, sugar, blackberries.
Roll out pastry, cut into 4 squares. Put peeled, cored apples, centres filled with sugar and blackberries, on to squares. Brush pastry with water, seal over apples, flute. Cook on baking sheet for 30 minutes. Lower heat to Gas Mark 4, 350°F. (180°C.) for a further 20 minutes.

TUESDAY

Mushroom Soup 1 onion, 6 oz. (150 g.) mushrooms, 1 oz. (25 g.) butter, 1¼ pints (7½ dl.) chicken stock, seasoning, chopped parsley.
Fry chopped onion and finely chopped mushrooms in butter. Add chicken stock, seasoning, simmer for 10 minutes. Add chopped parsley.

Potato Pancakes, to serve with cold beef 8 oz. (200 g.) raw potatoes, 2 oz. (50 g.) flour, 1 egg, seasoning, milk, fat for frying.
Grate peeled potatoes into a basin. Add flour, egg, seasoning, enough milk to make a thick batter. Drop spoonfuls in hot shallow fat; fry steadily, turning once, until brown and cooked. Slice cold beef and arrange round the pancakes.

Bread and Butter Pudding butter, 3–4 thin slices bread, 2 oz. (50 g.) sultanas, 1 oz. (25 g.) chopped candied peel, ½–1 oz. (15–25 g.) chopped glacé cherries, grated rind of 1 orange, 3 egg yolks, 2 oz. (50 g.) sugar, ¾ pint (4½ dl.) hot milk, few tablespoons cream.
Butter bread, cut into triangles, put into dish with sultanas, peel, cherries, orange rind. Blend egg yolks (put whites in covered basin for Thursday) with sugar, milk, cream. Strain over bread and butter. Bake for 45 minutes in coolest part of very moderate oven, Gas Mark 3, 325°F. (170°C.).

FRIDAY

Tomato Omelettes allow 1½–2 eggs per person. Beat lightly with seasoning, add 1 tablespoon water to each 2 eggs. Heat butter in omelette pan, add eggs. Cook until lightly set. Fry sliced tomatoes lightly, season. Put in omelettes before folding. Serve with:

Marrow Scones 8 oz. (¼ kilo) peeled marrow, 6 oz. (150 g.) self-raising flour, 1 level teaspoon baking powder, good pinch salt and pepper, 1 oz. (25 g.) margarine, milk. To serve: butter, cheese.
Steam marrow until very tender. Sieve flour with baking powder. Add salt, pepper, rub in margarine, add marrow and enough milk to make a soft rolling consistency. Roll out to neat round about ½ inch (1 cm.) thick. Mark in triangles. Bake on greased baking sheet at top of a hot oven, Gas Mark 7, 425°F. (220°C.), for approximately 12–15 minutes. Serve hot; split and top with butter and cheese.

Butterscotch Pancakes 4 oz. (100 g.) flour, pinch salt, 1 egg, ½ pint (3 dl.) milk, fat for frying, 3 oz. (75 g.) butter, 4 oz. (100 g.) brown sugar, juice of 2 oranges.
Make batter with flour, salt, egg, milk. Cook pancakes, fold into triangles, put in shallow dish. Heat butter and sugar in pan, stir until sugar is dissolved, add orange juice. Pour over pancakes; heat. Picture page 66.

SATURDAY

Devilled Mince-Collop 1 onion, 2 oz. (50 g.) fat, 1 teaspoon curry powder, shake cayenne pepper, 1 oz. (25 g.) flour, ½ pint (3 dl.) brown stock, 1 teaspoon Worcestershire sauce, 1 tablespoon chutney, 1 lb. (½ kilo) minced beef.
Fry chopped onion in fat. Add curry powder, cayenne pepper, flour, cook for 2 or 3 minutes. Gradually stir in stock, Worcestershire sauce and chutney. Bring to boil, stir well, cook until a thickened sauce; add minced beef. Cover pan, simmer gently for approximately 1 hour, stirring from time to time.

Herb-flavoured Potatoes cream potatoes until white and fluffy, beat in chopped parsley, chopped chives and pinch fresh lemon thyme.

Rosy Pears 4 tablespoons redcurrant jelly, ¼ pint (1½ dl.) water, ¼ pint (1½ dl.) red wine, 2 oz. (50 g.) sugar, firm pears. To serve: cream.
Make syrup with jelly, water, wine and sugar. (Use lemon juice and water in place of wine, if wished.) Peel and core pears but leave whole. Simmer gently in syrup until tender. Lift into shallow serving dish, pour over syrup. Serve cold with cream.

Making pancakes, Butterscotch pancakes, recipe on this page

Week 25

Fillets of veal must be cooked with plenty of fat, so be as generous as possible with the butter. Ideally you should use at least 3 oz. (75 g.). You can mix this with a little olive oil, or use margarine if preferred (Sunday's menu). *Buy one extra* fillet of veal and *one extra* pork chop for Tuesday's menu and, as both veal and pork are highly perishable, store carefully (as near the freezing compartment of the refrigerator as possible). A generous sized pâté is made for Thursday, this makes an excellent standby for supper or picnics. If preferred use half quantities and cook for just under 1 hour.

For your shopping list the main meals need:
8 eggs, nearly 3½ pints (nearly 2 litres) milk, 3 oz. (75 g.) Cheddar or other cooking cheese.
Sunday, Monday, Tuesday and Wednesday need:
Veal fillets, bacon rashers, pork chops.
Sherry (optional), thick cream, ice cream (optional).
Potatoes (some large), onions, mushrooms, marrow, tomatoes, watercress, parsley, green vegetable, red cabbage, spring onions, fresh fruit, cooking apples, oranges.
Thursday, Friday and Saturday need:
Pigs' and lambs' liver, bacon rashers, whiting, shrimps or prawns, ice cream.
Potatoes (some large), salad ingredients, runner beans, celery, lemon.

Sunday

Veal, Mushroom and Onion Bake 4 fillets veal, butter, 3 onions, 4 oz. (100 g.) mushrooms.
Fry veal in butter for 2–3 minutes on each side, lift on to a plate. Fry thinly sliced onions and thickly sliced mushrooms. Place a layer of mushroom and onion mixture at bottom of an ovenproof dish, top with veal and more mushrooms and onions, bake for approximately 20 minutes towards top of a moderately hot oven, Gas Mark 6, 400°F. (200°C.).

Savoury Marrow 1 marrow, melted butter, tomatoes, breadcrumbs.
Peel marrow, cut into pieces. Steam until just tender, put in ovenproof dish, cover with little melted butter, thin slices tomato, breadcrumbs, heat through for about 15 minutes in the oven.

Cheese, Fresh Fruit put Brie or Camembert cheese in the ice-making compartment of the refrigerator for a short time so it is lightly chilled. Serve with fruit, or with:

Sherry Apple Drops mix together 4 oz. (100 g.) plain flour, pinch salt, 1 egg, ¼ pint (1½ dl.) milk, 2 tablespoons sherry and 2 large peeled and grated apples. Drop small spoonfuls into hot fat, fry until crisp and brown. Dust with sugar and sprinkle with sherry, serve hot.

Wednesday

Grilled Pork Chops brush lean part of chops with little melted fat so it does not become dry, snip fat round the edge to encourage it to crisp. Cook quickly on both sides under a hot grill, lower heat to make sure pork is cooked right through.

Barbecue Sauce 1 onion, 1 oz. (25 g.) fat, 4 tomatoes, 1 teaspoon Tabasco or chilli sauce, ¼ pint (1½ dl.) stock, 1 level teaspoon cornflour, seasoning.
Fry finely chopped onion in fat. Add skinned chopped tomatoes, Tabasco or chilli sauce and the stock blended with cornflour. Simmer until sauce is clear, but it need not be smooth; season highly.

Padded Pudding 2 level tablespoons custard powder, 1–2 oz. (25–50 g.) sugar, 1 pint (6 dl.) milk, 2 oz. (50 g.) fine cake crumbs (or half cake crumbs and half chopped nuts). For topping: whipped cream, glacé cherries, nuts.
Make 1 pint (6 dl.) custard using custard powder, sugar, milk. When custard is thickened, add cake crumbs or crumbs and nuts. Put into glasses. Top with whipped cream, glacé cherries and nuts.

Thursday

Liver Pâté Loaf 1 lb. (½ kilo) pigs' liver, 8 oz. (200 g.) lambs' liver, 12 oz. (300 g.) fairly fat bacon rashers, 1½ oz. (40 g.) butter, 1½ oz. (40 g.) flour, ⅓ pint (2 dl.) milk, 2 gherkins, pinch dried herbs, seasoning, 2 eggs, 2 bay leaves.
For this particular pâté you mince all the liver, but dice half the bacon finely (if preferred the bacon could be minced also). Make a thick sauce with the butter, flour and milk, add the liver and diced bacon, the diced gherkins, herbs, seasoning and beaten eggs. Grease a mould or tin well, put in the bay leaves then the rest of the bacon and add the pâté mixture. Cover with well greased paper or foil. Stand in a dish of cold water and bake in the centre of a slow to very moderate oven, Gas Mark 2–3, 300–325°F. (150–170°C.), for 1¼–1½ hours. Cool in the container with a weight on top and keep well wrapped to prevent drying. Serve with salad as a main dish or a sustaining hors d'oeuvre. Serves up to 14 as an hors d'oeuvre or 6–7 as a main dish.

Coffee Bake 2 oz. (50 g.) margarine, 2 oz. (50 g.) sugar, 2 eggs, 2 oz. (50 g.) self-raising flour, just over ¼ pint (1½ dl.) strong coffee. To serve: ice cream.
Cream margarine and sugar, add egg yolks, flour, coffee. Lastly fold in stiffly beaten egg whites. Pour into pie dish, stand in dish of cold water, bake for approximately 40 minutes in coolest part of oven. Mixture separates to give coffee sauce at base. Serve with ice cream.

Orange and grape cocktail, Creamed blanquette of veal,
Brazilian meringue, recipes on page 80

MONDAY

Corned Beef Roll *suet crust pastry:* 10 oz. (250 g.) self-raising flour (or plain flour with 3 teaspoons baking powder), good pinch salt, 5 oz. (125 g.) shredded suet, water to mix, 12 oz. (300 g.) corned beef, 2–3 bacon rashers, 2 large onions, 2 tablespoons stock or water, seasoning, little fat. To garnish: watercress, chopped parsley.

Make the suet crust pastry by sieving the flour or flour and baking powder with the salt, add the suet and enough water to make a soft rolling consistency. Roll out to a neat oblong. Dice the corned beef, bacon rashers and onions, mix with the stock or water and seasoning. Put on to the pastry. Turn in the edges, then roll neatly. Lift the pastry roll on to very well greased foil and wrap loosely, then lift on to a baking tray. Bake in the centre of a moderately hot to hot oven, Gas Mark 6–7, 400–425°F. (200–220°C.) for 25 minutes, then reduce the heat to very moderate for a further 35 minutes. Garnish with watercress and a little chopped parsley. Serve the roll with jacket potatoes, baked halved tomatoes and a green vegetable, see the picture page 82.

Either make gravy to serve with the roll, or heat a can of tomato soup and flavour with Worcestershire sauce and serve as gravy.

Follow this substantial meal with cheese and fresh fruit.

TUESDAY

Paprika Meat Balls 8 oz. (¼ kilo) minced veal, 8 oz. (¼ kilo) minced pork, 1 oz. (25 g.) margarine, 1 oz. (25 g.) flour, ¼ pint (1½ dl.) plus 2 tablespoons milk, ½–1 tablespoon paprika, 1 egg, 1 pint (6 dl.) chicken or beef stock.

Ideally use veal and pork (see Introduction), but other minced meat may be used. Make a thick sauce with margarine, flour, ¼ pint (1½ dl.) milk. Blend paprika with the 2 tablespoons milk, stir into thickened sauce. Gradually add meat, together with beaten egg. Form into small balls, simmer gently in stock for approximately 10–12 minutes. Lift out, put on hot dish, thicken liquid to form a gravy.

Red Cabbage cook shredded red cabbage as green cabbage. When cooked, either mix with a little cream and few caraway seeds or toss with grated apple and chopped spring onion.

Orange Compote 4 oranges, sugar, cream or ice cream. Cut peel and white pith away from oranges. Pile sliced orange into glasses. Sprinkle with a little sugar. Serve very cold with cream or ice cream.

FRIDAY

Curried Whiting Fillets 4 whiting, 1 oz. (25 g.) flour, good pinch salt, 1 teaspoon curry powder, fat for frying. Fillet fish. Mix flour with salt and curry powder. Coat whiting with this, fry until crisp and golden.

Potato Balls large potatoes, fat for frying.
Peel potatoes, either cut into balls with a vegetable scoop or into large dice. Fry until crisp and golden brown.

Cheese Puffs 3 oz. (75 g.) finely grated Cheddar cheese, 2 oz. (50 g.) breadcrumbs, 2 eggs, ½ pint (3 dl.) milk, ½–1 teaspoon made-mustard, salt and pepper.
Mix cheese with breadcrumbs. Blend egg yolks with milk, mustard, salt and pepper, pour over cheese and crumbs. Leave to stand for approximately 15 minutes. Fold in stiffly beaten egg whites. Put into 4 individual ovenproof dishes. Bake for 20 minutes in a moderate oven, Gas Mark 4, 350°F. (180°C.), until crisp and golden brown.
To vary: put the mixture in one 6–7-inch (15–18-cm.) soufflé dish as the picture page 75. Allow 25–30 minutes cooking time at the temperature above.

SATURDAY

Macaroni Pie 1½ oz. (40 g.) fat, 1½ oz. (40 g.) flour, 1 pint (6 dl.) milk, seasoning, 2–4 oz. (50–100 g.) shrimps or prawns, small can pink salmon, 3 oz. (75 g.) cooked macaroni, breadcrumbs.
Make a white sauce with fat, flour and milk; season well. Add shelled shrimps or prawns, flaked salmon and macaroni. Put into a pie dish, cover with breadcrumbs, heat through in centre of a moderately hot oven, Gas Mark 6, 400°F. (200°C.), for 20–25 minutes.

Bean and Celery Salad cook sliced runner beans; drain well. Mix with chopped raw celery, mayonnaise. Serve on green salad.

Treacle Tart shortcrust pastry*, 4 tablespoons golden syrup, 2 tablespoons breadcrumbs, 1 tablespoon lemon juice.
Line an ovenproof dish with pastry. Prick and bake 'blind' for about 10 minutes towards top of oven. Mix syrup with breadcrumbs and lemon juice. Spread over half-baked pastry, return to the oven for a further 20–25 minutes until golden.
*5 oz. (125 g.) pastry is enough for a 7–8-inch (18–20-cm.) shallow dish, 6 oz. (150 g.) pastry for an 8–9-inch (20–23-cm.) shallow dish.

WEEK 26

SUNDAY

One of the traditional British dishes that has remained popular for centuries is a jugged hare. The name originated because the food was cooked slowly in a deep jug. The same recipe can be used for rabbit, but shorten the cooking time.

Baked cooking apples look very interesting when decorated with almonds, etc. (see Sunday's menu). The cored apples may be filled with sugar or jam before cooking.

For your shopping list the main meals need:
11 eggs, 3 or 3½ pints (1¾ or 2 litres) milk, about 4 oz. (100 g.) Cheddar or other cooking cheese (if making cheese sauce for Monday).

Sunday, Monday, Tuesday and Wednesday need:
Rabbit or hare, lamb chops, cooked ham (wrap well, store carefully).
Port wine or red wine, thick cream, little rum (optional).
Potatoes, onions, carrots, parsley, root vegetables (optional) — see Monday's menu, spinach, chives, mint, tomatoes, sweetcorn (optional), garlic, cooking apples, dessert pears, lemons, bananas (choose firm fruit).

Thursday, Friday and Saturday need:
Small chickens, sausagemeat, cod (store carefully), stewing steak.
Sherry, thick cream, chocolate (plain or milk).
Potatoes, large tomatoes, onions (preferably small), celery, parsley, lemons, rhubarb, fresh fruit.

Jugged Rabbit or Hare 1 rabbit or hare, 2 onions, 2 carrots, 2 oz. (50 g.) fat, 2 oz. (50 g.) flour, 1¼ pints (7½ dl.) brown stock, blood of rabbit or hare, 2 bay leaves, seasoning, 2 tablespoons redcurrant jelly, ¼–½ pint (1½–3 dl.) port wine or red wine.
Soak jointed rabbit or hare for 30 minutes in cold water. Fry chopped onions and sliced carrots in fat, stir in flour, cook for several minutes, gradually add stock with blood. Add meat to sauce with bay leaves, seasoning, and liver of rabbit or hare; simmer for about 1 hour. Lift joints into casserole, add jelly and wine to sauce, heat for few minutes, then sieve sauce and liver. Pour over meat, cover, cook for 2 hours for rabbit, 3 hours for hare in a cool oven, Gas Mark 1, 275°F. (140°C.). Serve with redcurrant jelly and Forcemeat Balls.

Forcemeat Balls 4 oz. (100 g.) breadcrumbs, 2 tablespoons chopped parsley, 1 teaspoon mixed herbs, salt, pepper, 2 oz. (50 g.) shredded suet or melted margarine, egg yolk.
Combine all ingredients; bind with egg yolk. Form into small balls, cook in oven for 40 minutes.

Apple Porcupines Bake apples as page 11. Remove skins, brush with beaten egg white, sprinkle with sugar, press blanched almonds into fruit, brown for a time in the oven.

WEDNESDAY

Creamed Ham and Eggs 4 eggs, 4 large or 8 small slices ham, creamed potatoes or corn, 1 oz. (25 g.) margarine, 1 oz. (25 g.) flour, ½ pint (3 dl.) milk, 4 tablespoons cream, seasoning. Recipe for sauce, page 5.
Hard boil eggs, shell and halve. Roll slices of ham. Put eggs and ham into an ovenproof dish in a border of creamed potatoes or corn. Cover with cream sauce made with margarine, flour, milk, cream, seasoning. Heat for 20 minutes in the oven at Gas Mark 5, 375°F. (190°C.).

Garlic Bread make slits in a French loaf. Cream 2 oz. (50 g.) butter with 1–3 crushed cloves of garlic, spread in the slits. Wrap in foil, heat for 15 minutes in the oven.

Baked Bananas 2–3 oz. (50–75 g.) butter, 2–3 oz. (50–75 g.) sugar, little rum (optional), 4 halved large or 8 small bananas.
Put butter and sugar in an ovenproof dish. Heat until butter melts. Add little rum, if wished. Turn bananas in this, bake for 20 minutes.

THURSDAY

Spatchcock Chicken 2 small chickens, melted butter, little seasoning, little lemon juice, finely grated lemon rind, paprika.
Have chickens split, but not cut, into halves. Brush with melted butter, add little seasoning and lemon juice, grill steadily. When nearly cooked, brush with more butter and sprinkle lightly with very finely grated lemon rind and paprika.

Grilled Stuffed Tomatoes halve and scoop centres out of 4 large tomatoes, chop, mix with 4 oz. (100 g.) sausagemeat. Put into seasoned tomato halves, grill steadily.

Velvet Mousse 3 eggs, 3 oz. (75 g.) castor sugar, 3 tablespoons sherry, 1 teaspoon powdered gelatine, 2 tablespoons hot water, ¼ pint (1½ dl.) whipped cream. To serve: grated chocolate.
Beat egg yolks and sugar until very thick and creamy. Add sherry and beat again over hot water. Dissolve gelatine in the hot water, gradually stir into egg yolks. Remove from heat, beat until cold, then fold in whipped cream and stiffly beaten egg whites. Serve in glasses, topped with grated chocolate.

MONDAY

Savoury Pancakes either chop left-over rabbit or hare finely and reheat to use as pancake filling, or make a thick cheese sauce, mix with diced cooked root vegetables, put into hot pancakes and roll firmly. Pancake recipe page 23.

Creamed Spinach 1½–2 lb. (¾–1 kilo) fresh spinach, salt, 1 oz. (25 g.) butter, 1 oz. (25 g.) flour, ¼ pint (1½ dl.) milk, little grated nutmeg.
Cook spinach with a little salt until soft. Sieve or chop finely, add to a white sauce made with butter, flour, milk. Beat well, re-season, add a little grated nutmeg.

Pear and Raspberry Condé 3 oz. (75 g.) rice, 1 pint (6 dl.) milk, 1 oz. (25 g.) sugar, little whipped cream, 4 small ripe dessert pears, ¼ pint (1½ dl.) water, 1 level teaspoon cornflour, 3 tablespoons raspberry jam, juice of 1 lemon.
Cook rice in milk with sugar in a double pan until soft *or* use canned rice. Cool, add little whipped cream. Put into a shallow dish. Peel and core pears. Arrange on rice, coat with glaze.
To make glaze: blend water with cornflour, simmer with other ingredients until thick and clear; cool.

TUESDAY

Lamb Chops 1½ tablespoons oil, ¾ tablespoon vinegar, 2 teaspoons each chopped chives, mint and parsley, 4 lamb chops.
Blend oil and vinegar with chives, mint and parsley. Pour on to a flat dish, leave chops soaking in this for 30 minutes, turning once. Grill chops.

Tomato Rice 1 lb. (½ kilo) tomatoes, water, seasoning, 4 oz. (100 g.) long grain rice.
Skin tomatoes, chop and measure pulp; add enough water to give 1 pint (6 dl.) pulp. Put into a pan, season well. Add rice and cook until tender.

Lemon Sponge 3 oz. (75 g.) margarine, 2 oz. (50 g.) sugar, grated rind of 1 lemon, 2 tablespoons lemon marmalade, 1 egg, 2 tablespoons lemon juice, 4 oz. (100 g.) self-raising flour. To serve: lemon marmalade.
Cream margarine, sugar, lemon rind and marmalade. Add egg beaten with lemon juice, then flour. Put into a greased basin, cover with greased paper or foil, steam for 1¼ hours. Turn out, serve with hot lemon marmalade.

FRIDAY

Cod Thermidor 1–1¼ lb. (½–⅝ kilo) cod steaks, seasoning, 1 oz. (25 g.) butter, 1 oz. (25 g.) flour, ½ pint (3 dl.) milk, 1–2 teaspoons made-mustard, 1 egg, 3 tablespoons cream or extra milk, juice of ½ a lemon, few breadcrumbs.
Divide fish into 1-inch (2½-cm) squares, removing all skin. Season fish, steam on a plate over boiling water for 5 minutes only. Make a sauce with butter, flour, milk, stir in mustard, egg beaten with cream or extra milk, lemon juice; add cod. Put into a hot ovenproof dish, top with breadcrumbs and heat for 20 minutes in coolest part of a moderately hot oven, Gas Mark 5, 375°F. (190°C.).

Oven-fried Potatoes grease baking sheet, put in oven to become very hot. Peel and slice potatoes, put on hot sheet, brush with melted fat, cook in hottest part of oven for 20–30 minutes, depending on thickness.

Rhubarb Cornflour Mould 1 lb. (½ kilo) rhubarb, juice of ½ lemon, 3 oz. (75 g.) sugar, ½ pint (3 dl.) water, 1¼ oz. (35 g.) cornflour, 4 tablespoons cold water.
Cook rhubarb with lemon juice, sugar, ½ pint (3 dl.) water until very soft. Blend cornflour with water; stir into rhubarb. Cook until thickened and smooth. Pour into a mould, turn out when set and cold.

SATURDAY

Steak and Onion Pie 1–1¼ lb. (½–⅝ kilo) stewing steak, about 12 small onions or 3 large onions, seasoning, 1½ oz. (40 g.) flour, 2 oz. (50 g.) fat, 1¼ pints (7½ dl.) brown stock or water and 2 stock cubes, 6 oz. (150 g.) shortcrust pastry, see page 10, or 6 oz. (150 g.) flaky pastry, see page 137. To glaze: 1 egg, 1 tablespoon water. To garnish: parsley.
Dice the steak, peel small onions, peel and slice large onions. Coat the meat and onions in seasoned flour, fry for a few minutes in the hot fat. Blend in the stock or water and stock cubes, bring to the boil, stir until thickened, lower heat, cover pan and simmer for 1¼–1½ hours. Meanwhile, make the pastry: lift the meat and onions, together with ¼ pint (1½ dl.) of the gravy into a pie dish (save the rest of the gravy for the celery, below). Cool slightly, cover with the pastry. Flake the edges, decorate with pastry leaves, brush with beaten egg and water. Bake for 15–20 minutes in the centre of a *hot oven* for *shortcrust pastry*, or a *very hot oven* for *flaky pastry*, lower the heat to moderate and complete the cooking for another 20–25 minutes; garnish with parsley, see picture page 42.

Casserole of Celery wash and dice 12 oz. (300 g.) celery, put into casserole, cover with rest of gravy (above) and a lid. Cook in coolest part of oven for 35 minutes.

Serve cheese and fresh fruit at the end of the meal.

WEEK 27

If you like really mild bacon soak overnight or buy green bacon or sweet-cure bacon. If you prefer it slightly salted, soak for a few hours only (see Sunday's menu). Spaghetti makes an economical and substantial main dish with an interesting sauce and the cheese topping provides essential protein.

For your shopping list the main meals need:
5 eggs, 3 pints (1¾ litres) milk, 8–10 oz. (200–250 g.) Cheddar or other cooking cheese.
Sunday and Monday need:
Collar of bacon, bacon rasher, cream (thick or thin). Potatoes, parsley, onions, garlic, tomatoes, bunch mixed herbs (optional), damsons.
Tuesday and Wednesday need:
Thick cream (optional), plain chocolate, coffee ice cream. Tomatoes, lettuce, celery, parsley, mixed vegetables, marrow, lemon, dessert apples, blackberries.
Thursday needs:
Small chicken.
Potatoes, onions, red pepper (optional), mushrooms (optional), parsley, runner beans, spring onions or chives, lemon, fruit for fruit salad.
Friday and Saturday need:
Cod, sausages, bacon rashers.
Potatoes, tomatoes (some large), garlic, green pepper, parsley, mushrooms (optional), chives, oranges.

SUNDAY

Boiled Collar Bacon piece collar bacon, 1 onion, bay leaf (optional), few peppercorns, chopped parsley.
Soak bacon in cold water for several hours, unless lightly cured. Put into fresh cold water, add onion, bay leaf, few peppercorns. Simmer steadily, allowing 35–40 minutes per lb. (½ kilo) and 35–40 minutes over, as collar is an economical but solid piece of bacon. Skin bacon, sprinkle with chopped parsley.

Gherkin and Parsley Sauce 1 oz. (25 g.) fat, 1 oz. (25 g.) flour, just over ¼ pint (1½ dl.) milk, ¼ pint (1½ dl.) bacon stock, seasoning, 3 small gherkins, 1 tablespoon chopped parsley, see page 5 for sauce recipe.
Make sauce with fat, flour, milk, stock, add seasoning, chopped gherkins, parsley. (Save ½ pint (3 dl.) bacon stock for Monday.)

Damson Charlotte cook 1½ lb. (¾ kilo) damsons in *little* water, sugar to taste, remove stones or sieve. Remove crusts from 6 large slices bread, cut into fingers. Fry until golden brown in hot margarine. Put one-third in dish, sprinkle with brown sugar, little cinnamon. Add half damson pulp, layer of bread, rest of pulp, final layer of bread, sugar, cinnamon. Bake in centre of very moderate oven, Gas Mark 3, 325°F. (170°C.), for 45 minutes.

WEDNESDAY

Vegetable Stuffed Marrow 1 lb. (½ kilo) mixed vegetables, seasoning, 1 marrow, 1 oz. (25 g.) butter, 3–4 oz. (75–100 g.) grated cheese, 1–2 oz. (25–50 g.) breadcrumbs.
Cook the vegetables – sliced runner beans, sprigs cauliflower, diced young swedes, etc. – in salted water. Peel marrow, cut into 1-inch (2½-cm.) rings, removing seeds. Steam until tender, strain, put into ovenproof dish. Mix vegetables with the butter, half the grated cheese, season well and put into centre of marrow rings, top with remainder of the grated cheese and breadcrumbs, brown under grill. Serve with:

Cheese Sauce make a sauce with 1 oz. (25 g.) butter, 1 oz. (25 g.) flour, ½ pint (3 dl.) milk, seasoning, 3 oz. (75 g.) grated Cheddar cheese.

Coffee Creams ¼ pint (1½ dl.) thick cream or evaporated milk, 2 oz. (50 g.) plain chocolate, coffee ice cream. Whip cream or evaporated milk lightly, see page 86. Add chocolate cut into small pieces. Arrange the coffee ice cream and the chocolate-flavoured cream in glasses.

THURSDAY

Chicken Pilau 1 small chicken, 1½ pints (9 dl.) chicken stock, 2 onions, 2 oz. (50 g.) fat, 4–6 oz. (100–150 g.) rice, seasoning, additional flavouring (see below). To garnish: chopped parsley, paprika.
Boil chicken until tender; dice meat neatly. Measure required amount of stock. Fry sliced onions in fat until just tender; add rice (amount depending on size of family) and stock. Simmer steadily until rice is nearly tender, add pieces of chicken, season well, heat together. Add to rice any of the following: 1 diced red pepper; 1–2 oz. (25–50 g.) blanched shredded almonds; grated lemon rind; 2 oz. (50 g.) mushrooms. Pile high to serve. Garnish with parsley and paprika.

Piquant Beans cook sliced runner beans and toss with chopped spring onion or chives and lemon juice before serving.

Autumn Fruit Salad make a syrup with 3–4 oz. (75–100 g.) sugar, ½ pint (3 dl.) water, flavouring with pared rind of an orange. Simmer for 5 minutes, strain over segments of orange, sliced dessert pears, plums, greengage plums, damsons, damson plums, apples, blackberries.

MONDAY

Spaghetti Milanaise 1 rasher bacon, 1 large onion, 1–2 garlic cloves, 2 tablespoons oil, 6 large tomatoes, seasoning, good pinch sugar, ½ pint (3 dl.) bacon stock, bunch mixed herbs or pinch dried herbs, 6–8 oz. (150–200 g.) spaghetti, grated cheese.
Fry chopped bacon, chopped onion and crushed garlic in oil. Add skinned tomatoes, seasoning, sugar, bacon stock, herbs. Simmer ½ hour, sieve if wished. Cook the spaghetti in 3–4 pints (2–2½ litres) boiling salted water, strain. Serve on a hot dish, top with the tomato sauce and grated cheese.

Vanilla Egg Fluff packet vanilla blancmange, 2 oz. (50 g.) sugar, 1 pint (6 dl.) milk, 1 egg, 1 tablespoon cream, few drops vanilla essence, 1–2 oz. (25–50 g.) sugar.
Make up blancmange with sugar and milk. When thickened, beat in egg yolk blended with cream. Heat slowly for 2–3 minutes, put into 4 glasses, allow to set. Whisk egg white until very stiff, fold in vanilla essence and sugar. Pile over sweet and serve.

TUESDAY

Cold Boiled Bacon arrange slices of bacon on a serving dish with tomato, lettuce, etc., serve with:

Celery and Apple Salad small head celery, 2–3 eating apples, mayonnaise, squeeze lemon juice, chopped parsley.
Chop celery finely. Mix with diced apples, mayonnaise, lemon juice and parsley. This is a substantial salad to take the place of potatoes.

Blackberry Pudding 4 oz. (100 g.) shredded suet, 8 oz. (200 g.) self-raising flour, pinch salt, water to bind, blackberries, sugar.
Add suet to the flour, sieved with salt. Bind with water. Roll out until very thin making a round; cut out one-quarter of round for lid. Re-roll the small portion to fit over basin as a lid. Line sides of a pudding basin with pastry, fill with blackberries and sugar. Top with pastry lid. Cover pudding top with greased paper or foil, steam for 2 hours.

FRIDAY

Casserole of Cod 1 lb. (½ kilo) smoked cod, 3 tomatoes, 1 oz. (25 g.) margarine, 1 garlic clove, 1 green pepper, ½ pint (3 dl.) fish sauce, see page 5, 1 tablespoon chopped parsley, ½–1 teaspoon paprika, breadcrumbs and extra margarine for topping.
Poach cod, then flake. Fry sliced tomatoes in margarine, add crushed garlic and diced pepper. Make sauce, then mix in fish, parsley and paprika. Put in a casserole, top with tomato mixture, breadcrumbs and extra margarine. Bake in a moderately hot oven, Gas Mark 5–6, 375–400°F. (190–200°C.), for 30 minutes.

Orange Meringue Pie 6 oz. (150 g.) sweet shortcrust pastry, see page 89, 1 oz. (25 g.) cornflour, 3 oranges, 4 oz. (100 g.) sugar, 1 oz. (25 g.) butter, 2 eggs.
Line deep flan ring or sandwich tin with pastry. Bake 'blind' in hot oven until *just* golden, see page 10. Blend cornflour with orange juice, make up to ½ pint (3 dl.) with water, grated rind from oranges and half sugar. Cook in pan until thickened, stir well. Add butter and beaten egg yolks; put into flan case. Whisk egg whites until stiff, fold in rest of sugar, pile over orange mixture. Put in coolest part of oven when dishing up casserole. Lower heat to Gas Mark 3, 325°F. (170°C.), cook for 20 minutes. To serve cold, use 4 oz. (100 g.) sugar for meringue. Set earlier in day for 1 hour in oven Gas Mark ½, 250°F. (130°C.)

SATURDAY

Sausage Whirls 8 large sausages, mustard or chutney, 8 rashers bacon, mushrooms (optional).
Split sausages, spread with mustard or chutney. Put the halves together; grill for 5–10 minutes. Wrap each sausage in bacon. Grill with mushrooms, if wished, until the bacon is crisp.

Chive Tomatoes halve tomatoes, top with margarine, chopped chives, seasoning, grill with sausage whirls.

Almond Mousse 2 oz. (50 g.) almonds, 2 eggs, 2 oz. (50 g.) sugar, few drops almond essence, ½ oz. (15 g.) powdered gelatine, ¼ pint (1½ dl.) very hot water, just *under* ¾ pint (4½ dl.) milk. To decorate: blanched almonds.
Blanch almonds in boiling water, remove skins, chop. Beat egg yolks with sugar and almond essence until thick and creamy. Dissolve gelatine in the hot water; whisk into egg yolks, add milk, chopped almonds. Let mixture cool and stiffen slightly, fold in stiffly beaten egg whites. Pile into a shallow glass dish, decorate with blanched almonds.

Liver pâté loaf, recipe on page 68

 Week 28

To make a deep sponge use 6 oz. (150 g.) margarine, 6 oz. (150 g.) castor sugar, 3 eggs, 6 oz. (150 g.) self-raising flour, 1 oz. (25 g.) cornflour and 1 tablespoon warm water. Follow method of mixing page 39, but bake for 1–1¼ hours in the centre of a very moderate oven, Gas Mark 3, 325°F. (170°C.).

For your shopping list the main meals need:
8–11 eggs, 1 pint (generous ½ litre) milk, 6 oz. (150 g.) Cheddar plus 4–6 oz. (100–150 g.) Danish Blue cheese.

Sunday and Monday need:
Joint lamb, cream (thick or thin).
Potatoes, mint, turnips, swedes, beans, celery (optional), chives, spring or ordinary onions, lettuce, cooking apples, lemon, Victoria plums.

Tuesday and Wednesday need:
Minced beef, halibut (store carefully).
Rolls, deep plain sponge (if not making this), thick cream, peanut brittle or French almond rock.
Potatoes, tomatoes, spring onions (if ordinary onions used earlier in week), green vegetables, parsley, apple, grapefruit, lemon (optional), dessert pears (use canned pears when these are not available).

Thursday, Friday and Saturday need:
Sweetbreads, bacon (either rashers or small pieces).
Potatoes, onions, carrots, swedes, runner beans, green salad ingredients, tomatoes, parsley, *large* cooking apples, dried apricots, orange, lemon.

 Sunday

Roast Lamb choose leg, shoulder, breast or loin. With leg or shoulder, remove bone to make cavity for stuffing; with loin, slit skin, insert stuffing into pocket; with breasts, remove bones, spread meat with stuffing, roll firmly.

Mint Stuffing (4–6 people) 2 good tablespoons chopped mint, 4 oz. (100 g.) breadcrumbs, 2 oz. (50 g.) melted margarine, seasoning, pinch sugar, 1 oz. (25 g.) raisins (optional), 2 egg yolks.
Add chopped mint to the breadcrumbs, melted margarine, seasoning, sugar, raisins. Bind with egg yolks (save whites for sweet). Weigh meat after stuffing, allow a good 20 minutes per lb. (½ kilo) and 20 minutes over in a hot oven, Gas Mark 7, 425°F. (220°C.). Serve with a mixture of diced turnips, swedes, beans; redcurrant jelly, thickened gravy.

Lemon Apple Whip good 1 lb. (½ kilo) apples, grated rind and juice 1 lemon, 2 oz. (50 g.) sugar, water, 2 egg whites. To serve: cream.
Cook apples with lemon rind and juice, sugar and just enough water to prevent fruit burning. Beat or sieve to a smooth purée. Fold in the stiffly beaten egg whites. Serve in glasses with cream.

Wednesday

Halibut Meunière slices halibut, seasoning, flour, pinch celery salt, pinch cayenne pepper, butter, squeeze lemon juice or few drops vinegar, chopped parsley.
Coat halibut in seasoned flour, adding celery salt and cayenne pepper. Fry steadily in hot butter until just cooked, put on a hot serving dish. Add lemon juice or vinegar to butter remaining in the pan, with little chopped parsley. Pour over the fish before serving. (Cheaper cod cutlets or fresh haddock could be used.)

French Fried Potatoes cut potatoes in slices, fry until golden in hot fat. Take out of pan, reheat fat, fry again for 1–2 minutes before serving. This makes certain they are crisp. Drain on absorbent paper.

Crispy Pear Fingers 1 deep plain sponge (made or bought), ¼ pint (1½ dl.) thick cream, sugar, 2 large or 4 small halved pears, water, apricot jam, 2–4 oz. (50–100 g.) peanut brittle or French almond rock.
Cut through centre of sponge to give 2 thinner layers. (Wrap and save half for Sunday.) Whip cream, add sugar to taste. Cook pears with sugar and water until soft, drain and cool. Spread sponge with jam, half the cream, half the crushed sweetmeat, the pears then a final layer of cream and brittle or rock.

Thursday

Braised Sweetbreads 1½ lb. (¾ kilo) sweetbreads, 2 onions, 2 carrots, 2 oz. (50 g.) fat, 1 oz. (25 g.) flour, ¾ pint (4½ dl.) brown stock, seasoning.
Sweetbreads shrink in cooking, so allow approximately 1½ lb. (¾ kilo). If using less (as they are expensive), cook extra vegetables. Blanch sweetbreads: put into cold water, boil for several minutes, strain, remove skins. Fry sliced onions and carrots in fat, add sweetbreads and flour. Stir well together, gradually adding stock, seasoning. Bring to boil, stir until smooth. Cover pan, lower heat, simmer gently for 1 hour, or put in covered casserole and cook a little longer. Serve in a border of:

Duchesse Potatoes 1–1½ lb. (½–¾ kilo) peeled potatoes, 1–2 oz. (25–50 g.) margarine, 1 egg yolk, seasoning.
Cook potatoes until tender. Mash, add margarine and egg yolk (save white for Saturday). Season well, pipe or form into rose or pyramid shapes on greased baking tray. Put towards top of oven to brown.

Stuffed Apples core and slit skins of 4 large cooking apples. Put in a dish with 2 tablespoons syrup, 4 tablespoons water. Fill centres with syrup, sultanas, breadcrumbs. Bake for 1¼ hours in centre of very moderate oven, Gas Mark 3, 325°F. (170°C.).

MONDAY

Minted Lamb slice lamb neatly; top each slice with a little mint stuffing, if any left, or make a thick mint sauce and use this.

Spiced Potato Salad boil potatoes in their jackets, peel while hot and dice. Mix with few capers, chopped gherkins, chopped celery (optional), chopped chives, spring onions or grated onion. Toss in a little vinegar, oil, seasoning. Serve on lettuce.

Victoria Plum Cake 4 oz. (100 g.) breadcrumbs, 2 oz. (50 g.) sugar, 2 tablespoons shredded suet, 1 lb. ($\frac{1}{2}$ kilo) Victoria plums, sugar or honey.
Mix breadcrumbs with sugar and suet. Grease sides and base of a 7-inch (18-cm.) soufflé dish or cake tin. Press two-thirds of crumb mixture against sides and bottom. Halve or quarter plums, put into dish with sugar or honey but no water. Cover with rest of the crumb mixture. Bake for 1 hour in a very moderate oven, Gas Mark 3, 325°F. (170°C.), until crisp. Turn out of the dish very carefully.

TUESDAY

Grapefruit serve cold, or if the day is chilly, top halved grapefruit with a little butter and brown sugar and heat under the grill.

Tomato Beef Cutlets 4 large tomatoes, 1 small apple, 1 tablespoon grated or finely chopped spring onion, 8–12 oz. (200–300 g.) good quality minced beef, 2 tablespoons breadcrumbs, seasoning, beaten egg, crisp breadcrumbs, fat for frying. To serve: fried potatoes, green vegetables.
Skin and chop tomatoes, add to the grated or finely chopped apple and spring onion. Mix with minced beef, breadcrumbs, seasoning. Form into cutlet shapes, dip in beaten egg and crisp breadcrumbs and fry steadily, since the meat is uncooked, until crisp and golden brown. Serve with fried potatoes and green vegetables.

Cheese and Garlic Rolls split rolls, butter, sprinkle with garlic salt. Warm in the oven for a few minutes. Serve with cheese.

FRIDAY

Cheese and Julienne Salad peel carrots, swedes, potatoes, cut into matchstick shapes, slice beans, cook until just tender. Add to diced Cheddar and Blue cheese, blend with mayonnaise. Pile on green salad.

Fruit and Honey Pudding 2 oz. (50 g.) margarine, 1 oz. (25 g.) sugar, 2 tablespoons honey, 1 egg, 4 oz. (100 g.) self-raising flour, $\frac{1}{2}$ teaspoon cinnamon, 4 oz. (100 g.) mixed dried fruit, milk. For the sauce: 4 oz. (100 g.) mixed dried fruit, 2 tablespoons honey, $\frac{1}{4}$ pint ($1\frac{1}{2}$ dl.) water.
Cream margarine, sugar and honey until soft. Add egg, flour sieved with cinnamon, dried fruit. Add sufficient milk to make a soft dropping consistency. Steam for approximately $1\frac{1}{4}$–$1\frac{1}{2}$ hours. Turn out, serve with honey fruit sauce, made by simmering dried fruit with honey and water for a few minutes only until fruit is plump and juicy.

*soak apricots (see Saturday).

SATURDAY

Egg and Bacon Hotpot 8 oz. ($\frac{1}{4}$ kilo) bacon, 4 tomatoes, 1 egg, 2 egg yolks (save whites for sweet), $\frac{3}{4}$ pint ($4\frac{1}{2}$ dl.) milk, 2 oz. (50 g.) breadcrumbs, 1 tablespoon chopped parsley, seasoning.
Fry diced bacon until crisp and sliced tomatoes until soft. Arrange in a casserole. Beat together egg and egg yolks, milk, breadcrumbs, parsley, seasoning. Pour over bacon mixture, set in a very moderate oven, Gas Mark 3, 325°F. (170°C.) for 45 minutes.

*Dried Apricot Sponge 8 oz. ($\frac{1}{4}$ kilo) dried apricots, juice of 1 orange, juice of 1 lemon, 2 tablespoons sugar, sponge cake (from Wednesday), 1 teaspoon powdered gelatine, 2 tablespoons hot water, 3 egg whites, chopped nuts.
Soak apricots overnight in enough water to cover. Cook in the water until tender, adding orange and lemon juice and sugar. Sieve or beat until smooth. While warm, spread a thin layer over the sponge cake to moisten. Dissolve gelatine in hot water, add to rest of hot apricot purée, allow to cool. Fold in stiffly beaten egg whites. Pile over sponge. Sprinkle with chopped nuts before serving.
Economy Note: to save eggs use 1 whole egg and 1 egg yolk only in the hotpot, and 2 egg whites only in the dessert.

SUNDAY

Celery is used in several dishes throughout the week. Stand the head of celery upright in a little cold water in a cool place and you will find it keeps very fresh. Choose Parmesan cheese for coating the meat (Saturday); this is the strongest cooking cheese and one does not need too much. If you are too generous with the cheese in this recipe it forms a greasy coating.

For your shopping list the main meals need:
6 or 7 eggs, generous 4½ pints (generous 2½ litres) milk, 1½–2 oz. (40–50 g.) Parmesan cheese, 2–3 oz. (50–75 g.) Cheddar or other cooking cheese.

Sunday and Monday need:
Topside, frankfurters, little sherry, thick cream, macaroon biscuit, peanut butter, rice krispies.
Potatoes, celery, onion, herbs, tomatoes, lemon, bananas, dessert apple, pear, orange, grapefruit, plums.

Tuesday, Wednesday and Thursday need:
Pork chops, lambs' hearts, minced beef (store very carefully), ice cream, thick cream.
Potatoes, green beans, spring onions or chives, lettuce, mushrooms, parsley, onions, aubergine (optional), tomatoes, tiny bananas, fresh pineapple (optional), lemon, orange, damsons.

Friday and Saturday need:
Trout, lamb or mutton cutlets.
Sponge cakes, fruit juice or sherry.
Potatoes, parsley, carrots, swede, cauliflower, runner beans, lemon (optional), plums.

Sherry Tomato Cocktail flavour canned or bottled tomato juice with 1–2 tablespoons sherry and a little Worcestershire sauce. Serve cold in cocktail glasses.

Celery Steak 2½ lb. (1¼ kilo) topside (enough for Monday also), 2 thin slices bread, fat for frying, about 3 oz. (75 g.) chopped celery, 1 onion, 1 teaspoon chopped fresh herbs, grated rind of ½ lemon.
Cut meat to make a pocket through centre. Dice bread, fry in hot fat until golden. Mix with chopped celery, chopped onion, herbs, lemon rind. Press mixture into pocket in the beef. Put into either greased foil or a covered roasting tin. Cook for 1 hour in a hot oven, Gas Mark 7, 425°F. (220°C.). Cut slices downwards to serve.

Scotch Mist 1 jelly (any flavour), ¼ pint (1½ dl.) hot water, ¾ pint (4½ dl.) cold milk, ¼ pint (1½ dl.) thick cream, 1 macaroon biscuit, 1 tablespoon desiccated coconut, 1 tablespoon finely diced glacé cherries, sugar. Dissolve jelly in the very hot water. When cold, add cold milk; pour into serving dish. Leave to set. Whip cream lightly, add crumbled macaroon biscuit, coconut, cherries, sprinkling of sugar. Pile this colourful mixture over the set milk jelly.

WEDNESDAY

Stuffed Lambs' Hearts 4 small lambs' hearts, 2 oz. (50 g.) mushrooms, 2 stalks celery, 2 oz. (50 g.) fat, little chopped parsley, 2 tablespoons breadcrumbs, seasoning.
Wash, split hearts, soak in cold water, dry well. Chop mushrooms and celery, toss in half the fat, add parsley, crumbs and seasoning. Press into the hearts. Skewer or tie together, top with fat or wrap each heart in well greased foil. Bake for approximately 1½ hours in a moderate oven, Gas Mark 4, 350°F. (180°C.). Save any fat in tin or foil as basis for gravy.

Daisy Pudding knob of butter, 6 oz. (150 g.) castor sugar, 8 glacé cherries, 2 oz. (50 g.) blanched almonds, 3 oz. (75 g.) margarine, 5 oz. (125 g.) self-raising flour, grated rind and juice of 1 orange and 1 lemon, 2 egg yolks, milk, 2 teaspoons cornflour.
Butter oblong or square tin at bottom, sprinkle with 1 oz. (25 g.) sugar. Top with cherries and half the almonds to look like flowers (save rest of almonds for Friday). Rub margarine into sieved flour, add 3 oz. (75 g.) sugar, fruit rinds, egg yolks and enough milk to make a sticky consistency, put in tin. Bake for 45 minutes in a moderate oven. Turn out, serve with a sauce made by blending fruit juices, plus water to make ½ pint (3 dl.), the cornflour and remaining sugar. Simmer until thickened.

THURSDAY

Moussaka 2 large onions, 2 oz. (50 g.) fat, 1½ lb. (¾ kilo) raw potatoes or 1 lb. (½ kilo) potatoes and 1 large aubergine, 2 large tomatoes, seasoning. For the sauce: 1 oz. (25 g.) butter, 1 oz. (25 g.) flour, good ½ pint (3 dl.) milk, 2–3 oz. (50–75 g.) grated cheese, seasoning, 2 egg yolks, ¾–1 lb. (⅜–½ kilo) minced meat.
Fry sliced onions in fat for a few minutes. Remove, then fry sliced potatoes or potatoes and sliced aubergine. Mix with onions, sliced tomatoes, seasoning. Make cheese sauce with butter, flour, milk, cheese, season well, add egg yolks. Season meat. Arrange vegetables, meat and sauce in layers in a casserole, ending with potato. Cover, bake in centre of very moderate oven, Gas Mark 3, 325°F. (170°C.) for 1½ hours.

Tossed Green Beans toss cooked beans in mayonnaise flavoured with very little cayenne pepper, very finely chopped raw celery.

Vanilla Cream with Damson Sauce make vanilla-flavoured blancmange in usual way, folding in a little whipped cream as mixture cools. Turn out. Coat with Damson Sauce made by cooking damsons with rather more water than usual, beating, sieving and adding sugar to taste.

MONDAY

Steak and Frankfurter Puff meat left over from Sunday, few frankfurter sausages, knob of fat, tomatoes, 4 oz. (100 g.) flour, pinch salt, 2 egg yolks, ½ pint (3 dl.) milk and water, 1 teaspoon chopped fresh herbs.
Dice meat and sausages. Heat in a knob of fat in baking dish with sliced or halved tomatoes. Make a batter with flour, salt, egg yolks (whites needed for biscuits), milk and water; flavour with herbs. Pour over hot meat, bake for 25–30 minutes towards top of a hot oven, Gas Mark 7, 425°F. (220°C.); reducing heat after 15 minutes if necessary.

Fruit Salad make syrup with 3 oz. (75 g.) sugar and just over ¼ pint (1½ dl.) water. Flavour with shredded lemon rind and juice left from Sunday. Cool, strain over sliced bananas, apple, pear, orange, grapefruit, plums. Serve with:

Peanut Macaroons 2 oz. (50 g.) peanut butter, 3 oz. (75 g.) castor sugar, 3 oz. (75 g.) rice krispies, 2 egg whites.
Cream peanut butter, castor sugar, add rice krispies and whipped egg whites. Grease a baking tin well. Put spoonfuls of mixture on tin, bake for 12–15 minutes in centre of a very moderate oven, Gas Mark 3, 325°F. (170°C.). Store in an airtight tin.

TUESDAY

Tropical Pork Chops 4 pork chops, fat for frying, 4 pineapple rings, 4 tiny bananas.
Fry chops until cooked through to centre. Keep hot, then fry pineapple rings and bananas. Top chops with fruit, serve with:

Green Bean Salad toss hot cooked beans in a well seasoned oil and vinegar dressing, add chopped spring onion or chives. Cool, serve on shredded lettuce.

Baked Alaska 4 eggs, block ice cream, fruit salad, 4–8 oz. (100–200 g.) sugar.
Separate eggs (cover yolks with a little cold water, use 2 on Wednesday, 2 on Thursday). Put ice cream into an ovenproof dish, adding any fruit salad left from previous day or fresh or canned fruit, or put ice cream on sponge cake. Whisk egg whites until very stiff indeed. Use 4–8 oz. (100–200 g.) sugar as preferred. Gradually whip in half the sugar, fold in the rest. Pile over ice cream, covering this completely. Put for 3–5 minutes only in a very hot oven, Gas Mark 9, 475°F. (240°C.), until tipped with golden brown. This can be done immediately before the meal as this sweet will stand.

FRIDAY

Trout and Almonds 4 fresh or frozen trout, 2 oz. (50 g.) butter or margarine, 1 oz. (25 g.) blanched almonds, little chopped parsley (optional), few drops vinegar or lemon juice, seasoning. To garnish: parsley.
Fresh or frozen trout are equally suitable for this dish and frozen trout need not be defrosted, although cooking time is shorter if you do defrost them (always at room temperature). Fry the fish in the hot butter or margarine. Meanwhile, chop, flake or cut the almonds into shreds (see picture page 19). Lift the fish on to a hot dish, brown the almonds in the butter or margarine remaining in pan, add the parsley (optional), vinegar or lemon juice and season well. Spoon over the fish and serve garnished with parsley.

Plum Tart 8–10 oz. (200–250 g.) short or sweet short-crust pastry, pages 10 and 89, cornflour, flour or semolina, plums, sugar. To serve: custard sauce.
Line a pie plate with half the pastry, sprinkle with corn-flour, flour or semolina to absorb juice. Put on the plums, with sugar but no water; cover with pastry. Bake in centre of a hot oven, Gas Mark 6–7, 400–425°F. (200–220°C.), for 20–25 minutes, then lower heat to moderate, Gas Mark 4, 350°F. (180°C.), for a further 15–20 minutes. Serve with custard sauce, making an extra pint for trifle on Saturday.

SATURDAY

Fried Parmesan Cutlets lamb or mutton cutlets, milk or egg, soft breadcrumbs, grated Parmesan cheese, fat for frying.
Coat lamb cutlets with milk or egg and soft breadcrumbs mixed with the Parmesan cheese. If using mutton cutlets, steam for 15 minutes, then coat. Fry steadily until meat is tender and the outside crisp and golden. Serve in a border of:

Mixed Vegetables cooked diced potatoes, carrots, swede, cauliflower, runner beans.

Trifle sponge cakes, jam, fresh fruit juice or sherry, 1 pint sweetened hot custard.
Split the sponge cakes, spread with jam. Soak either with a little fresh fruit juice or sherry, pour on the hot custard. Allow to set. If wished, the sponge cake may be set in jelly first, then cold custard poured on top.

Note. It is suggested that extra custard is cooked on Friday in readiness for Saturday's trifle. Either make trifle on Friday or reheat custard for a few minutes on Saturday, whisking it well. Whipped cream may be added to the trifle, plus glacé cherries, nuts, etc.

WEEK 30

SUNDAY

The Cherry Queen of Puddings (Sunday) is generally served as a hot dish; if you prefer it cold then increase the amount of sugar in the meringue to 4 oz. (100 g.) and set the meringue for an hour in a very cool oven, this makes sure the meringue remains crisp.

For your shopping list the main meals need:
10 or 11 eggs, 3½ pints (2 litres) milk, approximately 2 oz. (50 g.) Cheddar or other cooking cheese.

Sunday, Monday and Tuesday need:
Stewing beef (cut in thin slices), cooked ham.
Burgundy (or other red wine).
Potatoes, parsley, mixed herbs (optional), onion, root vegetables, green pepper, tomatoes, watercress, chives, green vegetable, lemon, dried figs, rhubarb.

Wednesday and Thursday need:
Lean stewing veal, bacon rashers, minced beef (store carefully).
Sherry (preferably dry), brandy (optional), thick cream, plain chocolate, pistachio nuts.
Potatoes, onions, parsley, runner beans, large oranges, grapes, lemon, cooking apples.

Friday and Saturday need:
Fresh haddock, cooked tongue, bacon rashers.
Thick cream.
Potatoes, spinach, tomatoes, parsley, mushrooms, bananas, orange, autumn fruits (including pears) for pie.

Burgundy Beef Olives 3 oz. (75 g.) breadcrumbs, 1 tablespoon chopped parsley, 1 teaspoon chopped fresh herbs or pinch dried herbs, 1 onion, 1 oz. (25 g.) suet or margarine, seasoning, little milk, 8 small slices stewing beef, 1 oz. (25 g.) fat, 1 oz. (25 g.) flour, ½ pint (3 dl.) brown stock, ¼ pint (1½ dl.) Burgundy.
Make stuffing with breadcrumbs, herbs, chopped onion and suet or margarine, seasoning, little milk to bind. Spread on beef; roll tightly, secure with cocktail sticks or cotton. Fry in fat, lift into casserole. Stir flour into fat, cook for several minutes. Add stock, Burgundy, seasoning. Bring to boil, cook until thickened. Pour over meat, cover, cook in centre of cool oven, Gas Mark 2, 300°F. (150°C.) for 2 hours. Serve with creamed potatoes (cook extra for Tuesday) and diced root vegetables.

Cherry Queen of Puddings medium can cherries, 2 eggs, 3 oz. (75 g.) sugar, ½ pint (3 dl.) milk, 2 oz. (50 g.) fine breadcrumbs.
Grease a pie dish, put layer of drained cherries at bottom. Beat egg yolks with 1 oz. (25 g.) sugar, mix with milk. Add to crumbs, pour over cherries, bake for 45 minutes until custard is set. Whisk egg whites until very stiff, fold in remaining sugar. Pile meringue over custard, return to oven until crisp and golden brown (approximately ½ hour).

WEDNESDAY

Orange and Grape Cocktails halve 2 large oranges, remove pulp, mix with de-seeded grapes and dry sherry. Fill orange cases with the fruit. Chill lightly. Picture page 67.

Creamed Blanquette of Veal cut 1½ lb. (¾ kilo) veal in pieces. Put in a pan with ½ pint (3 dl.) chicken stock, 2 onions, 1 bay leaf and the juice and thinly pared rind from ½ lemon. Season and simmer for 1¼ hours. Remove the onions, bay leaf and lemon strips. Heat 2 oz. (50 g.) butter in a second pan, stir in 2 oz. (50 g.) flour, blend in ½ pint (3 dl.) milk. Bring to the boil, cook until thickened. Blend the veal and stock into this sauce. Whisk 2 egg yolks, 3 tablespoons sherry or brandy and 3 tablespoons thick cream together, blend slowly into veal mixture. Season and serve on a bed of cooked rice, as picture page 67, or with creamed potatoes. Garnish with paprika, lemon, parsley and bacon rolls.

Brazilian Meringues whisk 2 egg whites until stiff, whisk in 2 oz. (50 g.) castor sugar; fold in 2 oz. (50 g.) sugar. Pipe into 4 nest shapes and 4 small rounds on an oiled tin. Dry out as page 25. Fill nests with whipped cream, top with rounds, melted chocolate and chopped pistachio nuts, see page 67.

THURSDAY

Onionburgers 3 large onions, fat for frying, 12 oz. (300 g.) minced beef, seasoning, 2 tablespoons rolled oats.
Slice onions thinly, fry until just tender, put aside half and keep warm. Chop rest and mix with minced beef, seasoning and rolled oats. Form into flat cakes, fry or grill for approximately 8–10 minutes (or bake in oven for approximately 20–25 minutes). Top with onion rings, serve.

Bean Bake 1 lb. (½ kilo) runner beans, can mushroom soup.
Cook beans *lightly*, strain, mix with soup, heat through in the oven.

Eve's Pudding apples, little water, sugar. For the sponge: 2 oz. (50 g.) margarine, 3 oz. (75 g.) sugar, 1 egg, 3 oz. (75 g.) self-raising flour, 2 tablespoons milk. To serve: cream.
Half fill pie dish with thinly sliced apple, very little water, sugar to taste. Cover, heat for 15–20 minutes in centre of moderate oven, Gas Mark 5, 375°F. (190°C.). Top with sponge made by creaming margarine and sugar, then adding egg, flour, milk. Return to centre of oven for approximately 40 minutes, lowering heat after 30 minutes if becoming too brown. Serve with cream.

MONDAY

Ham and Egg Mould 6–8 oz. (150–200 g.) cooked ham, 2–3 hard-boiled eggs, 1 oz. (25 g.) margarine, 1 oz. (25 g.) flour, ¼ pint (1½ dl.) milk, seasoning, 1 egg.
Dice or mince ham, mix with chopped hard-boiled eggs and sauce made with margarine, flour, milk and seasoning. Add egg. Put into a basin, steam for 30 minutes, turn out, serve hot or cold.

Tomato Pepper Salad slice raw green pepper and tomatoes thinly, toss in a little oil, vinegar and seasoning. Serve on a bed of crisp watercress.

Lemon Rice 2 oz. (50 g.) round grain rice, 1 pint (6 dl.) milk, 1–2 oz. (25–50 g.) sugar, grated rind of 1 lemon, lemon curd.
Cook rice in milk with sugar and lemon rind (save lemon juice for Tuesday). A double saucepan is ideal for cooking this. When rice is soft, put into a serving dish. Serve hot or cold, topped with lemon curd.

TUESDAY

Pork Loaf can pork luncheon meat, tomatoes, little chopped chives, fat.
Open can of meat, put in an ovenproof dish, top with slices of tomato, chives and very little fat. Heat in a moderate oven, Gas Mark 5, 375°F. (190°C.), for 25–30 minutes. Serve with a green vegetable and Potato Cakes.

Potato Cakes 1 oz. (25 g.) flour, 1 tablespoon chopped parsley, 1 egg, mashed potato, well seasoned flour.
Add flour, parsley, yolk of egg to mashed potato cooked on Sunday. Form into cakes, dip in the egg white and seasoned flour and put on a hot greased baking sheet. Bake towards top of oven until crisp and brown.

Fig and Rhubarb Crumble 2–4 oz. (50–100 g.) chopped dried figs, juice of 1 lemon, little water, 1 lb. (½ kilo) rhubarb, sugar. For the crumble: 1½ oz. (40 g.) margarine, 3 oz. (75 g,) flour, 2–3 oz. (50–75 g.) sugar.
Soak figs in lemon juice (from Monday) for several hours, adding very little water. Put in pie dish with diced rhubarb, sugar to taste. Top with crumble made by rubbing margarine into flour, then adding sugar. Press on top of fruit and bake for 35–40 minutes in coolest part of the oven.

FRIDAY

Anchovy and Haddock Fish Cakes 1 lb. (½ kilo) cooked fresh haddock (or other white fish), good 8 oz. (200 g.) creamed potatoes, 1 teaspoon anchovy essence, 1 beaten egg, little milk, seasoned flour, crisp breadcrumbs, fat for frying. To serve: creamed spinach.
Flake fish, mix with potatoes, anchovy essence, half the egg. Form into flat cakes, mix remaining egg with a little milk, coat cakes in seasoned flour, then in egg and crisp breadcrumbs. Fry until crisp and golden brown. Serve with creamed spinach.

Banana Nutmeg Creams 4 large ripe bananas, ¾ pint (4½ dl.) milk, juice of 1 orange, ½ oz. (15 g.) powdered gelatine, 4 tablespoons very hot water, 1–2 tablespoons sugar or honey, whipped cream, grated nutmeg.
Mash bananas, add milk, blend thoroughly, gradually stir in orange juice. Dissolve gelatine in the very hot water, add to banana mixture, together with sugar or honey. Spoon into a dish. When set, top with lightly whipped cream and grated nutmeg.

SATURDAY

Tongue and Bacon Rolls 2–3 large tomatoes, 2 tablespoons crisp breadcrumbs, 1 tablespoon chopped parsley, seasoning, 1 oz. (25 g.) margarine, 4 large thin slices cooked tongue, 4 long streaky rashers bacon.
Skin and chop tomatoes, blend with breadcrumbs, parsley, seasoning, margarine. Divide stuffing between slices of tongue, roll firmly then wrap a rasher of bacon round each tongue roll. Put into an uncovered dish and bake in a moderately hot oven, Gas Mark 6, 400°F. (200°C.), until bacon is crisp and golden.

Savoury Mushrooms arrange well seasoned mushrooms in a dish in oven, top with a little milk, margarine and grated cheese. Bake for approximately 15 minutes.

Autumn Pie fruit (see below), sugar, water, pastry to cover.
Mix any autumn fruits, including sliced pears, together, put into a pie dish with sugar and a little water. Top with pastry and cook until pastry is crisp and golden brown. Sprinkle with sugar.
To make a good fruit pie: fill pie dish *generously* with fruit, avoid using too much liquid in the dish. Use 6 oz. (150 g.) pastry (short, sweet shortcrust or flaky) to cover 1½–2-pint (1–1¼-litre) pie dish.

Corned beef roll, recipe on page 69

Week 31

Sunday

To make the crackling of pork really crisp, rub with oil (or melted lard) before cooking. Some people like to sprinkle it with salt also, but this is purely a matter of personal taste.

The stuffing for the pork (Sunday) is an interesting adaptation of the familiar sage and onion.

The sauce in which liver is cooked (Tuesday) not only gives interesting flavour, but keeps liver moist.

For your shopping list the main meals need:
2 eggs, 1¾ pints (1 litre) milk, 10 oz. (250 g.) Cheddar or other cooking cheese plus about 3–4 oz. (75–100 g.) cream cheese.

Sunday and Monday need:
Loin pork, roasting chicken, sausagemeat (store carefully).
Potatoes, onions, sage (optional), green salad ingredients, parsley, dessert apples, lemon, fresh fruit.

Tuesday, Wednesday and Thursday need:
Liver (lambs', calf's or ox liver – see recipe).
Potatoes (some large), onions, garlic (optional), tomatoes (some large), parsley, globe artichokes, carrot, chives (optional), oranges, fresh fruit.

Friday and Saturday need:
White fish, rabbit, fat bacon rashers (or bacon pieces). Coffee ice cream, plain chocolate.
Potatoes, onions, green tomatoes, large plums or prunes.

Apple Stuffed Loin of Pork 4 good sized dessert apples, 2 onions, 2 oz. (50 g.) breadcrumbs, seasoning, 1 teaspoon fresh or ½ teaspoon dried sage, 1 oz. (25 g.) melted margarine, little oil, piece loin of pork.
Wipe but do not peel apples, grate coarsely, mix with grated onions, breadcrumbs, seasoning, sage, melted margarine. Slit fat of meat downwards, press stuffing into pocket, brush fat with a little oil to encourage crisping, put in roasting tin. Cook for 25 minutes per lb. (½ kilo), 25 minutes over (weight to include stuffing) in a hot oven, Gas Mark 6–7, 400–425°F. (200–220°C.).

Roasted Onions put peeled onions round joint and cook for 1–1¼ hours depending on size.

Coconut Flan 5–6 oz. (125–150 g.) short or sweet shortcrust pastry, see pages 10 and 89, small can condensed milk, 4 oz. (100 g.) desiccated coconut, grated rind and juice of 1 lemon, lemon marmalade or apricot jam.
Line flan tin with pastry, bake 'blind' for 10–15 minutes until set but not browned. Mix milk with coconut, lemon rind and juice. Cover pastry with thin layer marmalade or jam, then coconut mixture, return to oven to brown pastry and filling, lowering heat to moderate, Gas Mark 5, 375°F. (190°C.).

Wednesday

Manhattan Chicken breast and wings of chicken, seasoning, flour, fat or butter, ½ pint (3 dl.) chicken stock, concentrated tomato purée, 1 tablespoon chopped parsley.
Cut breast and wings of chicken left from Monday into neat pieces, coat in a little seasoned flour, fry in hot fat or butter until pale golden brown. Lift on to a plate, then add chicken stock to fat and flour mixture remaining in pan, bring to boil. When thickened, add tomato purée to flavour, seasoning, chopped parsley. Return chicken to sauce, cover, simmer gently until tender. Serve with:
Potato Sticks cut peeled potatoes into matchstick shapes, fry in hot fat or oil until tender, lift out, reheat fat, plunge potatoes into this again, fry for 1–2 minutes until crisp. Drain on kitchen paper.

Nut Rarebit 4 oz. (100 g.) grated Cheddar cheese, 1 tablespoon chopped nuts, seasoning, 1 teaspoon made-mustard, 1 tablespoon milk, buttered toast.
Prepare before the meal, so quick browning only is necessary. Mix cheese, nuts, seasoning, mustard, milk. Spread on slices of buttered toast, brown steadily under a hot grill.

Thursday

Artichokes Vinaigrette trim leaves and stems from 4 globe artichokes. Simmer in salted water until tender (about 25 minutes). Cool, remove centre and fill with well seasoned oil and vinegar, see picture page 106.

Macaroni Cheese 3–4 oz. (75–100 g.) macaroni, seasoning, 1½ oz. (40 g.) margarine, 1½ oz. (40 g.) flour, ¾ pint (4½ dl.) milk, 3–4 oz. (75–100 g.) grated cheese. For the topping: grated cheese, breadcrumbs, little margarine.
Cook macaroni in 2 pints (1¼ litres) boiling salted water, strain. Meanwhile, make sauce with margarine, flour, milk, seasoning, grated cheese. Add macaroni to sauce, put into ovenproof dish, top with grated cheese, breadcrumbs and a little margarine. Heat through and brown in coolest part of a moderately hot oven, Gas Mark 6, 400°F. (200°C.), for 25 minutes. Serve with:

Stuffed Tomatoes scoop out centres of large tomatoes, chop pulp, mix with little grated raw carrot, few chopped chives or grated onion, seasoning and a knob of margarine. Pile mixture back into tomato cases, bake for approximately 15 minutes.

Follow with fresh fruit.

Bacon and cheese pies, recipe on page 15

MONDAY

Piquant Chicken Legs 1 small roasting chicken, 8 oz. (200 g.) sausagemeat, 1 egg, crisp crumbs, fat for frying. To serve: green salad.
Remove legs from chicken*, cut into 4 joints, press a thin layer of sausagemeat round each joint. Dip in beaten egg and crumbs, fry steadily until crisp and brown. Either continue frying slowly, or transfer to an uncovered dish and bake in a moderate oven, Gas Mark 5, 375°F. (190°C.), for 35–40 minutes. Serve with green salad and Fried Rice.
*Reserve breast and wings for Wednesday.

Fried Rice 4–6 oz. (100–150 g.) long grain rice, seasoning, fat, chopped parsley.
Boil rice until tender but not too soft. Season well, strain, spread on a plate, allow to dry, then toss in a little hot fat until golden. Mix with chopped parsley.

Cheese, Fruit when home-grown pears are plentiful and not too expensive they are delicious served with a real cream or cottage cheese.

TUESDAY

Liver Provençal 2 onions, 1–2 garlic cloves (optional), fat for frying, medium sized can tomatoes *or* 4 large tomatoes plus ¼ pint (1½ dl.) water, seasoning, 1 lb. (½ kilo) liver.
Make a sauce by frying chopped onions and chopped garlic, add canned tomatoes or skinned, chopped tomatoes with water. Season well. When a fairly smooth sauce, pour over the sliced seasoned liver; cover. If using lambs' or calves' liver, bake for only 30 minutes in a very moderate oven, Gas Mark 3, 325°F. (170°C.); if using ox liver, bake for 1 hour.

Foil Baked Potatoes scrub large potatoes, wrap each in greased foil, bake for 1–1½ hours, depending on size.

Baked Oranges 2 oz. (50 g.) sugar, 2 tablespoons plus ½ pint (3 dl.) water, 4 oranges.
Make a caramel with sugar and 2 tablespoons water. When golden brown, add ½ pint (3 dl.) water, stir until caramel has dissolved in this. Put into a fairly deep casserole, add whole peeled oranges, cook for approximately 25–30 minutes. Serve hot or cold.

FRIDAY

Grilled Fish and Egg Sauce steaks or portions of white fish, melted margarine, pinch celery salt, pinch paprika, seasoning. For the sauce: 1 oz. (25 g.) margarine, 1 oz. (25 g.) flour, ½ pint (3 dl.) milk, 1 egg, 1 tablespoon vinegar.
Brush fish with a little melted margarine, to which should be added a pinch celery salt and paprika as well as ordinary seasoning. Grill steadily until golden brown on either side. Meanwhile, make a white sauce with margarine, flour, milk. When thickened add the beaten egg mixed with vinegar and seasoning. Cook very slowly without boiling for 2–3 minutes.

Czech Dumplings if fresh plums are available, split, remove stones and fill with cream cheese. Otherwise use plump soaked but not cooked prunes. Coat each plum or prune with a wafer-thin layer of suet pastry, simmer in boiling salted water for 20–25 minutes. Drain, roll in sugar to which is added a good pinch cinnamon.
Note. Suet crust pastry made with 6 oz. (150 g.) self-raising flour, pinch salt, 3 oz. (75 g.) shredded suet and water to mix, will cover about 12 large plums or prunes.

SATURDAY

Rabbit Pie 1 rabbit, 1–2 onions, 1–2 rashers fat bacon, seasoning, 1½ pints (9 dl.) water, 1 oz. (25 g.) margarine, 1 oz. (25 g.) flour, ¼ pint (1½ dl.) milk, ¼ pint (1½ dl.) rabbit stock, 6 oz. (150 g.) shortcrust or flaky pastry, see pages 10 and 137.
Simmer jointed rabbit with chopped onions, diced bacon, seasoning and water until tender. Lift out rabbit, put into pie dish, cover with sauce made with margarine, flour, milk, rabbit stock, seasoning. Top with pastry, bake in hot oven, Gas Mark 7, 425°F. (220°C.), until pastry is golden brown, lower heat to ensure rabbit is heated through.

Braised Green Tomatoes 1 oz. (25 g.) dripping or fat, 1 oz. (25 g.) flour, good ½ pint (3 dl.) water or rabbit stock, 1 beef stock cube, 1 lb. (½ kilo) green tomatoes.
Make a sauce with dripping or fat, flour, water (or in this case, rabbit stock) and stock cube. Put in the tomatoes, simmer gently in covered pan until soft but unbroken.

Coffee Chocolate Sundaes top coffee ice cream with chocolate sauce and chopped nuts. To make sauce, melt 4 oz. (100 g.) plain chocolate with 2–3 tablespoons milk in a basin over hot water.

Week 32

Topside is a roasting joint which appeals to many families, not only because it is cheaper than sirloin or rib but because it is an exceptionally lean piece of beef. I prefer to roast topside more slowly than when cooking sirloin, etc. This means you cannot roast potatoes but if you raise the oven temperature for the final cooking time (see Sunday's menu) you cook small puddings well.

For your shopping list the main meals need:
12 eggs, 2½ pints (nearly 1½ litres) milk, 6 oz. (150 g.) Cheddar or other cooking cheese.
Sunday, Monday, Tuesday and Wednesday need:
Topside beef, bacon rashers, cooked ham, loin lamb (store carefully).
Crème de menthe, cream (thick or thin) or ice cream. French bread.
Potatoes, green vegetables, swedes, parsley, onions, cooked beetroot (store carefully), cabbage (preferably white), carrot (optional), celery (optional), tomatoes, garlic (optional), marrow, red or green pepper, aubergine (optional), dessert apples, lemons.
Thursday, Friday and Saturday need:
Tripe, sausagemeat (store carefully).
Macaroon biscuits, cream (thick or thin) – optional.
Potatoes (some large), spinach, parsley, celeriac, onion, tomatoes, dates, apples.

Sunday

Roast Topside of Beef try slower roasting to give very tender flavour to this joint. Cover outside with a little fat and allow 35 minutes per lb. (½ kilo) and 35 minutes over in centre of oven at Gas Mark 4, 350°F. (180°C.). Serve with a green vegetable, mashed swedes and jacket potatoes.

Yorkshire Pudding 3 oz. (75 g.) flour, pinch salt, 1 egg, ¼ pint (1½ dl.) milk, 4 tablespoons water, 1 teaspoon chopped parsley, pinch mixed herbs.
Since oven is too cool for cooking large Yorkshire Pudding, put mixture in small patty tins, which means raising temperature of oven for the last 20–25 minutes only. Switch or turn heat to Gas Mark 7, 425°F. (220°C.). Grease 6–9 small patty tins, heat well. Make a batter* with flour, salt, egg, milk, water, add parsley and herbs. Pour into hot tins, bake at top of oven for 15 minutes, or until firm.
*double amount of plain batter can be made and half stored in screw-topped jar in refrigerator for Tuesday.

Crème de Menthe Jellies make an ordinary lemon jelly, using 2 tablespoons less water than usual. Stir in 2 tablespoons crème de menthe, pour into mould rinsed out in cold water. When set, turn out, serve with cream or ice cream.

Wednesday

Stuffed Loin of Lamb piece loin of lamb. For the stuffing: 1–2 tablespoons chopped parsley, grated rind and juice 1 lemon, 4 oz. (100 g.) breadcrumbs, 2 oz. (50 g.) shredded suet, 1 egg, seasoning.
Make a slit in the fat of the loin to give a 'pocket', pack with lemon parsley stuffing. To make the stuffing add parsley, lemon rind and juice to breadcrumbs, stir in suet, egg and seasoning. Cook as timing page 54. Always weigh meat after stuffing.

Ratatouille 2 onions, 4 large tomatoes, 2 tablespoons oil, 1–2 crushed garlic cloves (optional), 1 small marrow, 1 red or green pepper, 1 small aubergine (optional), seasoning, chopped parsley.
Fry sliced onions and skinned tomatoes in oil, add garlic if wished. Add diced peeled marrow, chopped red or green pepper and for a special occasion, the sliced aubergine (egg plant). Season well, add no liquid. Either cook in tightly covered casserole in coolest part of oven, or in saucepan. Top with chopped parsley.

Blackcurrant Whip use either a can blackcurrants and drain off syrup, or blackcurrant pie filling. Mash or crush fruit, mix with small can whipped evaporated milk. To whip milk, boil can for 15 minutes, open, and when milk is cold, whisk vigorously.

Thursday

Tripe Mornay 1½ lb. (¾ kilo) tripe, seasoning, 1 oz. (25 g.) margarine, 1 oz. (25 g.) flour, ½ pint (3 dl.) milk, 3 tablespoons tripe stock, 3 oz. (75 g.) grated cheese. To garnish: creamed spinach.
Blanch tripe by bringing to the boil and simmering for 5 minutes; throw away the water. Cut tripe into neat fingers, simmer in fresh salted water for approximately 45 minutes. Make a cheese sauce with margarine, flour, milk, stock, stir in grated cheese and seasoning. Strain tripe into hot dish, top with sauce, garnish with creamed spinach.

Potato Whirls cream cooked potatoes, form into whirls with large pipe. Brown under grill for a few minutes. Cook extra potatoes and mash for Friday.

Date and Walnut Sponge 3 oz. (75 g.) margarine, 3 oz. (75 g.) sugar, 1 egg, 4 oz. (100 g.) self-raising flour, 4 oz. (100 g.) chopped dates, 1 oz. (25 g.) chopped walnuts, milk.
Cream margarine with sugar, add egg, fold in flour, dates and nuts. Add milk to make a sticky consistency. Put into a greased basin, top with greased foil, steam for 1½ hours.

MONDAY

Beef Rolls 12 oz. (300 g.) cooked beef, 2 rashers bacon or little cooked ham, seasoning, little chopped parsley, pinch mixed herbs, little chopped onion, 1 egg, 8 oz. (200 g.) shortcrust pastry, see page 10, milk.

Mince or chop beef with bacon or ham, season well, add parsley, herbs and onion. Bind with egg. Roll out pastry to an oblong, spread with meat mixture, roll up (like a Swiss roll). Brush with milk, bake for 30—35 minutes in centre of hot oven, Gas Mark 7, 425°F. (220°C.), reducing heat slightly after 20 minutes. Cut into neat slices to serve.

Spiced Hot Beetroot 1 oz. (25 g.) butter, 1 tablespoon vinegar, pinch each of sugar, salt, cayenne pepper, mustard, mixed spice, 1—2 teaspoons Worcestershire sauce, 1—2 beetroots.

Heat butter with vinegar, seasonings, spice and Worcestershire sauce. Dice beetroot and heat in this.

Maple Syrup Mould make a blancmange or cornflour mould. Turn out, top with mock maple syrup made by heating 2 tablespoons golden syrup and 2 tablespoons brown sugar.

TUESDAY

Bean Chowder 2 large onions, 1 oz. (25 g.) margarine, 2 rashers bacon, 1 large potato, large can beans in tomato sauce, ½ pint (3 dl.) water, seasoning. To serve: French bread.

Fry chopped onions in margarine until tender but not browned. Towards end of cooking time add chopped bacon and potato cut into ¼-inch (½-cm.) dice. Add beans, water, season well, simmer until potato is cooked and mixture hot. Serve in soup bowls with crusty French bread.

Ham and Apple Coleslaw ½ small cabbage, 1—2 dessert apples, 4—6 oz. (100—150 g.) diced ham, mayonnaise.

Shred cabbage finely, mix with peeled, chopped apples, diced ham and mayonnaise. (Grated raw carrot, chopped celery can also be added, if wished.) Picture page 91.

Lemon Pineapple Fritters if using batter stored from Sunday, pour into basin and beat in 1 oz. (25 g.) extra flour; if making fresh, use 4 oz. (100 g.) flour to same amount of egg, milk and water. Add grated rind 1 lemon, 2 tablespoons lemon juice. Dip rings canned pineapple in little flour, coat in batter, fry until crisp and brown, roll in sugar and serve.

FRIDAY

Potato and Tuna Nests chopped parsley, potatoes left from Thursday, 1 egg, 2 tablespoons milk, seasoning, medium can tuna.

Add parsley to potatoes from Thursday or cook and mash specially, form into 4 nest shapes. Blend egg, milk and seasoning with tuna, fill nests, heat in a moderately hot oven, Gas Mark 5, 375°F. (190°C.), for 20 minutes.

Scalloped Celeriac (celery root) peel, slice, boil in salted water for 15—20 minutes; strain, put in an oven-proof serving dish with a little butter and top of the milk between each layer. Heat in oven for 20—30 minutes, until the top is pale gold.

Macaroon Sweet Omelette 4 eggs, 2 tablespoons milk or cream, ½ tablespoon sugar, 2 macaroon biscuits, 1 oz. (25 g.) butter, sweetened apple purée.

Separate eggs, beat yolks with milk or cream, sugar and crushed macaroon biscuits, fold in stiffly beaten egg whites. Heat butter in omelette pan, cook mixture for few minutes until set underneath. Put pan under grill or in oven to set on top. Fill with thin apple purée.

SATURDAY

Guy Fawkes or Rocket Patties 1 lb. (½ kilo) sausage-meat, 2 teaspoons grated onion, 2 tomatoes, 1 table-spoon breadcrumbs, 1 beaten egg, crisp breadcrumbs, little fat.

Mix sausagemeat with onion, skinned finely chopped tomatoes, breadcrumbs. Form into 8 croquettes, brush with beaten egg, roll in crisp breadcrumbs, fry, bake or grill. Insert wooden skewers gently into base, stand the 'rockets' up in a tall container.

Stuffed Potatoes bake potatoes in jackets, scoop out centre pulp, mash with seasoning, little butter or margarine and grated cheese. Pile back in potato halves, heat in oven until golden brown.

Spiced Fruit Fingers 3 oz. (75 g.) margarine, 5 oz. (125 g.) self-raising flour, 1 teaspoon mixed spice, 4 oz. (100 g.) brown sugar, 6 oz. (150 g.) mixed dried fruit, 1 egg. To serve: castor sugar.

Rub margarine into flour sieved with spice. Add sugar, fruit and egg to bind. Press into a 7-inch (18-cm.) well greased tin, bake in centre of a moderate oven, Gas Mark 5, 375°F. (190°C.) until golden brown — approximately 30 minutes. Cut into fingers, serve with castor sugar.

Week 33

The fresh taste of lemon with chicken makes a very pleasant change for Sunday's main dish. Simmer a young boiling fowl for 25–30 minutes per lb. (½ kilo) and 25–30 minutes over; a young roasting chicken for 15 minutes per lb. (½ kilo) and 15 minutes over.
A Fruit Cobbler (Sunday) makes a change from a pie, and you could make up extra scones for tea.
If using frozen shelled prawns (Thursday), allow to thaw out at room temperature. You will need to buy ¾ pint (4½ dl.) prawns (or shrimps) in shells to give enough when shelled.

For your shopping list the main meals need:
13–15 eggs, approximately 3½ pints (approximately 2 litres) milk, 12 oz. (300 g.) cottage or cream cheese but no Cheddar cheese.
Sunday, Monday and Tuesday need:
Chicken, pork chops (store carefully).
Thick cream, rose hip syrup, rennet.
Potatoes, onions, carrots, cauliflower, garlic, mixed salad ingredients, lemons, fruit for cobbler.
Wednesday, Thursday and Friday need:
Lambs' kidneys, bacon rashers, plaice, prawns (store very carefully).
Cornflakes, chocolate, cream (thick or thin).
Potatoes, onions, mixed root vegetables, parsley, celery, tomatoes, mixed dried fruits, oranges, lemons.
Saturday needs:
Stewing steak, lemon squash, potatoes, onions.

Sunday

Lemon Chicken 1 chicken, 1 bay leaf, 1–2 onions, 1–2 carrots, seasoning, little melted butter, juice and finely grated rind of 1 lemon.
Put chicken into cold water, add bay leaf, onions, carrots, season well, simmer until just tender. Lift on to a hot dish, brush with butter, sprinkle with lemon juice and rind. Put at top of a moderately hot oven, Gas Mark 6, 400°F. (200°C.), for 10–15 minutes to brown outside. (Save chicken stock for Tuesday).

Creamed Cauliflower divide cauliflower into small sprigs, boil until *just* tender in salted water, strain. Make ½ pint (3 dl.) white sauce, see page 5. Arrange layers of cauliflower and sauce in an ovenproof dish, top with a few breadcrumbs, put into oven for 10 minutes.

Fruit Cobbler put 1–1½ lb. (½–¾ kilo) prepared fruit in a dish with a little water and sugar to taste. Heat until softened slightly. Top with rounds of scone mixture and bake towards the top of a hot oven for 15–20 minutes, see picture page 98. Serve with cream.
To make scone mixture: sieve 4 oz. (100 g.) self-raising flour and a pinch salt, rub in 1 oz. (25 g.) margarine, add 1 oz. (25g.) sugar, bind with milk to a soft rolling consistency.

Wednesday

Braised Kidneys 8 lambs' kidneys, 1 onion, 2 rashers bacon, 1 oz. (25 g.) fat, ½ oz. (15 g.) flour, ½ pint (3 dl.) stock or water and beef stock cube, 1 tablespoon concentrated tomato purée, seasoning. To serve: mixed diced vegetables.
Wash, skin and halve kidneys. Fry chopped onion, chopped bacon in fat. Add flour, stock or water and stock cube, tomato purée, seasoning. Bring to boil, cook until thickened slightly, add kidneys, simmer gently for 15–20 minutes. Serve in a border of cooked mixed diced vegetables.

Compote Dried Fruit soak 8 oz. (¼ kilo) dried fruit in cold water overnight. Add sugar to taste, cook in a covered casserole in a slow oven, Gas Mark 2, 300°F. (150°C.), for 1 hour. Serve with:

Baked Custard 2 eggs, 1 oz. (25 g.) sugar, ¾ pint (4½ dl.) milk, grated nutmeg (optional).
Beat eggs with sugar, add warm milk, strain into an ovenproof dish. Stand this in another dish of cold water. Top with grated nutmeg if wished. Bake the custard for 1 hour in the coolest part of the oven.

Thursday

Plaice and Prawn Bake seasoning, 8 fillets plaice, 2 oz. (50 g.) prawns, 1 oz. (25 g.) margarine, 1 oz. (25 g.) breadcrumbs, 2 tablespoons chopped parsley, little extra margarine. To garnish: few prawns, parsley, lemon. To serve: jacket potatoes.
Well season fillets of plaice. Arrange 4 in a greased ovenproof dish. Mix prawns with margarine, breadcrumbs, seasoning and parsley, spread over the fillets. Top with rest of fillets, little margarine; bake above centre of a moderately hot oven, Gas Mark 5, 375°F. (190°C.), for 30 minutes. Garnish with a few prawns, parsley and lemon. Serve with jacket potatoes.

Choco-orange Flan 2 oz. (50 g.) butter, 3 oz. (75 g.) icing sugar, 1 oz. (25 g.) cocoa, 5 oz. (125 g.) crushed cornflakes, 1 pint (6 dl.) thick custard, 2 oranges, grated chocolate. To serve: cream.
Cream butter, icing sugar, add cocoa and cornflakes. Form into flan shape, leave in cool place to set. Make custard, add grated rind of oranges. When cold, pour custard into flan case, top with rings of fresh orange, grated chocolate. Serve with cream.
To make a thick custard: use 2 good tablespoons custard powder, 1 pint (6 dl.) milk, sugar to taste (do not have filling too sweet). Follow directions on tin or packet.

MONDAY

Pork Chops Provençal 1 onion, 1 garlic clove, 1 oz. (25 g.) fat, medium sized can tomatoes, seasoning, 4 tablespoons water, 4 pork chops.
Fry finely chopped onion and garlic in fat. Add tomatoes, seasoning and water. Arrange pork chops in this mixture and cook slowly for 20 minutes in a covered pan. Turn chops halfway through cooking.

Cherry Castles 2 oz. (50 g.) margarine, 2 oz. (50 g.) sugar, 1 egg, 4 oz. (100 g.) self-raising flour, 2–3 oz. (50–75 g.) chopped glacé cherries, 2 tablespoons milk.
Cream margarine with sugar. Add egg, flour, cherries and milk. Half fill greased dariole moulds (castle pudding tins), cover with greased greaseproof paper. Steam for 20 minutes. Serve with:

Rosy Sauce 2 level teaspoons cornflour, ¼ pint (1½ dl.) water, finely grated rind of 1 lemon, 2 tablespoons rose hip syrup, little sugar (optional).
Blend cornflour with water; bring to boil with the lemon rind. Cook until thickened, stirring all the time. (Save rest of lemon for Tuesday.) Remove pan from heat and stir in rose hip syrup, plus little extra sugar if required. Do not boil again.

TUESDAY

Chicken Broth remove from bones any small pieces of chicken left, rub vegetables cooked with chicken on Sunday through a sieve, return to stock together with 1–2 oz. (25–50 g.) long grain rice. Simmer steadily until rice is tender, add pieces of chicken, re-season. Serve topped with croûtons of crisp fried bread.

Stuffed Egg Salad 4–6 hard-boiled eggs, juice of 1 lemon, small can sardines, seasoning. To serve: mixed salad.
Shell eggs, halve, remove yolks. Mash yolks with lemon juice, sardines, little seasoning. Pile back into the white cases and serve on a bed of mixed salad.

Coffee Junkets ¼ pint (1½ dl.) strong coffee, ¾ pint (4½ dl.) milk, *or* 1 pint (6 dl.) milk flavoured with coffee essence, 1–2 oz. (25–50 g.) sugar, 1 teaspoon rennet. To serve: cream, chopped walnuts (optional).
Bring coffee and milk, or milk flavoured with coffee essence, to blood heat. Add sugar, rennet. Pour into sundae glasses; allow to set. Serve topped with cream and chopped walnuts if wished.

Soak dried fruit for tomorrow.

FRIDAY

Vegetable Roast 1 lb. (½ kilo) carrots, 1 large onion, 4 stalks celery, 2 oz. (50 g.) breadcrumbs, ¼ pint (1½ dl.) milk, 2 eggs, seasoning, 1 tablespoon chopped parsley, tomatoes.
Grate peeled carrots, mix with very finely chopped onion, celery, breadcrumbs, milk, eggs, seasoning, parsley. Put into a well greased loaf tin or ovenproof baking dish. Bake in centre of a moderate oven, Gas Mark 5, 375°F. (190°C.), for 45 minutes. Bake tomatoes in oven for the last 10–15 minutes. Turn out vegetable roast, arrange tomatoes round.

Feather Cheese Cake sweet shortcrust pastry*, 1 oz. (25 g.) cornflour, 12 oz. (300 g.) cottage or cream cheese, small can sweetened condensed milk, 3 eggs, 1 lemon.
Line 8-inch (20-cm.) flan ring or sandwich tin with a thin layer of pastry; bake 'blind' for 10 minutes. Mix cornflour with cottage or cream cheese, add condensed milk, egg yolks, grated rind and juice of lemon. Fold in stiffly beaten egg whites. Spoon carefully into half-baked pastry case, cook in cool oven, Gas Mark 2, 300°F. (150°C.), for 1 hour. Allow to cool in oven with heat off. (Serves 8 good portions.)
Sweet shortcrust pastry: sieve 6 oz. (150 g.) plain flour, pinch salt and rub in 3–3½ oz. (75–90 g.) butter or margarine; add 1 oz. (25 g.) sugar and bind with water or egg yolk and water.

SATURDAY

Steak and Onion Pudding 10 oz. (250 g.) self-raising flour, pinch salt, 5 oz. (125 g.) shredded suet, water to mix, 1¼ lb. (⅝ kilo) stewing steak, seasoned flour, 12 oz. (300 g.) onions, few tablespoons stock or water.
Make suet crust pastry with flour, salt, suet, cold water to mix. Use two-thirds to line a pudding basin. Fill with the diced stewing steak rolled in seasoned flour, sliced onions, stock or water. Cover with a suet crust lid, then greaseproof paper or greased foil. Steam for 3–4 hours.

Honeycomb Mould ¼ pint (1½ dl.) lemon squash, ¾ pint (4½ dl.) water, 2 oz. (50 g.) sugar, 1 egg, ½ oz. (15 g.) powdered gelatine, 2 tablespoons cold water.
Put lemon squash blended with water into a saucepan with sugar and egg yolk. Whisk over low heat until mixture thickens very slightly, but it should never boil. Soften gelatine in the cold water, add to mixture. When cold and beginning to thicken, add stiffly beaten egg white. Pour into a mould; allow to set.

Cheese pie, recipe on page 119

 Week 34

 Sunday

Tender plump pigeons (or squabs, as they often are called) are delicious as a main dish. They can be roasted but the method of cooking (in Sunday's menu) keeps them very moist.

Never cook chestnuts and sprouts in the same pan, otherwise the sprouts become a strange colour; cook separately and mix before serving.

If you have any clarified dripping, cook the mushrooms in this (for the savoury on Tuesday) as dripping gives them a very good flavour.

For your shopping list the main meals need:
7–8 eggs, 3½ pints (2 litres) milk, 8 oz. (200 g.) Cheddar or other cheese (see Thursday's salad).
Sunday, Monday, Tuesday, Wednesday and Thursday need:
Pigeons, minced steak (store carefully), middle or scrag end neck of lamb, cooked ham.
Port wine, ice cream, French almond rock or peanut brittle, capers, thin cream (optional).
Potatoes, sprouts, chestnuts, parsley, onions, tomato (optional), carrots, mushrooms (store carefully), peas, green salad ingredients (store carefully), lemon, oranges, melon (to be ripe by Wednesday), apple (dessert or cooking), fresh fruit.
Friday and Saturday need:
Whiting, stewing steak.
Potatoes, onions, parsley, cauliflower, cooking apples.

Salmis of Pigeon 2 large or 4 small pigeons, seasoning, 1½ oz. (40 g.) flour, 2 oz. (50 g.) fat, ¾ pint (4½ dl.) brown stock or water and stock cube, 2–3 tablespoons port wine, 2 tablespoons lemon juice, 1 tablespoon redcurrant jelly, few olives (optional).
Wash and dry pigeons. Coat in half the seasoned flour, fry for 5 minutes in fat, put into casserole. Add remaining flour to fat and cook for 2–3 minutes. Stir in brown stock or water and stock cube. Allow to thicken, add port wine, lemon juice and jelly. Season, pour over pigeons. Cover casserole and cook for 1½–2 hours in a very moderate oven. A few olives may be added. Serve with redcurrant jelly.

Sprouts and Chestnuts chestnuts, seasoning, sprouts, butter.
Split chestnuts, boil for 10 minutes, remove shells. Put in fresh boiling seasoned water, cook for 10 minutes. Cook sprouts separately in salted water. Strain sprouts and chestnuts, toss in butter.

Orange Brulée 1¼ oz. (35 g.) cornflour, 1 pint (6 dl.) milk, 1–2 oz. (25–50 g.) sugar, 2 oranges, brown sugar. Make cornflour mould, flavour with grated orange rinds. Pour into soufflé dish or heat-resisting serving dish, top with orange rings. Sprinkle with a layer of brown sugar, heat under low grill until crisp.

Wednesday

Thursday

Ham Rolls can celery hearts, 4 slices ham, mustard sauce, see below. To serve: peas.
Divide celery hearts into 4 good portions. Roll a slice of ham round each portion and arrange neatly in a long ovenproof dish. Cover with mustard sauce, see below, and heat for about 15 minutes in a moderately hot oven, Gas Mark 5–6, 375–400°F. (190–200°C.). Serve with cooked peas.

Mustard Sauce ½–1 level tablespoon dry mustard, 1 oz. (25 g.) flour, 1 oz. (25 g.) margarine, ½ pint (3 dl.) milk, seasoning.
Blend mustard with flour. Make a sauce with margarine, the mustard and flour mixture, milk and seasoning.

Melon Ginger make balls or dice ripe melon. Put into a bowl. Toss in sugar and powdered ginger or diced preserved ginger. Spoon into sundae glasses. Top with a little thin cream if wished.

Mulligatawny Soup 1 large onion, 1 apple, 1 large carrot, 2 oz. (50 g.) fat, 1 oz. (25 g.) flour, ½–1 level tablespoon curry powder, 1½ pints (9 dl.) lamb stock, good pinch sugar, few drops vinegar, 1 oz. (25 g.) sultanas, 1 tablespoon finely chopped sweet chutney.
Fry chopped onion, diced apple, carrot in fat. Stir in flour, curry powder and stock. Bring to the boil, cook until thickened slightly, then add sugar, vinegar, sultanas, chutney. Simmer together for 15–20 minutes.

Cheese Caesar Salad 8 oz. (200 g.) Cheddar, Cheshire or Lancashire cheese, 2–3 slices bread, 2 tablespoons oil, green salad. To garnish: anchovy fillets, hard-boiled eggs.
Dice cheese. Cut bread into small dice, fry in oil until crisp and golden; cool. Mix with diced cheese and serve on a bed of green salad. Garnish with anchovy fillets, sliced hard-boiled egg.

Fresh Fruit there should be many varieties of good apples available and these would follow the salad excellently; or serve bananas, sliced and topped with a little thin cream.

Coleslaw, recipe on page 87

MONDAY

Viennese Steaks 12 oz. (300 g.) minced meat, 1 tablespoon tomato ketchup, ½ tablespoon chopped parsley, seasoning, pinch mixed herbs, 1 egg, flour, fat for frying, onion rings.

Mix together minced meat, tomato ketchup, parsley, seasoning, herbs and egg yolk. Form into 4 flat cakes like pieces of steak. Flour well, fry until golden brown. Keep hot, top with rings of onion dipped in beaten egg white and flour and fried until crisp and golden.

Tomato Potato Cakes tomato ketchup *or* 1 tomato, 1 lb. (½ kilo) creamed potatoes, flour, fat for frying.

Add small amount of ketchup or the skinned, chopped tomato to creamed potatoes. Form into cakes, flour, fry until crisp and golden brown. Serve round the Viennese steaks. If frying in one pan, cook these before the meat and onions and keep hot.

Ice Cream Brittle crush a little French almond rock or peanut brittle and top portions of ice cream with this.

TUESDAY

Lamb and Caper Sauce middle or scrag end of neck of lamb, 3–4 onions, 4 carrots, water, seasoning, 1 oz. (25 g.) margarine, 1 oz. (25 g.) flour, ¼ pint (1½ dl.) milk, ¼ pint (1½ dl.) lamb stock, 2 teaspoons capers, little vinegar, chopped parsley.

Simmer lamb with whole onions, whole carrots, water to cover and seasoning until tender, approximately 1½ hours. Make a sauce with margarine, flour, milk, stock and seasoning. Add capers and little vinegar from bottle of capers. Lift lamb out of stock, arrange on a dish with vegetables, chopped parsley. (Save stock for Thursday; re-boil on Wednesday if you have no refrigerator.)

Vichy Carrots slice peeled carrots thinly, cook in well seasoned stock with small knob of butter or margarine, with lid off pan, so carrots absorb stock and become rather shiny. Serve topped with chopped parsley.

Mushrooms on Toast mushrooms, little fat, toast.

Cook mushrooms lightly in fat until tender. Put on ovenproof plate and keep warm in very low oven. Make toast at last minute, put mushrooms on top.

FRIDAY

Whiting Twists 4 small or 2 large whiting, beaten egg, crisp breadcrumbs, fat for frying.

Cut fish into fillets, remove heads and bones. Roll lightly, secure with wooden cocktail sticks. Coat with beaten egg and crumbs, fry in hot fat until crisp and golden brown.

Fried Potatoes cut potatoes into slices or chip shapes and fry once until tender, lift out of hot fat, reheat this, then fry potatoes again until really crisp and golden brown. Drain well on crumpled tissue or kitchen paper.

Cabinet Puddings 2 large slices bread, ¾ pint (4½ dl.) milk, 2 eggs, 2 oz. (50 g.) sugar, 3–4 oz. (75–100 g.) mixed dried fruit.

Remove crusts from bread, cut into dice. Heat ½ pint (3 dl.) milk, pour over bread and stand for short time. Beat eggs with remaining milk, stir into bread mixture with sugar. Grease dariole moulds very well, arrange dried fruit in bottom and round sides of these. Pour in egg custard mixture. Cover with greased greaseproof paper and steam for 25–30 minutes.

SATURDAY

Goulash 1 tablespoon flour, 1 tablespoon paprika, 1 lb. (½ kilo) stewing beef, 1 oz. (25 g.) fat, 2 large onions, medium can tomatoes, 12 oz. (300 g.) peeled potatoes, seasoning, chopped parsley.

Mix flour and paprika. Coat diced meat in this, fry in fat for a few minutes. Put on to a plate. Fry sliced onions for few minutes until softened slightly, add tomatoes, simmer for few minutes until a purée. Add the meat. Cover pan, simmer gently for 1 hour. Add sliced potatoes, seasoning, and continue cooking for a further ½ hour until potatoes are tender. Pile mixture into a hot dish, garnish with parsley. This is a very thick stew; take care it does not burn. Add a little water if necessary during cooking.

Crisp Topped Cauliflower 1 cauliflower, 1 hard-boiled egg, little chopped parsley, 2 tablespoons crisp breadcrumbs, 1 oz. (25 g.) margarine.

Cook cauliflower whole, strain. Toss chopped egg, parsley, crisp crumbs in margarine. Sprinkle over cauliflower and serve.

Apple Custard arrange layers of thick apple purée, sultanas and thick custard (see page 88) in sundae glasses, end with apple. Decorate with glacé cherries and angelica.

Week 35

Sunday

Puff pastry is used for Saturday's menu. Puff pastry made with 8 oz. (200 g.) flour, etc., or 1 lb. (½ kilo) ready-frozen puff pastry will make sufficient vol-au-vent cases for 4–6 people.

For your shopping list the main meals need:
5 eggs, approximately 2½ pints (approximately 1½ litres) milk, 5–7 oz. (125–175 g.) Cheddar or other cooking cheese — more if making cheese filling for Saturday, 1 tablespoon grated Parmesan cheese (optional), about 4 oz. (100 g.) cream cheese.

Sunday and Monday need:
Veal (see recipe for suggested cuts), thick cream.
Potatoes, peas, green salad ingredients, red cabbage (optional), parsley, lemon, fresh pineapple (optional), prunes (optional).

Tuesday, Wednesday and Thursday need:
Minced steak, liver (preferably lambs' or calves', but ox live can be used — optional), pig's fry (store carefully), fish fingers, potatoes, tomatoes, celery, carrot, green salad ingredients, cooking apples, lemon, dessert apple, bananas, oranges.

Friday and Saturday need:
Prawns, cooked ham or fish (both optional).
Red wine, cream (thick or thin) or ice cream.
Potatoes, mixed vegetables (optional), onions, prunes, pears, apples.

Roast Veal and Barbecue Sauce part of leg or loin or breast of veal, fat. For the sauce: 1 level tablespoon flour, good pinch salt, shake cayenne pepper, 2 teaspoons brown sugar, ½ teaspoon dry mustard, grated rind and juice of 1 lemon, 2 tablespoons tomato ketchup, ½ pint (3 dl.) water, 2 teaspoons Worcestershire sauce.
Put veal into roasting tin and cover with a generous amount of fat, for veal dries easily in cooking. Allow 25 minutes per lb. (½ kilo) and 25 minutes over in a hot oven, Gas Mark 7, 425–450°F. (220–230°C.). The heat may be lowered after 30–40 minutes cooking to moderately hot. Keep meat basted with fat during cooking and serve with the sauce, or, if preferred, baste with fat and a little sauce towards the end of the cooking time. To make the sauce, heat all the ingredients gently for 10–15 minutes.

Peas Indienne toss cooked peas in a little butter to which is added a good pinch of curry powder.

Pineapple Brulée 8 slices canned or fresh pineapple, 2 oz. (50 g.) flaked almonds, 1 oz. (25 g.) brown sugar, ¼ pint (1½ dl.) thick cream.
Put the pineapple slices on a flat ovenproof dish, top with the almonds and sugar and brown for 2–3 minutes under the grill. Top with whipped cream.

Wednesday

Pig's Fry 1–1½ lb. (½–¾ kilo) pig's fry, seasoning, flour, fat for frying.
Wash and dry pig's fry. Coat lightly in seasoned flour, fry until tender. Arrange on a hot dish.

Savoury Tomatoes slice tomatoes, sprinkle very lightly with a little paprika, celery salt and brown sugar. Fry until just tender. Arrange round pig's fry.

Spiced Apple Crisp cooking apples, honey, sugar or golden syrup, little water, 2 oz. (50 g.) margarine, 2 oz. (50 g.) sugar, ½–1 level teaspoon mixed spice, 1 level tablespoon golden syrup, 4 oz. (100 g.) rolled oats.
Half fill pie dish with thinly sliced apples. Add either honey, sugar or syrup to sweeten and very little water. Heat gently in oven for 15–20 minutes. Do not have heat too high, otherwise apples will dry on top. Thoroughly mix together margarine, sugar, spice, syrup and oats. Spread with a damp knife on top of apple. Return to oven, cook in a very moderate heat, Gas Mark 3, 325°F. (170°C.), until top is crisp and golden brown — 35–40 minutes.

Thursday

Sweet and Sour Fish Fingers 1 large carrot, 2 small gherkins, 1 lemon, ½ tablespoon cornflour or arrowroot, ¼ pint (1½ dl.) water, seasoning, 2 teaspoons honey or sugar, fish fingers. To serve: green salad.
Blend together grated carrot, gherkins cut into neat slices, grated rind and juice of lemon with cornflour or arrowroot. Add water, seasoning and honey or sugar. Put in a saucepan, allow to simmer. Taste and adjust sweetening and seasoning if necessary. Grill fish fingers until crisp and golden brown. Serve with the sauce and crisp green salad.

Fried Mixed Fruits 1 dessert apple, 2 oz. (50 g.) butter, 3–4 bananas, brown sugar, 2–3 oranges.
Fry cored but not peeled rings of apple in butter in a pan. Add halved bananas. Cook until golden brown, adding a little brown sugar to fruits. Put on a hot serving dish, then fry rings of fresh orange for a few minutes. This will keep hot while serving the first course.
*put prunes to soak overnight in weak well strained tea.

MONDAY

Cold Veal serve on a bed of green salad. Well drained cooked prunes and red cabbage form good accompaniments.

Potato Puffs 2 eggs, 1 lb. ($\frac{1}{2}$ kilo) mashed potatoes, little chopped parsley, 1 tablespoon grated Parmesan cheese or 2 tablespoons grated Cheddar cheese, seasoning, fat or oil for frying.
Add egg yolks to mashed potatoes, together with parsley, grated cheese. Season well, then fold in stiffly beaten egg whites. Drop dessertspoons of the mixture into hot fat or oil. Fry quickly until golden brown, drain well.

Cherry Coconut Meringue large can cherries, 2 eggs, 2–4 oz. (50–100 g.) castor sugar, 2 oz. (50 g.) desiccated coconut.
Put cherries into a pie dish and heat in very moderate oven, Gas Mark 3, 325°F. (170°C.). Whisk egg whites (save yolks for Tuesday) until really stiff. Fold in sugar and coconut. Spread over cherries and return to oven to brown lightly.

TUESDAY

Mexicano Pie 2 egg yolks (from Monday), 1 lb. ($\frac{1}{2}$ kilo) minced steak, 1 oz. (25 g.) flour, 4 oz. (100 g.) chopped liver *or* small can liver pâté, seasoning. Filling: canned sweetcorn, sliced tomato.
Mix egg yolks with steak, flour, liver – or use can liver pâté and a little extra flour. Add seasoning, form into a flan shape on an ovenproof serving plate or dish. Bake in a very moderate oven, Gas Mark 3, 325°F. (170°C.), for 1 hour. Fill with hot sweetcorn and tomato slices.

Braised Celery wash a head of celery, cut into convenient-sized pieces. Prepare as the recipe for braised leeks on page 110, but cook for 1 hour in a covered dish in the oven.

Caramel Ground Rice 4 oz. (100 g.) sugar, 3 tablespoons water, 1 pint (6 dl.) milk, 2 oz. (50 g.) ground rice.
Make a caramel with 3 oz. (75 g.) sugar and the water, see page 85. When golden brown, remove from heat, cool slightly, add milk. Stir over low heat until milk has absorbed caramel. Sprinkle ground rice and rest of sugar into liquid, cook gently for 5 minutes then transfer to a pie dish and cook for a good hour in coolest part of the oven.

FRIDAY

Prawn and Cheese Pancakes 4 oz. (100 g.) flour, pinch salt, 1 egg, $\frac{1}{2}$ pint (3 dl.) milk and water, fat for frying, 4 oz. (100 g.) shelled prawns, seasoning, $\frac{1}{2}$ pint (3 dl.) cheese sauce, see page 5.
Make a smooth pancake batter with the flour, salt, egg, milk and water. Heat a knob of fat in a pan, pour over enough batter to make a thin layer, cook for 2 minutes, turn or toss, and cook on the second side. Continue like this until all the pancakes are cooked. Keep warm, without rolling, on a hot dish over a pan of boiling water. Mix the prawns with hot, well seasoned cheese sauce. Fill the pancakes with this mixture and roll, see picture page 99.

***Prunes de Luxe** 8 oz. (200 g.) prunes, little sugar, 3 tablespoons red wine, few blanched almonds. To serve: ice cream or cream.
Simmer prunes (soaked last night) until tender in a little water. Add sugar and red wine. Arrange in a shallow dish, top with blanched almonds. Serve with ice cream or cream.

SATURDAY

Savoury Vol-au-Vents roll out home-made or frozen puff pastry and form into 2$\frac{1}{2}$-inch (6-cm.) vol-au-vent cases. Bake in a really very hot oven, Gas Mark 8–9, 450–475°F. (230–240°C.), for the first 10–15 minutes to make sure they rise. The moment the pastry begins to brown, lower heat until crisp through to centre. Fill with: mixed vegetables in cheese sauce; diced cooked ham in well flavoured white sauce; cooked flaked fish in a white or cheese sauce, see page 5.

Puff Pastry Use 8 oz. (200 g.) plain flour. Sieve this with a pinch salt then add a little lemon juice and enough cold water to make an *elastic* dough. Roll out to an oblong shape. Place 8 oz. (200 g.) slightly softened butter in the centre of the dough. Fold this to cover the butter, then turn, seal ends etc., as described under flaky pastry, page 137, but allow 7 rollings and 7 foldings.

Scalloped Onions and Potatoes onions, potatoes, margarine, seasoning, little milk (optional).
Arrange layers of equal quantities sliced peeled onions and potatoes in a well greased dish, add a little margarine, plenty of seasoning. Cook in coolest part of oven until tender and brown, about 1 hour. Add a little milk.

Fresh Fruit serve fresh pears and apples with soft cream cheese.
Put 4 oz. (100 g.) haricot beans to soak in cold water overnight.

Week 36

Oxtail Casserole (Sunday's menu) is one of the most satisfying of meals, particularly when haricot beans are added to the meat, etc.

Canned haricot beans could be used instead of the dried variety, add these to the casserole about 30 minutes before serving.

If you choose the shortcrust pastry for the Chocolate Roll (Monday) and Tomato Pie (Thursday) you can make one batch of pastry.

For your shopping list the main meals need:
13–17 eggs, generous 2 pints (1¼ litres) milk or 3 pints (1¾ litres) if serving custard, 6 oz. (150 g.) cream cheese, 3–4 oz. (75–100 g.) Cheddar or other cooking cheese.

Sunday and Monday need:
Oxtail, cream (thick or thin) – (optional).
Potatoes, carrots, leeks or onions, parsley, grapefruit, lemon, oranges.

Tuesday, Wednesday and Thursday need:
Liver (can be more economical pig's or ox liver), rabbit, bacon rashers.
Potatoes, tomatoes, green vegetable, onion (optional), parsley, watercress (store carefully), lemon, cooking apples.

Friday and Saturday need:
Whole plaice, salami, rollmop herrings, prawns or shrimps, ingredients for stuffing.
Potatoes, tomatoes, beetroot, carrots, parsley, lemon, tangerines or clementines.

Oxtail Casserole with Haricot Beans 4 oz. (100 g.) haricot beans, 2–2½ lb. (1–1¼ kilo) oxtail, seasoning, 1½ oz. (40 g.) flour, 1 oz. (25 g.) fat, 2–3 carrots, 2–3 leeks or onions, generous 1 pint (6 dl.) stock or water and 2 beef stock cubes.

Soak beans overnight in cold water. It is a good idea to prepare this casserole the day before if possible, and to remove excess fat before reheating. Cut oxtail into neat pieces, coat in half the seasoned flour. Fry in fat for a few minutes. Lift into casserole, fry sliced carrots, sliced leeks or onions in fat in pan, add to oxtail. Pour out all but 1 tablespoon fat from pan, blend in rest of flour, add stock or water and stock cubes. Bring to boil, cook until thickened, season well. Pour over oxtail; add drained beans. Cover casserole, cook for about 2½ hours (little less if reheating) in centre of very moderate oven, Gas Mark 3, 325°F. (170°C.), see picture page 59.

Fruit Cloud put into a saucepan grated rind of ½ grapefruit, 1 lemon, 2 oranges with 1 pint (6 dl.) water; simmer for 5 minutes. Strain, blend with 1 oz. (25 g.) cornflour. Return to pan with juice of the fruits and 2 oz. (50 g.) sugar. Cook until thickened, cool slightly; add 2 beaten egg yolks, *cook without boiling* for a few minutes, then cool. Fold in 2 stiffly whisked egg whites, spoon into glasses. Chill well.

Wednesday

Paprika Rabbit 1 jointed rabbit, ½–1 tablespoon paprika, 1 tablespoon flour, 1 oz. (25 g.) fat, water, seasoning, 1 rasher fat bacon, 1 onion (optional). For the sauce: 1 oz. (25 g.) margarine, 1 oz. (25 g.) flour, ½ pint (3 dl.) milk, ¼ pint (1½ dl.) rabbit stock. To garnish: wedges of lemon, chopped parsley.

Wash and dry rabbit. Blend paprika with flour. Coat rabbit in this, then fry in fat. Cover with cold water, add seasoning, diced bacon and sliced onion, if wished. Simmer gently until tender – approximately 1½ hours. Make a sauce with margarine, flour, milk, stock, seasoning. Drain rabbit from the liquid. Arrange on a hot dish, cover with sauce, garnish with wedges of lemon and parsley.

Milk Jelly 1 raspberry jelly, ¼ pint (1½ dl.) hot water, ¾ pint (4½ dl.) milk.
Dissolve jelly in the very hot water. When cool, add the cold milk. Pour into a mould, allow to set.

Jam Sauce heat 4 tablespoons raspberry jam with equal amount of water. Serve with the jelly.

Thursday

Tomato Pie 10 oz. (250 g.) shortcrust pastry, see page 10, seasoning, tomatoes, finely chopped bacon, 4 eggs. To glaze: milk or egg.
Roll out pastry, use half to line an 8–9-inch (20–23-cm.) pie plate. Cover with thick layer well seasoned tomatoes, sliced, a layer chopped bacon, another layer of tomato. Make 4 nest shapes in mixture, drop an egg in each. Season well. Put pastry cover lightly over top, seal edges, flute together with bottom pastry. Brush with milk or egg to glaze. Bake in centre of a hot oven, Gas Mark 7, 425°F. (220°C.) for 20–25 minutes, then lower heat to moderately hot, Gas Mark 5, 375°F. (190°C.), for a further 20 minutes.

Watercress Salad sprig some watercress and toss in oil and vinegar dressing.

Sultana Cobbler half fill a pie dish with sliced apples, little water and sugar. Cover, heat for 10–15 minutes. Dip rounds of bread in melted butter, then sugar, put on fruit. Top with sultanas. Bake for 15 minutes.

MONDAY

Corned Beef and Potato Omelette can corned beef, 8 oz. (100 g.) very smooth mashed potato, 3 eggs, ½ tablespoon chopped parsley, seasoning, 4 tablespoons top of the milk.
Slice the corned beef, put into a well greased dish, cover with foil, heat gently in oven. To make the omelette for 4: mix mashed potato with eggs, parsley, seasoning, top of the milk. Grease a shallow ovenproof dish, put in the potato mixture, bake towards top of a moderate oven, Gas Mark 5, 375°F. (190°C.), for 15–20 minutes until pale golden brown. Either serve in dish or turn out and fold like an omelette with corned beef slices around the hot dish.

Chocolate Roll 4–6 oz. (100–150 g.) short or sweet shortcrust pastry, see pages 10 and 89, 2 oz. (50 g.) stale cake or breadcrumbs, 2 oz. (50 g.) sweetened chocolate powder, 1 oz. (25 g.) margarine, 2–3 oz. (50–75 g.) sultanas. To serve: custard or cream.
Roll out pastry to thin oblong. Blend crumbs with chocolate powder, margarine, sultanas. Put mixture thinly over pastry, roll like a Swiss roll. Bake in a hot oven, Gas Mark 7, 425°F. (220°C.), for about 20 minutes, lower heat when omelette goes in, cook for a further 20 minutes. If serving hot, move to coolest part of oven when dishing up main course and turn heat very low. Serve hot with custard; cold with cream.

TUESDAY

Liver and Tomato Fritters 8–12 oz. (200–300 g.) liver, 2 tomatoes, little seasoning, 1 egg, 4 oz. (100 g.) flour, milk, fat for frying. To serve: green vegetable.
An excellent way of serving liver, particularly for children who may not like the rather strong taste. Mince or chop liver finely. Mix with skinned chopped tomatoes, seasoning, egg, flour and enough milk to make a thick batter. Drop spoonfuls into hot fat, fry quickly on either side until crisp and brown, lower heat to cook through to centre. Serve with a green vegetable.

Crumb Pudding 3 tablespoons golden syrup, 2 oz. (50 g.) breadcrumbs, 2 oz. (50 g.) sultanas, 2 oz. (50 g.) flour, 1 oz. (25 g.) shredded suet, 1 egg, milk to mix.
Put 2 tablespoons golden syrup into a greased basin. Mix remaining 1 tablespoon syrup with breadcrumbs, sultanas, add flour, suet, egg and milk to make a sticky consistency. Put into basin, cover with greased foil or paper and steam quickly for 1½ hours.

FRIDAY

Plaice Colbert whole plaice, stuffing, beaten egg, crisp breadcrumbs, fat or butter for frying or grilling.
Wash and dry fish, make a slit down centre. Put a knife under this on either side to make a pocket. Fill this with a stuffing. Dip fish in beaten egg and coat in crisp crumbs. Fry or grill until crisp and golden brown.

Lemon Butter grated rind of 1 lemon, 1 tablespoon lemon juice, 2 oz. (50 g.) butter, chopped watercress (optional).
Beat lemon rind and juice into butter. Add a little chopped watercress if wished. Chill, cut into neat pieces, serve on top of plaice.

Cream Cheese Fingers remove crusts from rather thick slices fresh bread. Cut bread into neat fingers. Coat on top and sides with cream cheese, roll in chopped nuts.

SATURDAY

Hors d'Oeuvre arrange a selection baked beans, hard-boiled eggs with anchovy fillets, slices tomato, salami, rollmop herrings, diced beetroot, prawns or shrimps on a large dish, serve with crisp toast.

Gnocchi 1 pint (6 dl.) water, ½ teaspoon salt, good shake pepper, 4 oz. (100 g.) semolina, 1 egg, grated cheese.
Bring water to boil, add salt, pepper. Gradually shake in semolina, cook for 10 minutes, stirring to prevent sticking. Add beaten egg, cool, press on lightly floured board, roll until ¾ inch (2 cm.) thick, cut in triangles or rounds. Put in an ovenproof dish, top with grated cheese, heat steadily under a moderately hot grill.

Fried Carrots parboil carrot balls (made with vegetable scoop) or slices. Drain well, fry in a little hot fat, toss in parsley. Serve cheese sauce with this if wished.

Fruit when tangerines, clementines, etc., make their appearance they are most refreshing.

Summer pudding, recipe on page 40
Fruit cobbler, recipe on page 88

WEEK 37

The method of cooking the duck (Sunday's menu) is ideal if you buy a large and older bird. The first stage extracts the fat, and the long cooking makes sure the flesh is tender. Allow a frozen duck to thaw out for at least 24 hours before cooking.

If you decide to use ½ pint (3 dl.) sweetened custard instead of whipped evaporated milk (Sunday's dessert), do not make this too thick.

A cheese dish (Cheese Puff, page 69, or Macaroni Cheese, page 84) could replace the tripe.

Note. If the egg whites are large when making meringues (Tuesday) use 110 g. not 100 g. sugar.

For your shopping list the main meals need:
7 eggs, 2½ or 3 pints (1½ or 1¾ litres) milk, 2–3 oz. (50–75 g.) Cheddar or other cooking cheese.
Sunday and Monday need:
Duck, sausages (store carefully), sherry (optional).
Potatoes, onions (some small), celery, cooked beetroot, carrot, cooking apples, cranberries (optional), oranges, bananas, lemon.
Tuesday, Wednesday, Thursday, Friday and Saturday need:
Stewing steak, tripe (store carefully), cooked ham (store carefully).
Potato crisps, ground almonds, brandy or rum (optional). Potatoes, onions, garlic, tomatoes, green pepper, parsley, salad ingredients, mixed vegetables, chestnuts, fruit for pancakes (optional).

Casserole of Duck and Celery 1 duck with giblets, 1 pint (6 dl.) water, 8 small onions, 1 head celery, seasoning, 1 oz. (25 g.) flour, 2 tablespoons sherry (optional). To serve: apple sauce or cranberry jelly.
Simmer giblets of duck in water until tender. Remove from stock, chop liver finely. Either cut duck into joints or use whole. Put in large pan over low heat for 10–15 minutes – this extracts surplus fat from skin. Place duck in a casserole, pour off all fat except 2 tablespoons, fry onions and chopped celery in this for 5–10 minutes. Lift out, stir well seasoned flour into fat remaining, add ¾ pint (4½ dl.) duck stock. Bring to boil, cook until thickened, add sherry if wished. Pour over duck and vegetables, add liver, cover casserole. Cook whole duck for 2 hours in very moderate oven, Gas Mark 3, 325°F. (170°C.), jointed duck for 1¼–1½ hours. Serve with Apple Sauce or Cranberry Jelly, see page 5.

Orange and Banana Flummery cut skin away from 2 large oranges to remove all white pith. Take out orange flesh, chop into small pieces. Slice 2–3 bananas, blend with ½ pint (3 dl.) sweetened whipped evaporated milk or custard, put into glasses and top with chopped nuts.

WEDNESDAY

Creamed Tripe and Onions 1½ lb. (¾ kilo) tripe, ½ pint (3 dl.) milk, ½ pint (3 dl.) water, 2–3 onions, seasoning, 1 level tablespoon cornflour or 2 tablespoons flour, 1 oz. (25 g.) margarine or butter. To garnish: paprika, chopped parsley.
Blanch tripe by bringing to the boil in water to cover, throw away water; cut tripe in neat pieces. Put in a pan with nearly all the milk, water and sliced onions, season lightly. Simmer gently for 45 minutes to 1 hour until tripe is tender. Blend the cornflour or flour with the remaining milk, stir into the tripe together with the margarine or butter. Cook gently until thickened, season well. Garnish with paprika and parsley.

Layer Pancakes egg yolks from Tuesday plus water to cover, 4 oz. (100 g.) flour, pinch salt, ⅓ pint (2 dl.) milk, juice of 1 lemon, fat for frying, fruit purée or jam.
Add egg yolks (plus the water used to cover them) to the flour sieved with the salt. Gradually beat in the milk, plus the lemon juice (rind used on Monday). Cook the pancakes in hot fat, see page 23, until crisp and brown. Sandwich together with hot fruit purée or jam to make a gâteau shape.

THURSDAY

Swedish Meat Balls 12 oz. (300 g.) stewing steak, 1 onion, 2 oz. (50 g.) breadcrumbs, seasoning, 1 tablespoon tomato ketchup, can tomato or mushroom soup, water. To serve: cooked diced vegetables.
Mince steak, mix with chopped onion, blend with breadcrumbs, seasoning, tomato ketchup. Form into walnut-sized balls. Put soup in a large pan, dilute with an equal quantity of water, simmer meat balls in this for approximately 30 minutes. Serve in a border of mixed vegetables.

Black Cap Pudding 3–4 tablespoons blackcurrant jam, 3 oz. (75 g.) margarine, 3 oz. (75 g.) castor sugar, 1 egg, 4 oz. (100 g.) self-raising flour, 2 tablespoons milk.
Put jam at the bottom of a greased basin. Cream margarine with sugar, add beaten egg, flour and milk. Put this over the jam, cover basin with greased paper or foil, steam for 1½ hours.

ONDAY

Sausages and Hunter's Salad sausages, 12 oz. (300 g.) boiled potatoes, small cooked beetroot, small packet frozen peas or canned peas, 1 raw carrot, little mayonnaise, grated onion (optional), hard-boiled eggs.
Bake, grill or fry the sausages, serve hot or cold. Dice potatoes, add to diced beetroot, cooked peas, grated carrot. Toss in a little mayonnaise, flavour with onion if desired. Garnish with slices of hard-boiled egg.

Apple Raisin Patties 8 oz. (200 g.) shortcrust pastry*, 3 oz. (75 g.) seedless raisins, 1 tablespoon honey, 1 large apple, grated rind of 1 lemon, pinch spice.
Roll out pastry thinly, cut into rounds about 4–5 inches (10–13 cm.) in diameter. Mix raisins, honey, peeled grated apple, lemon rind, spice. Put on half the pastry, brush edges with water, fold to make patty shapes. Flute edges together, bake above centre of a hot oven, Gas Mark 6–7, 400–425°F. (200–220°C.), for 20–25 minutes.
*4 oz. (100 g.) pastry needed for Friday, so fat could be rubbed into flour in readiness. Store in a cool place, recipe page 10.
If preferred, however, you could make the pastry completely. Wrap this carefully and store in the refrigerator or freezer.

UESDAY

Spanish Steak 2 lb. (1 kilo) stewing steak*, 2 onions, 1 garlic clove, 1 oz. (25 g.) fat, 3 tomatoes, 1 green pepper, ½ pint (3 dl.) stock, seasoning, little chopped parsley.
*Put 12 oz. (300 g.) steak in cool place for Thursday. Divide remaining steak into very thin fingers. Fry sliced onions and crushed garlic in the fat. Add skinned sliced tomatoes, diced green pepper and stock. Arrange fingers of steak in this mixture, season well. Simmer, either in a tightly covered pan or casserole, in very moderate oven, Gas Mark 3, 325°F. (170°C.) for 2 hours. Top with parsley. Serve with spaghetti and salad, see picture page 114.

Chestnut Meringues 8 oz. (¼ kilo) fresh chestnuts, few drops vanilla essence, 5 oz. (125 g.) castor sugar, 2 eggs.
Split the chestnuts, boil in water for 10 minutes, peel while warm. Put in a little fresh water with vanilla essence, 1 oz. (25 g.) sugar, and simmer until soft. Strain and sieve the nuts, to make a purée. Whisk egg whites until very stiff (cover yolks with cold water for Wednesday). Gradually beat in 2 oz. (50 g.) castor sugar, fold in remainder. Pile or pipe into 8 meringue shells on oiled or buttered tin, dry off in very slow oven, Gas Mark 0–¼, 225°F. (110°C.), for 2 hours. Sandwich the meringues with the chestnut purée.
To vary: use sweetened canned chestnut purée.

RIDAY

Breton Boats 4 oz. (100 g.) shortcrust pastry, see page 10, sardines, grated cheese.
Roll out pastry thinly, line 8 small boat-shaped tins (patty tins could be used) or form aluminium foil into boat shapes. Bake in a hot oven, Gas Mark 7, 425°F. (220°C.). Remove pastry from cases, put on an ovenproof dish, fill with mashed sardines. Top with a thick layer of grated cheese and return to oven.

Devilled Crisps roll potato crisps in celery salt and cayenne pepper, warm in oven.

Nut Bread and Butter Pudding 3 large slices bread and butter, 2 oz. (50 g.) chopped nuts, 2 eggs, 1–2 oz. (25–50 g.) sugar, ¾ pint (4½ dl.) milk.
Cut bread and butter into neat triangles, put in a pie dish with chopped nuts. Beat eggs with sugar, add hot milk, pour over bread and butter, allow to stand. Put in coolest part of oven, cook for 45 minutes to 1 hour. When Breton Boats are removed from oven, reduce to Gas Mark 2, 300°F. (150°C.), to prevent custard curdling.

ATURDAY

Ham and Corn Scallops 1 oz. (25 g.) margarine, 1 oz. (25 g.) flour, ½ pint (3 dl.) milk, seasoning, can sweetcorn, 8 oz. (200 g.) diced ham, breadcrumbs.
Make a white sauce with margarine, flour, milk and season well. Add corn, together with any liquid in can, and diced ham. Put into individual scallop dishes, top with a few breadcrumbs and brown under the grill.

Chocolate Truffles 4 oz. (100 g.) fine cake crumbs, 4 oz. (100 g.) ground almonds, 2 tablespoons chocolate powder, 2 tablespoons sieved icing sugar, 2 good tablespoons apricot jam, brandy or rum (optional). For the coating: icing sugar, chocolate powder.
Mix cake crumbs, ground almonds, chocolate powder, icing sugar. Moisten and blend with apricot jam. Add a few drops brandy or rum if wished. Roll into balls and coat with an equal quantity of icing sugar and chocolate powder. These take the place of a sweet and are excellent served with hot coffee. For a more substantial meal you can have cheese after the scallops and serve the truffles with coffee.

Week 38

Mutton is a meat that is better if roasted for a generous time, and the method of cooking for Sunday is ideal for this, for the foil keeps it moist. Choose a piece of loin or half leg or half shoulder or a best end of mutton.
The quantity of eggs, given below, assumes that 2 eggs are used on Tuesday for the topping of the Egg and Macaroni Cocottes and that either 4 or 8 eggs are used for poaching on Friday.

For your shopping list the main meals need:
9–13 eggs, 3½ pints (2 litres) milk, 10–12 oz. (250–300 g.) Cheddar or other cooking cheese.
Sunday, Monday and Tuesday need:
Mutton (see above for choice of joint).
Pickled red cabbage, marshmallows.
Potatoes, onions, garlic (optional), carrots, swedes, turnips, parsley, bananas, lemon, cooking apples.
Wednesday and Thursday need:
Minced beef, bacon rashers, sausages (store carefully).
Cooking dates.
Potatoes, onions, tomatoes, carrots, dessert apple, cooked beetroot, lettuce, lemon, cooking apples (optional).
Friday and Saturday need:
Cod steaks.
Anchovy paste.
Potatoes, onions, carrot, parsley, tomatoes, celery, citrus fruits, dessert apples.

Sunday

Foil Roasted Mutton brush a piece of foil with a little fat, sprinkle with 1–2 finely chopped onions and a crushed clove of garlic (optional). Add a joint of mutton, wrap into a neat parcel. Roast in a moderately hot oven, Gas Mark 5–6, 375–400°F. (190–200°C.), allowing 35 minutes per lb. (½ kilo) and 35 minutes over. Unwrap carefully, pour off some of the excess fat in the foil to use as a basis for gravy.

Vegetable Casserole arrange thin slices of potato, carrot, swede and a little turnip in a casserole. Add a knob of margarine, seasoning and water to cover. Cover the casserole, cook in coolest part of oven for 1¼–1½ hours; strain. Toss vegetables in chopped parsley.

Princess Pudding 1 pint (6 dl.) thick, well sweetened custard, see page 88, 2–3 bananas, 1 egg, grated rind of 1 lemon, 2 tablespoons cake crumbs, 2 tablespoons lemon curd, 1 oz. (25 g.) castor sugar.
Cool custard slightly, add sliced bananas, beaten egg yolk, lemon rind (save juice for Monday), cake crumbs and lemon curd. Put into a pie dish. Whisk egg white stiffly, fold in sugar, pile over custard. Put in oven when meat, etc., comes out; reduce heat to very moderate, cook for 15–20 minutes.

Wednesday

Shepherd's Pie 1 lb. (½ kilo) potatoes, 1½ oz. (40 g.) margarine, little milk, seasoning, 2 onions, 2 tomatoes, 1 oz. (25 g.) fat, 8 oz. (200 g.) raw minced beef, ¼ pint (1½ dl.) stock or water and ½ stock cube, pinch mixed herbs, medium can baked beans.
Peel, cook and mash potatoes with half the margarine, the milk and seasoning. Fry chopped onions and tomatoes in the fat. Add beef and stock, or water and stock cube. Simmer for a few minutes until a thickish mixture, add seasoning, herbs and baked beans. Put into an ovenproof dish, top with the potatoes and rest of the margarine. Bake for 35 minutes in centre of a moderate oven, Gas Mark 5, 375°F. (190°C.), until brown.

Mixed Salad serve grated raw carrot, diced dessert apple, diced beetroot, sliced tomatoes on a bed of lettuce.

Date and Lemon Tart 12 oz. (300 g.) shortcrust pastry*, see page 10, 12 oz. (300 g.) cooking dates, grated rind and juice of 1 lemon, 2 tablespoons water, ½ oz. (15 g.) margarine, 1 tablespoon brown sugar.
*save half pastry for Thursday. Roll out remainder, line a large pie plate, bake 'blind' for 15 minutes in a hot oven, Gas Mark 6, 400°F. (200°C.). Chop dates, simmer with rest of ingredients for 5 minutes, spoon over pastry, cook for a further 10–15 minutes until pastry is crisp.

Thursday

Bacon and Sausage Toad-in-the-Hole 2–3 rashers long streaky bacon, ½–1 lb. (¼–½ kilo) sausages, 4 oz. (100 g.) flour, pinch salt, 1 egg, ½ pint (3 dl.) milk and water.
Cut bacon into pieces, put with sausages into a Yorkshire pudding tin. Heat for 10 minutes towards top of a hot oven, Gas Mark 6, 400°F. (200°C.). Make a batter with flour, salt, egg, milk and water, pour over sausages and bacon. Cook for 15 minutes in hot oven, then lower heat to moderately hot, Gas Mark 5, 375°F. (190°C.), so batter cooks without becoming over-brown.

Bramble Roll pastry from Wednesday, bramble jelly or little bramble jelly plus 2 grated apples, sugar (optional). To serve: custard.
Roll out pastry, spread with bramble jelly or a little jelly and the grated apple. Add sugar if wished. Roll like a Swiss roll, bake in centre of oven for approximately 40 minutes. Cut into slices, serve with custard.

MONDAY

Mutton Hash and Pickled Red Cabbage approximately 12 oz. (300 g.) cooked mutton, 1 lb. (½ kilo) potatoes, 2 onions, knob of dripping, seasoning, chopped parsley. To serve: pickled red cabbage.
Mince the cooked mutton. Cook and mash potatoes. Slice onions very thinly. Heat dripping in a frying pan, toss onions in this until soft but unbrowned, mix with potatoes and meat, season well and press mixture into pan to form a firm layer. Heat gently until bottom is set into a crisp brown skin, put a palette knife underneath, fold over like an omelette, tip on to hot dish. Top with chopped parsley, serve with pickled red cabbage.

Marshmallow Surprise 1½ lb. (¾ kilo) apples, lemon juice (from Sunday), sugar or honey, marshmallows.
Cook apples until a smooth thick purée, adding lemon juice with sugar or honey to sweeten. Put 1 lb. (½ kilo) only* into a pie dish, top with marshmallows and melt these under the grill. Serve hot or cold.
*save rest for Tuesday.

TUESDAY

Egg and Macaroni Cocottes 3–4 oz. (75–100 g.) macaroni, seasoning, 1 oz. (25 g.) margarine, 1 oz. (25 g.) flour, ½ pint (3 dl.) milk, ¼ pint (1½ dl.) macaroni water, 3–4 oz. (75–100 g.) grated cheese. For the topping: hard-boiled eggs, grated cheese.
Cook macaroni in boiling salted water, strain. Mix with cheese sauce made with margarine, flour, milk, macaroni water, grated cheese, seasoning. Put into individual ovenproof dishes, top with sliced hard-boiled eggs and a layer of grated cheese. Heat for a few minutes only until cheese has melted.

Raisin Puffs 4 oz. (100 g.) self-raising flour, pinch salt, 1 egg, ½ pint (3 dl.) apple purée (from Monday), 4 oz. (100 g.) seedless raisins, 2 oz. (50 g.) fat.
Mix together flour, salt, egg and apple purée. Add raisins, allow to stand in the mixture to make these moist and plump. Heat fat in pan, drop in spoonfuls of mixture. Cook for 3 minutes on each side until brown, lower heat; cook for a further 2–3 minutes.

FRIDAY

Golden Fish Soup 5 cod steaks (see below), 1 onion, 1 large carrot, 1 oz. (25 g.) margarine, 1 pint (6 dl.) water, 8 oz. (200 g.) diced potato, seasoning, milk (optional), chopped parsley.
Buy 5 cod steaks, keep 4 in a cool place for Saturday. Fry diced onion, grated carrot in margarine. Add water and potato, simmer for approximately 10 minutes. Cut 1 cod steak into neat pieces, add to soup, season very well and continue cooking for a further 5–10 minutes until fish is just tender but unbroken, add a little milk if wished. Serve in hot soup cups topped with chopped parsley.

Savoury Poached Eggs poach eggs, serve on toast spread with butter and anchovy paste.

Fresh Fruit serve a good selection of citrus fruits, e.g. tangerines, as well as apples, etc.

SATURDAY

Baked Cod Steaks 4 cod steaks, margarine, seasoning, breadcrumbs, chopped parsley.
Put fish into a well greased dish. Brush with a little melted margarine, season well, cover with breadcrumbs and chopped parsley. Bake towards the top of a moderate oven, Gas Mark 5, 375°F. (190°C.), for 25 minutes.

Vegetable Hotpot arrange layers of wafer-thin peeled potato and onion and tomato in an ovenproof dish, seasoning each layer well. End with potato, brush with a little melted margarine, add no water. Cover and bake for approximately 1 hour. Towards end of cooking time, remove lid to brown.

Celery Rarebit 1 head celery, seasoning, 1 oz. (25 g.) margarine, 1 oz. (25 g.) flour, 4 tablespoons celery water, 2 tablespoons milk, 1 teaspoon made-mustard, 6 oz. (150 g.) grated Cheddar cheese, hot buttered toast.
Wash celery, take out centre heart for a salad, cut outer stalks into neat lengths, simmer in salted water until tender. Drain carefully. Make a *very* thick sauce with margarine, flour, celery water. Add milk, seasoning, mustard, cheese. Arrange hot celery on hot buttered toast, cover with rarebit mixture, brown under grill.

WEEK 39

SUNDAY

Marzipan is not only good for icing cakes but a very delicious filling for pears (Sunday's menu). The recipe for making marzipan follows the main recipe.
Braised Steak (Wednesday) is a warming and relatively economical main dish. Vegetables may be added to the meat, etc., or the meat cooked without these. The Herb Dumplings can be varied by adding mustard, a little grated horseradish or horseradish cream, etc. The picture on page 107 shows Braised Steak and Dumplings, as recipe for Wednesday, but larger quantities have been used so the dish serves up to 8 people.

For your shopping list the main meals need:
18 or 20 eggs (if using these in Hamburgers), 2½ pints (nearly 1½ litres) milk, 3 or 6 oz. (75 or 150 g.) Cheddar or other cooking cheese (if using this in Hamburgers).
Sunday, Monday and Tuesday need:
Pork chops, sausages, lambs' or calfs' or pigs' liver (store carefully), bacon rashers.
Cornflakes, ingredients for marzipan (optional).
Potatoes, onions, parsley, celery, dessert apples, dessert pears, dried apricots, tangerines.
Wednesday, Thursday, Friday and Saturday need:
Stewing steak, beef, bacon rashers.
Lemon marmalade or lemon curd, thin cream.
Potatoes, onions, carrots, parsley, tomatoes, mushrooms, spinach.

Crisp Coated Pork Chops pork chops, seasoning, flour, milk, cornflakes, dessert apples.
Dip the chops in well seasoned flour, toss in milk and crushed cornflakes. Put into a greased baking dish and bake for approximately 35 minutes in the centre of a moderately hot oven, Gas Mark 6, 400°F. (200°C.). Towards the end of the cooking time, apple rings (i.e. cored but not peeled dessert apples) can be put in the dish to cook and serve with the chops.

Marzipan and Pear Dumplings 4 dessert pears, marzipan (or apricot jam), 8 oz. (200 g.) short or sweet shortcrust pastry, pages 10 and 89.
Peel and core pears. Try to keep them whole. Press a little marzipan (or apricot jam) in centre of each pear. Roll out pastry very thinly, cut into 4 squares. Cover each pear with pastry and bake for approximately 30 minutes towards the top of the oven.
Soak apricots for Monday.
To make marzipan: mix 2 oz. (50 g.) ground almonds, 1 oz. (25 g.) castor and 1 oz. (25 g.) sieved icing sugar. Bind with a little milk or sherry (it is not worth using an egg for this quantity).
The above gives a fairly modest filling for the pears; double the quantities if you like a lot of marzipan.

WEDNESDAY

Braised Steak 2–3 onions, 2–3 carrots, 1 lb. (½ kilo) stewing steak, seasoning, 1 oz. (25 g.) flour, 2 oz. (50 g.) fat, 1 pint (6 dl.) brown stock or water and stock cube, good pinch herbs.
Peel and slice onions and carrots. Cut steak into neat pieces, coat with the well seasoned flour. Fry steak in the fat, together with the vegetables, until meat is golden on the outside. Gradually stir in stock, or water and stock cube, bring to boil, cook until a smooth sauce. Add seasoning and herbs. Put lid on pan to cover tightly and simmer very gently for nearly 2 hours, see picture page 107.

Herb Dumplings 3 oz. (75 g.) self-raising flour, good pinch salt, 1–1½ oz. (25–40 g.) shredded suet, 2 teaspoons chopped parsley, good pinch mixed dried herbs, water.
Mix flour, salt, suet, parsley, herbs; bind with water. With floured hands, form into small walnut-sized balls. Lift lid from steak pan; if gravy is rather thick, stir in a little water, drop dumplings on top of boiling liquid, cook for good 15 minutes.

Lemon Knight's Fritters make sandwiches of bread, butter, lemon marmalade or lemon curd. Cut in neat fingers. Beat an egg with a little milk, dip fingers in this, fry in hot margarine until crisp and golden brown.

THURSDAY

Tomato and Mushroom Omelettes 4 tomatoes, 2 oz. (50 g.) mushrooms, little margarine, 6 eggs, seasoning, 2–3 tablespoons water, 2 oz. (50 g.) butter.
Skin and slice tomatoes, fry with sliced mushrooms in a little margarine. Beat eggs (this quantity is needed for 4 people) with seasoning, add water. Unless you have a large omelette pan, cook half the mixture in 1 oz. (25 g.) butter, fill with tomatoes and mushrooms, fold; make a second omelette, fill and serve at once.

Coconut Rice Crumble 2 oz. (50 g.) round rice, 1 oz. (25 g.) desiccated coconut, 1 oz. (25 g.) sugar, 1 pint (6 dl.) milk. For the crumble: 1 oz. (25 g.) margarine, 2 oz. (50 g.) sugar, 2 oz. (50 g.) flour, 1 oz. (25 g.) desiccated coconut. To serve: cream (optional).
Cook rice, coconut and sugar in the milk until rice is tender. It is better to do this in a double saucepan. When cooked, put in a hot pie dish. Make crumble by adding margarine and sugar to flour, then add coconut. Sprinkle over top of hot rice, bake towards top of a moderate oven, Gas Mark 5, 375°F. (190°C.), for 20–25 minutes. Serve with cream, if liked.

MONDAY

Penny-Wise Mixed Grill for an economical grill, serve a sausage, a rasher of bacon, a thin slice of liver for each person. When the meat is nearly cooked, fry an egg and arrange with the bacon, etc., on the serving dish.

Lyonnaise Potatoes approximately 1 lb. (½ kilo) potatoes, seasoning, just over 8 oz. (¼ kilo) onions, knob of fat, chopped parsley.
Cook potatoes lightly in salted water so they may be sliced thickly without breaking. Peel and slice onions, fry in fat until tender. Add potatoes, season mixture and finish cooking onions and potatoes together. Serve topped with parsley.

Apricot Pudding 6–8 oz. (150–200 g.) dried apricots, water, stale bread, sugar, little cornflour.
Soak apricots in cold water overnight. Line sides and bottom of a pudding basin with fingers of stale bread. Simmer fruit with sugar to taste until tender. Put well drained apricots into bread-lined basin, cover with more bread, put a weight on top, leave for several hours. It is better made the day before. Serve with apricot juice thickened with a little cornflour, as a sauce.

TUESDAY

Sardine and Egg Slices cover large slices of toast with mashed sardines, top with either scrambled or poached egg. Serve with hot baked beans in tomato sauce to make a more substantial meal.

Tangerines in Caramel Sauce 3 oz. (75 g.) sugar, 3 tablespoons water, 4 tangerines, good ¼ pint (1½ dl.) water.
Make a caramel sauce by stirring sugar and 3 tablespoons water in a strong pan over heat. When sugar is dissolved, allow to boil steadily until a golden caramel. Remove from heat. Take peel from the tangerines, simmer this in the water for 5 minutes. Add strained liquid to the caramel, heat together until blended. Cut tangerines in slices, put in a dish and cover with the cold caramel sauce.

Cheese serve cheese with celery, biscuits or French bread at the end of this light but satisfying meal.

FRIDAY

Salmon à la King 1 oz. (25 g.) margarine, 1 oz. (25 g.) flour, ½ pint (3 dl.) milk, seasoning, small can sweetcorn, 8–12 oz. (200–300 g.) can salmon. To serve: creamed spinach.
Make a white sauce with margarine, flour, milk, seasoning, add canned corn and the salmon (cheaper pink salmon can be used). Heat gently and serve in a border of creamed spinach and Cheese Croûtons.

Cheese Croûtons toast bread, top with butter and grated cheese, brown for 1 minute under grill, cut into neat squares.

Grandmother's Bread Pudding 8 oz. (200 g.) stale brown or white bread, 2 oz. (50 g.) shredded suet, 6 oz. (150 g.) dried fruit, 2 tablespoons orange marmalade, 2 oz. (50 g.) brown sugar, grated nutmeg, 1 egg, sugar for topping.
Pour cold water over bread, allow to stand for 30 minutes; strain bread, pressing firmly to extract surplus moisture. Mix with suet, dried fruit, marmalade, sugar, nutmeg and egg. Put into either a greased pie dish or shallow tin, bake for 1¼ hours in centre of a very moderate oven, Gas Mark 3, 325°F. (170°C.). Turn on to hot dish, dredge with sugar.

SATURDAY

Layered Hamburgers 12 oz. (300 g.) beef*, 2 rashers bacon, 1 onion, 1 medium potato, seasoning, pinch mixed herbs, fat for frying, hard-boiled eggs or cheese.
*choose stewing steak for economy; fresh brisket, rump or buttock steak for prime flavour.
Mince beef, bacon and onion. Mix with grated potato, seasoning and herbs. Form into 8 thin cakes. Bake, grill or fry until tender. Sandwich with sliced hard-boiled eggs or cheese.

Luxury Custard Tarts 5–6 oz. (125–150 g.) short or sweet shortcrust pastry, see pages 10 and 89, 2 eggs, ½–1 oz. (15–25 g.) sugar, just under ½ pint (3 dl.) milk, 4–5 tablespoons thin cream, grated nutmeg (optional).
Line 8 or 9 deep patty tins with pastry, bake 'blind' in a hot oven, Gas Mark 7, 425°F. (220°C.), for 10 minutes. Beat eggs with sugar, add the hot milk and cream. Strain hot custard into hot pastry cases. Return to oven, lowering heat to very moderate, Gas Mark 3, 325°F. (170°C.). Continue cooking for a further 25–30 minutes until set.
To vary: you can top custard tarts with grated nutmeg before baking, if wished.

Artichokes vinaigrette, recipe on page 84

WEEK 40

SUNDAY

The recipes from Sunday to Tuesday would be very suitable for a Christmas menu. The stuffings suggested for the capon would be suitable for turkey. Serve with Bread or Cranberry Sauce, recipes page 5.

For your shopping list the main meals need:
9–10 eggs*, 1–2 pints (generous ½–1¼ litres) milk, plus milk for bread sauce, 4 oz. (100 g.) cream cheese, 4–5 oz. (100–125 g.) Cheddar or other cooking cheese.
*Plus extra if making sponge cake for Monday and Christmas pudding (this is best made several weeks before Christmas).
Sunday, Monday and Tuesday need:
Capon, fat bacon rashers (optional), sausagemeat, ham or boiled bacon, tongue, sherry, Tia Maria, thick cream, sponge cake (unless making this).
Potatoes, onions, celery, parsley, cooked beetroot, salad ingredients, root vegetables, cranberries (optional), oranges, dessert apples, chestnuts, fruit (dried and fresh for Tuesday's Fruit Salad).
Wednesday and Thursday need:
Lamb chops, tongue, claret, potatoes, carrots, watercress, onions, tomatoes, parsley.
Friday and Saturday need:
Haddock cutlets or fillet, minced beef (store carefully), plain chocolate, ice cream, potatoes, tomatoes, mushrooms (optional), green vegetable or peas, carrots, onion.

Roast Capon weigh capon *after* stuffing. Allow 15 minutes per lb. (½ kilo) and 15 minutes over. Cook in a hot oven, Gas Mark 7, 425°F. (220°C.); lower heat to moderately hot, Gas Mark 5, 375°F. (190°C.), after the first 45 minutes. Cover breast with plenty of fat bacon, butter or fat.
Stuffings: (a) mix 1 lb. (½ kilo) sausagemeat with chopped raw capon liver, pinch mixed herbs, 2 egg yolks. (b) celery stuffing: chop 2 large onions, half head celery, few celery leaves and a little parsley. Toss in 2 oz. (50 g.) margarine. Add 3 oz. (75 g.) cooked long grain rice, seasoning, pinch mixed herbs.

Orange Christmas Pudding Christmas pudding recipe, page 120, juice of 1 orange. For the sauce: finely grated rind of 2 large oranges, 4 oz. (100 g.) butter, 6 oz. (150 g.) icing sugar, 2 tablespoons orange juice.
Remove covers of pudding on Christmas Eve. Prick pudding, pour orange juice over; this will soak into pudding. Re-cover on Christmas morning and cook for 2 hours. Serve with orange sauce made by creaming grated orange rind, butter and sieved icing sugar. Gradually beat in orange juice.

Mince Pies (*see recipe on Tuesday*) put these in oven when dishing up main course, serve with sherry-flavoured custard.

WEDNESDAY

THURSDAY

Lamb Chops in Claret 4 lamb chops, fat, 1 level tablespoon flour, ¼ pint (1½ dl.) stock, ¼ pint (1½ dl.) claret, seasoning, pinch garlic salt, 10 oz. (250 g.) raisins.
Brown both sides of chops in a little fat in a pan, lift out on to a hot dish. Then add flour blended with stock and claret (or use all stock). Thicken slightly, adding seasoning, garlic salt, raisins. Return chops to pan, cover, cook steadily for 15 minutes.

Potato Balls add a little grated raw carrot to mashed potatoes, form into balls. Arrange round chops and sauce, garnish with watercress.

Christmas Pudding Fritters slice pudding, dip in egg, beaten with a little milk, fry in hot margarine.

Casserole of Tongue 1 lb. (½ kilo) potatoes, 2 large onions, 4 tomatoes, seasoning, margarine, diced tongue. Boil potatoes and onions until the vegetables are soft. Slice potatoes thickly, onions thinly. Arrange half potatoes, 1 sliced onion, 2 sliced tomatoes in a shallow casserole, season, add a little melted margarine. Add a layer of diced tongue, more sliced tomatoes, remaining onion and potatoes and little margarine, bake in centre of a moderate oven, Gas Mark 5, 375°F. (190°C.) for 35 minutes.

Macedoine of Vegetables cook diced mixed root vegetables in salted water, strain, toss in margarine and chopped parsley.

Cheese Tartlets 5–6 oz. (125–150 g.) shortcrust pastry (see below), 2 oz. (50 g.) grated Cheddar cheese, 2 eggs, seasoning.
Line 8 or 9 patty tins with thin shortcrust pastry. Add cheese to beaten eggs, season; spoon into pastry. Put in centre of oven for 15–20 minutes, raising temperature to hot, Gas Mark 7, 425°F. (220°C.). Serve hot.
To make shortcrust pastry: sieve 8 oz. (200 g.) plain flour with a pinch of salt. Rub in 4 oz. (100 g.) fat – this can be margarine, cooking fat, butter or lard. Add cold water to bind. You will need from 2 tablespoons water for 8 oz. (200 g.) flour.

Braised steak and herb dumplings, recipe on page 104

MONDAY

Cold Buffet and Salads dice chicken, gherkins, celery, eating apple, cooked potatoes. Bind with mayonnaise and capers. Serve on a bed of sliced beetroot. Blend 4 oz. (100 g.) cream cheese, 2 chopped hard-boiled eggs, little horseradish cream. Spread on sliced ham or boiled bacon, roll into cornet shapes (so filling shows), arrange on mixed salad. Serve sliced tongue on Russian salad: made by blending cooked root vegetables with mayonnaise.

Tipsy Cake split a sponge cake, recipe page 39, into three layers; spread the first layer with jam and chopped nuts, put on plate, soak liberally with sherry. Add second layer of sponge, spread with jam, nuts, soak with sherry, add top layer, spread with nuts, then jam and soak well with sherry. Coat cake with custard or cream, decorate with glacé cherries, nuts, angelica.

Chocolate Meringues (make before Christmas) whisk 2 egg whites until very stiff. Sieve ½ tablespoon cocoa with 4 oz. (110 g. not 100 g.) castor sugar. Gradually beat half this into egg whites, fold in rest. Form into about 8 neat rounds on an oiled baking sheet. Dry out in very cool oven, Gas Mark ¼, 225°F. (110°C.), for several hours, cool, store in airtight tin. Sandwich together with whipped cream flavoured with Tia Maria.

TUESDAY

Braised Chicken and Chestnuts chicken, seasoning, water, 8 oz. (200 g.) chestnuts, 2 onions, 2 oz. (50 g.) fat, 1½ oz. (40 g.) flour, boiled bacon, stuffing.
Remove all flesh from chicken bones, simmer bones in salted water to give 1 pint (6 dl.) stock. Boil split chestnuts for 10 minutes, remove skins while warm. Fry sliced onions in fat, add chestnuts, cook until golden. Lift into casserole, stir flour into fat remaining, cook for several minutes, blend in stock, boil, then cook until thickened. Season well, add diced chicken, any diced boiled bacon or pieces of stuffing left. Cover casserole, cook for 1 hour in a very moderate oven, Gas Mark 3, 325°F. (170°C.).

Christmas Fruit Salad add nuts, stoned dates, diced dessert figs to diced fruit, moisten with orange juice.

Mince Pies 12 oz. (300 g.) short, sweet shortcrust or flaky pastry, pages 10, 89 and 137, about 10–12 oz. (250–300 g.) mincemeat, see page 112.
Roll out the pastry, cut out about 18 rounds to fit patty tins. Put in the mincemeat. Cut out 18 smaller rounds for the lids. Brush the edges of the pastry with water, put on the 'lids', seal firmly. Make slits in the tops, bake in the centre of a hot oven, *or* a very hot oven for flaky pastry, for 15–20 minutes, reducing heat after 10–12 minutes if necessary.

FRIDAY

Haddock au Gratin cutlets or pieces fresh haddock fillet, melted margarine, fine breadcrumbs, grated cheese. To serve: tomatoes and/or mushrooms, jacket potatoes, green vegetables or peas.
Grill haddock, basting with melted margarine. When nearly cooked, top with a few breadcrumbs, little grated cheese and a little more melted margarine. Brown for 2–3 minutes under grill. Serve with grilled tomatoes and/or mushrooms, jacket potatoes, a green vegetable or peas.

Coffee Chocolate Bake 2 oz. (50 g.) margarine, 3 oz. (75 g.) castor sugar, 2 eggs, 3 oz. (75 g.) self-raising flour, ½ oz. (15 g.) cocoa, ⅓ pint (2 dl.) strong black coffee.
Cream margarine and sugar until soft, add yolks of eggs, flour sieved with cocoa. Add black coffee – the mixture will probably curdle, but this does not matter. Lastly fold in stiffly beaten egg whites. Pour into a lightly greased pie dish – stand this in another dish of cold water. Bake for approximately 45 minutes in the centre of a moderate oven, Gas Mark 4–5, 350–375°F. (180–190°C.). Serve at once.

SATURDAY

Harlequin Pinwheels 8 oz. (¼ kilo) minced beef, 2 large carrots, 1 onion, 1 oz. (25 g.) fat, small can baked beans, 8 oz. (200 g.) shortcrust pastry, milk or beaten egg.
Toss uncooked beef, grated raw carrots, grated onion in the fat, mix with baked beans. Roll pastry to an oblong, spread with meat mixture, roll up like a Swiss roll. Lift on to a greased baking tin, brush with milk or beaten egg, bake for 25 minutes in the centre of a hot oven, Gas Mark 6–7, 400–425°F. (200–220°C.); lower heat to moderate, Gas Mark 5, 375°F. (190°C.), for a further 30 minutes. Slice to serve. See Thursday for pastry recipe.

Peppermint Chocolate Sundae 2–3 oz. (50–75 g.) chocolate, 3 tablespoons water, few drops peppermint essence, ice cream.
Melt chocolate with water and peppermint essence in a basin over hot water. Pour over ice cream just before serving.
Soak salt beef overnight in saucepan of cold water for following Sunday.

WEEK 41

The emphasis this week is on the minimum of shopping and really satisfying meals for cold weather. Remember salted meats shrink in cooking. 4 lb. (2 kilos) brisket (before cooking) would provide generous helpings for 4 people (Sunday) with some left for Monday and for another meal.

The pears for the dessert on Friday should be peeled but left whole if possible.

For your shopping list the main meals need:
8–9 eggs, generous 3 pints (generous 1¾ litres) milk, 3–4 oz. (75–100 g.) Cheddar or other cheese.
Sunday, Monday and Tuesday need:
Salted brisket, pickled herrings.
Gingernut biscuits.
Potatoes, carrots, onions (some large), parsley, watercress, cooked beetroot, celery, melon, cooking apples, dates, dessert apple, bananas.
Wednesday, Thursday, Friday and Saturday need:
Breasts of lamb, bacon rashers, frankfurters.
Tomato juice, block ice cream, thick cream, thin cream (optional).
Potatoes, parsley, onions, leeks, tomatoes, green vegetables, dried apricot, lemon, dessert pears, fresh fruits.

Boiled Brisket Beef salt beef, carrots, onions, pepper. Lift salt beef from water used for soaking — fresh beef does not need to be soaked. Put into saucepan, cover with fresh cold water, add whole carrots, onions and pepper, but no salt with salt beef. Bring liquid to boil, 'skim', lower heat, cover pan, simmer gently, allowing 30 minutes per lb. (½ kilo), 30 minutes over; add dumplings 20 minutes before end of cooking time.

Parsley Dumplings pinch salt, shake pepper, 2 oz. (50 g.) shredded suet, 2 tablespoons chopped parsley, 4 oz. (100 g.) self-raising flour, water.
Add salt, pepper, suet, parsley to the flour, bind with water, make into 8 small balls; add to liquid in pan, cook steadily. Serve beef with vegetables and dumplings round.

Jellied Melon Slices halve small melon lengthways, remove seeds, put halves on a flat dish, make sure they are level. Make up a 1-pint (6-dl.) jelly, pour into the two centre hollows — any jelly left should be allowed to set, whisked and arranged round melon slices. When jelly has set, cut the melon into slices for serving.

WEDNESDAY

Apricot Stuffed Breasts of Lamb ¼ pint (1½ dl.) boiling water, 6 oz. (150 g.) dried apricots, 2 oz. (50 g.) breadcrumbs, 2 oz. (50 g.) finely chopped celery, 2 teaspoons chopped parsley, 1 small onion, 2 breasts of lamb.
Pour boiling water over chopped apricots; leave for 30 minutes, add breadcrumbs, celery, parsley, grated onion. Mix well, spread over meat and roll. Weigh meat, roast for 25 minutes per lb. (½ kilo) and 25 minutes over in a moderately hot oven, Gas Mark 5–6, 375–400°F. (190–200°C.). Serve with creamed potatoes and Braised Leeks.

Braised Leeks 4 large or 8 small leeks, 1–1½ oz. (25–40 g.) fat, 1 rasher bacon, 1 oz. (25 g.) flour, ¾ pint (4½ dl.) brown stock or water and stock cube, seasoning, pinch mixed herbs.
Wash the leeks, trim green ends. Dry, fry in the fat with the chopped bacon for a few minutes. Lift out leeks, stir in the flour and the stock or water and stock cube. Bring to boil, thicken, add seasoning, herbs and leeks. Cover pan, simmer for 40 minutes.

Jiffy Butterscotch Sundae heat 3 oz. (75 g.) brown sugar and 1 oz. (25 g.) butter for 3 minutes in a saucepan, cool for a few minutes, beat into a block of ice cream. Spoon into glasses, top with whipped cream and nuts.

THURSDAY

Tomato Broth 1 onion, 1 oz. (25 g.) margarine, 1 pint (6 dl.) canned or bottled tomato juice, ½ pint (3 dl.) water, 1 oz. (25 g.) rice, seasoning, chopped parsley.
Peel and chop onion finely, fry in margarine for 3 minutes, add tomato juice, water, bring to boil, add rice. Cook for 20 minutes, season, top with parsley.

Savoury Bread and Butter Pudding 3 rashers bacon, butter, 4 slices bread, 3 oz. (75 g.) grated cheese, 2 eggs, seasoning, ¾ pint (4½ dl.) milk. To serve: tomatoes.
Chop bacon, fry until crisp. Butter bread, cut into triangles, arrange in a pie dish with the bacon and grated cheese. Beat eggs with seasoning, beat in hot milk; strain over bread and butter. Bake for 45–55 minutes in in centre of very moderate oven, Gas Mark 3, 325°F. (170°C.), until set and golden brown. Serve with baked tomatoes.

Date and Pineapple Ring small can pineapple, 1 pineapple jelly, ¼ pint (1½ dl.) thin cream or evaporated milk, 2 oz. (50 g.) dessert dates, 1 oz. (25 g.) desiccated coconut, ice cream (optional).
Strain fruit, chop. Measure syrup, add water to give ½ pint (3 dl.). Dissolve jelly in heated liquid; cool, add rest of ingredients. Pour into ring mould to set. Turn out, serve with ice cream (optional).

MONDAY

Beef Stuffed Onions 4 large onions, salt, 2 oz. (50 g.) breadcrumbs, 12 oz. (300 g.) chopped or minced cooked beef, pinch sage, 1 egg, fat or margarine.
Skin onions, boil gently in salted water for 25 minutes; remove, take out centre pulp. Put outer onion cases into greased casserole. Chop onion pulp finely, mix with breadcrumbs, beef, sage, egg. Pile mixture back into onion cases, brush each with a little melted fat or margarine. Bake in a moderately hot oven, Gas Mark 6, 400°F. (200°C.), for 30 minutes.

Savoury Scalloped Potatoes peel and slice 1 lb. ($\frac{1}{2}$ kilo) potatoes, arrange layers in ovenproof dish, adding to each layer seasoning, little melted margarine, light sprinkling mixed herbs. Add $\frac{1}{2}$ pint (3 dl.) milk. Cook in coolest part of oven for 1 hour. Garnish with chopped parsley.

Ginger Crumb Pie 1 lb. ($\frac{1}{2}$ kilo) apples, water, sugar, few dates, 2 oz. (50 g.) margarine, 2 oz. (50 g.) sugar, 4 oz. (100 g.) gingernut crumbs.
Cook apples with very little water, sugar, chopped dates until tender; put in pie dish. Cream margarine, sugar, add crumbs, press over apple. Brown in oven for 25 minutes – lower heat to moderate when main course comes out.

TUESDAY

Pickled Herring Salad jar pickled (rollmop) herrings (about 8 fillets), watercress, cooked beetroot, 2 dessert apples, little celery, hard-boiled eggs.
Drain herrings, arrange on a bed of watercress. Dice beetroot, peeled apples, celery, arrange round herrings with sliced hard-boiled eggs.

Herb Rusks 1 oz. (25 g.) fat, seasoning, 4 oz. (100 g.) self-raising flour, 1 level teaspoon mixed herbs, milk. To serve: butter.
Rub fat into well seasoned flour, add herbs. Bind with milk to a rolling consistency, roll out to a round $\frac{1}{4}$ inch ($\frac{1}{2}$ cm.) in thickness. Cut into 8 triangles. Bake on an ungreased tin for 10 minutes towards top of hot oven, until brown. Split through centre while hot, return to oven with cut sides uppermost for a further 5 minutes. Serve with butter.

Queen Mab's Pudding 2 oz. (50 g.) margarine or shredded suet, 2 oz. (50 g.) sugar, 2 eggs, 3 oz. (75 g.) self-raising flour, 3 large bananas, $\frac{1}{4}$ pint ($1\frac{1}{2}$ dl.) milk. To serve: custard.
Cream margarine or mix suet with sugar. Add beaten eggs, flour (wholemeal often used), sliced bananas, milk. Put in greased basin, cover, steam for $1\frac{1}{4}$ hours. Serve with hot, pouring custard.

FRIDAY

Bean and Cheese Popovers 4 oz. (100 g.) flour, pinch salt, 1 egg, $\frac{1}{3}$ pint (2 dl.) milk, seasoning, can beans in tomato sauce, grated cheese.
Make a rather thick batter with flour, salt, egg and milk, season well. Grease and heat rather deep patty tins, pour in batter, cook for approximately 15 minutes towards top of a hot oven, Gas Mark 7–8, 425–450°F. (220–230°C.). Heat beans. Dish up popovers, fill with beans, top with grated cheese.

Mincemeat Baked Pears 2 tablespoons golden syrup, juice and grated rind of 1 lemon, 2 tablespoons water, 4 large firm, ripe pears, mincemeat.
Put syrup, lemon juice and rind and water into a dish. Heat for about 10 minutes in oven. Peel and core pears, press mincemeat in centre of each pear. Stand pears in lemon syrup and baste well with this. Put into oven when popovers come out, reducing heat to moderate, Gas Mark 4, 350°F. (180°C.). Baste with lemon syrup to keep fruit a good colour.

SATURDAY

Mushroom and Frankfurter Casserole 8 small frankfurters, medium can mushroom soup. To serve: jacket potatoes, green vegetables.
Put frankfurters in a casserole, top with the mushroom soup. Cover and heat for 30 minutes in a very moderate oven, Gas Mark 3, 325°F. (170°C.). Serve with jacket potatoes and green vegetables.

Fresh Fruit and Cheese serve fresh fruits with Cheddar, Cheshire or Caerphilly cheese.

WEEK 42

SUNDAY

To make mincemeat for Sunday's dessert: blend 4 oz. (100 g.) of each of the following, shredded suet, brown sugar, grated apple, chopped crystallised peel, chopped blanched almonds, with 1 lb. (½ kilo) mixed dried fruit, shake grated nutmeg, mixed spice, 4 tablespoons whisky or brandy, grated rind and juice of 1 lemon. Put into jars, seal down and store in a dry place. I have not given quantities for pastry, etc., for Thursday's dessert since these tarts are good for teatime too. 5–6 oz. (125–150 g.) shortcrust pastry will give you at least 12 tarts.

For your shopping list the main meals need:
12 eggs, ½ or 1½ pints (generous ¼ or nearly 1 litre) milk – if making custard on Tuesday, 8 oz. (200 g.) Cheddar or other cooking cheese.

Sunday, Monday and Tuesday need:
Steaks, hare or rabbit, ham or bacon rashers (thick). Ingredients for mincemeat, redcurrant jelly, port wine, thick or thin cream (optional).
Potatoes, mushrooms, tomatoes, peas, green salad ingredients, onions, sprouts, carrots, watercress (store carefully), dried figs, oranges, cooking apples.

Wednesday, Thursday, Friday and Saturday need:
Slices (fillets) veal, sausagemeat (store carefully), neck of lamb, lambs' kidneys, little bacon (optional).
Cornflakes, thick or thin cream, potatoes, green vegetables or salad ingredients, parsley, cauliflower, tomatoes, carrots, turnip, swede, onions, lemons, apricots.

Oven Baked Steaks Garni cut pieces of foil large enough to wrap each fillet steak or piece of rump steak – the steak should be 1 inch (2½ cm.) thick. Butter the foil, put one steak on each piece of foil, add 2 sliced mushrooms, 1 sliced tomato, seasoning. Wrap steaks, put on a baking tray. Cook for 15–20 minutes for underdone steak, 25 minutes for medium cooked, 30–35 minutes for well done steak in a hot oven, Gas Mark 7, 425°F. (220°C.). Unwrap steaks carefully so no juice is wasted. Serve with jacket potatoes, cooked peas and green salad.
If preferred the steaks may be cooked in foil without mushrooms and tomatoes and served with a tomato salad as the picture page 115.
To give the crisp outside to the steaks that many people like, open the foil and put the baking tray under a very hot grill for 1–2 minutes.

Hawaiian Mince Pies 8 oz. (200 g.) sweet shortcrust pastry, see page 89, mincemeat, see Introduction, canned pineapple.
Use just over half the pastry to line deep patty tins. Fill with mincemeat and chopped, well drained pineapple. Cover with rounds made from the rest of the pastry, seal edges, slit pastry on top. Bake just above centre of a hot oven for 15–20 minutes. Serve hot or cold.
Soak figs for Monday (see below).

WEDNESDAY

Escalopes of Veal 4 thin slices veal, seasoning, flour, beaten egg, crumbs, butter or butter and oil, ½ lemon, little finely chopped parsley, 1 hard-boiled egg. To serve: green vegetables or green salad.
Coat slices of veal in seasoned flour, then egg and crumbs. Fry in hot butter or butter and oil until both sides are golden brown and crisp; lower heat and cook gently through. Garnish with rings of lemon, topped with parsley and hard-boiled egg. Serve with green vegetables or green salad and Fried Rice.

Fried Rice boil 4 oz. (100 g.) long grain rice in salted water until just tender. Strain and dry on kitchen paper, fry in a little hot oil or fat until golden.

Fresh Apricot Compote 2–3 oz. (50–75 g.) sugar, juice of ½ lemon, ⅓ pint (2 dl.) water, 1 lb. (½ kilo) apricots.
Make syrup of sugar, lemon juice, water. Put apricots into this and poach slowly until tender but unbroken. Picture, page 122.

THURSDAY

Sausagemeat Patties and Baked Eggs 1 tablespoon tomato ketchup, 2 teaspoons chopped parsley, pinch mixed herbs, ¾–1 lb. (⅜–½ kilo) sausagemeat, seasoning, flour, 4 eggs, little butter. To serve: cauliflower, creamed potatoes.
Mix ketchup, parsley, herbs with sausagemeat. Form into 4 round flat cakes, toss in seasoned flour, bake for 20 minutes in a hot oven. Break eggs into buttered dishes, cook for 10 minutes. Serve with cauliflower and creamed potatoes. If preferred, patties and eggs may be fried.

Redcurrant Crispies shortcrust pastry, see page 10, redcurrant jelly, cornflakes. To serve: cream.
Line patty tins with shortcrust pastry, bake 'blind' for 8 minutes in a hot oven, Gas Mark 6–7, 400–425°F. (200–220°C.); put in a little redcurrant jelly and cover top with finely crushed cornflakes. Return to oven for a further 5 minutes. Serve hot or cold, with cream.

MONDAY

Stuffed Roast Hare or Rabbit young hare or rabbit, melted fat. For the sage and onion stuffing: 2–3 large onions, 3–4 oz. (75–100 g.) breadcrumbs, ½–1 tea-spoon powdered sage, seasoning, 1–2 oz. (25–50 g.) shredded suet or margarine.
You must choose a young hare or rabbit to roast well. Wash and dry thoroughly. Cook head and liver to make stock for gravy. Stuff body with sage and onion stuffing, brush the hare or rabbit with melted fat. Weigh, and roast rabbit for 25 minutes per lb. (½ kilo) and 25 minutes over – allow 30 minutes per lb. (½ kilo) and 30 minutes over for hare – in a moderately hot oven, Gas Mark 6, 400°F. (200°C.). Serve with thickened gravy, redcurrant jelly, roast potatoes, sprouts. Serve legs, fleshy parts of back, save rest for soup. To make stuffing: boil onions for 20 minutes or until half-cooked. Drain, chop, and mix with breadcrumbs, sage, seasoning and suet or margarine. Bind with a little onion stock.

Orange Figs take 8–12 oz. (200–300 g.) dried figs, soaked overnight with finely grated rind and juice of 2 oranges, or small can orange juice, and enough water to cover. Simmer, adding sugar to taste, until tender.

TUESDAY

Game Soup left-over hare or rabbit, 1¼ pints (7½ dl.) water, mixed herbs, seasoning, 2 onions, 1 carrot, 1½ oz. (40 g.) fat, 1 oz. (25 g.) flour, 3 tablespoons port wine, 1 tablespoon redcurrant jelly, croûtons bread.
Remove flesh from game, simmer bones with water, herbs and seasoning for at least 1 hour (or 15 minutes in a pressure cooker); strain stock. Toss diced vegetables in fat, stir in flour, then blend in the stock. Bring to the boil, cook until thickened, simmer for 15 minutes. Add wine, jelly, game flesh, season well, heat gently for 10 minutes. Top with croûtons.

Fried Bacon and Cheese fry thick rashers bacon. Just before serving, add 4 slices Cheddar cheese; leave until cheese begins to soften. Garnish with watercress and tomatoes.

Apple Brownie 4 oz. (100 g.) brown breadcrumbs, 1 oz. (25 g.) brown sugar, 1 oz. (25 g.) shredded suet, ½–1 teaspoon mixed spice, 1 lb. (½ kilo) apples, 3 oz. (75 g.) sultanas, 2–4 tablespoons golden syrup.
Mix crumbs, sugar, suet, spice. Peel apples, slice thinly, mix with sultanas, syrup. Put layers of crumb mixture and apple mixture into greased basin, end with crumbs. Cover with greased foil or paper, steam for 1½ hours. Serve with custard sauce or cream.

FRIDAY

Fluffy Cheese Eggs 4 slices buttered toast, 4 eggs, pinch salt, pepper, grated cheese. To serve: tomatoes.
Put toast on to an ovenproof dish. Whisk egg whites with salt, pepper, form nest shapes on toast, drop egg yolks in centre, top with grated cheese. Set for 7–10 minutes in a moderate oven, Gas Mark 5, 375°F. (190°C.), serve with baked tomatoes.

Caramel Mousse with Cream Sauce 6 oz. (150 g.) sugar, water, ½ oz. (15 g.) powdered gelatine, 2 eggs, ¼ pint (1½ dl.) cream (thick or thin).
Make a caramel sauce with 5 oz. (125 g.) sugar and 5 tablespoons water, add ½ pint (3 dl.) water, heat until caramel has dissolved in this; remove 2 tablespoonsful. Stir in gelatine, softened in 4 tablespoons water, cool, then whisk on to egg yolks, beaten with remaining sugar. Allow mixture to stiffen slightly, fold in beaten egg whites, pile into a shallow dish. Add the 2 tablespoons caramel to the cream, serve with the mousse.

SATURDAY

Blanquette of Lamb 8–12 pieces middle or scrag end neck of lamb, 1 pint (6 dl.) water, 4–6 carrots, 1 turnip, 1 swede, seasoning, 1 oz. (25 g.) margarine, 1 oz. (25 g.) flour, ½ pint (3 dl.) milk. To garnish: chopped parsley.
Cook lamb with water, carrots, sliced turnip, diced swede for 1¼ hours; season well. Make a white sauce with margarine, flour, milk. Stir into lamb mixture and cook for a further 15 minutes. Garnish with chopped parsley. Serve with boiled potatoes and Glazed Onions.

Glazed Onions boil 4–8 even-sized onions in salted water. When tender but unbroken, strain and toss in a little hot fat until pale golden.

Bengal Toasts 4 slices bread, butter, 2–4 lambs' kidneys, little bacon (optional), seasoning, pinch curry powder, ½ tablespoon chutney, lemon.
Toast and butter the bread. Fry skinned sliced kidneys in a little butter, adding little chopped bacon if desired, seasoning, curry powder and chutney. Pile on toast, garnish with wedge of lemon.

Spanish steak and spaghetti, recipe on page 101

WEEK 43

Lancashire Hotpot is a very well known British dish, and the recipe for Wednesday's menu gives the best known method of making this. Beetroot or pickled cabbage is an excellent accompaniment to the hotpot.

For your shopping list the main meals need:
9–10 eggs, nearly 1½ pints (nearly 1 litre) milk, 2–4 oz. (50–100 g.) Cheddar or Parmesan cheese, 4–6 oz. (100–150 g.) cream cheese (or half cream and half cottage cheese).

Sunday and Monday need:
Joint pork, Swiss roll, thick cream.
Potatoes, onions (small), tomatoes (small), mushrooms, red pepper, Seville oranges, prunes.

Tuesday and Wednesday need:
Calf's head, middle or scrag end neck of mutton.
Marshmallows, potatoes, carrots, onions, turnip, parsley, lettuce, cooked beetroot, fresh apricots (optional), plums, cooking apples (optional).

Thursday, Friday and Saturday need:
Minced beef, prawns, sausagemeat (store all of these very carefully), tomato purée (optional), red wine, chocolate sponge (if not making this), thick cream, coffee ice cream, rum.
Potatoes, onions, carrots, mushrooms, tomatoes, lettuce or endive, watercress, green pepper, peas, aubergines, parsley, lemon.

SUNDAY

Roast Pork with Seville Sauce joint of pork, little melted fat or oil, seasoning, 2 Seville oranges, ¾ pint (4½ dl.) brown stock, 1 oz. (25 g.) flour, sugar.
Rub scored fat or skin of pork with little melted fat or oil, sprinkle lightly with salt. Roast for 25 minutes per lb. (½ kilo) and 25 minutes over in a hot oven, Gas Mark 7, 425°F. (220°C.). Remove peel from oranges, shred finely, soak in stock for 1 hour, then simmer in same stock for 15 minutes. Blend flour into 1 oz. (25 g.) fat from meat, cook for 2–3 minutes, then add orange peel, stock. Bring to boil, cook for 10 minutes, adding seasoning, juice from oranges, sugar to taste.

Golden Sponge Roll Swiss roll, small can halved peaches, 1 level teaspoon cornflour or arrowroot, 1 tablespoon sieved or smooth apricot jam. To decorate: cream, nuts.
Moisten slices of Swiss roll with a little syrup from peaches. Arrange a halved peach on each slice. Blend ¼ pint (1½ dl.) peach syrup with cornflour or arrowroot and jam. Boil until thick and clear, cool slightly, brush over peaches. Decorate with cream and nuts.

WEDNESDAY

Lancashire Hotpot 1–1½ lb. (½–¾ kilo) potatoes, 2 large onions, 1–1½ lb. (½–¾ kilo) middle or scrag end neck of mutton, seasoning, little margarine, stock or water and stock cube.
Peel potatoes, cut into ¼-inch (½-cm.) slices; slice onions thinly. Divide mutton into neat joints. Put layers of well seasoned vegetables and meat into a casserole, ending with a layer of potatoes. Cover with a little margarine and add enough stock or water and stock cube to come halfway up the casserole. Put on lid or cover with foil, cook for approximately 1½ hours in the centre of a very moderate oven, Gas Mark 3, 325°F. (170°C.). Remove lid or foil; leave a further 30 minutes to brown potatoes.

Beetroot Relish little vinegar, 1 oz. (25 g.) seedless raisins, seasoning, 1 beetroot.
Boil vinegar, pour over raisins, cool, add to the well seasoned sliced beetroot.

Marshmallow Pie cook plums, or plums and apples, adding water and a very little sugar, until soft but unbroken. Put into a pie dish, cover with marshmallows. Heat under a low grill until these melt slightly.

THURSDAY

Spaghetti Bolognese 1 onion, 1 carrot, 1–2 oz. (25–50 g.) fat or oil, 8–12 oz. (200–300 g.) minced raw beef, 1–2 oz. (25–50 g.) mushrooms, 3 tomatoes or 1–2 tablespoons tomato purée, ½ pint (3 dl.) beef stock, seasoning, pinch herbs, little red wine, approximately 6 oz. (150 g.) spaghetti, 3 pints (1⅔ litres) water, grated Parmesan or Cheddar cheese.
Make sauce: fry finely chopped onion and carrot in fat or oil, add minced beef, chopped mushrooms, skinned chopped tomatoes or tomato purée, stock, seasoning, herbs. Simmer steadily in a covered pan, stirring from time to time, for 1 hour. Taste and add extra seasoning if desired, together with a little red wine. Cook spaghetti in the boiling salted water, drain, put on to a hot dish, top with the meat sauce. Serve with the grated cheese.

Green Salad mix shredded lettuce, or endive, watercress, sliced green pepper with a little oil, vinegar and seasoning.

Mocha Gâteau split a chocolate sponge, fill with little whipped cream. Top with coffee ice cream and serve with *Mocha Sauce*, made by heating 1 oz. (25 g.) butter, 1 oz. (25 g.) sugar, 1 tablespoon golden syrup, 1 oz. (25 g.) cocoa and 3 tablespoons strong coffee.

To make your own Chocolate Sponge follow the recipe on page 39, but omit 1 tablespoon flour and use 1 tablespoon sieved cocoa instead.

MONDAY

Kebabs with Pepper Rice cooked pork from Sunday, 4–8 small onions, seasoning, good $\frac{1}{2}$ pint (3 dl.) water, 4 small firm tomatoes, 4–8 mushrooms, oil or fat, 1 red pepper, 1 oz. (25 g.) margarine, 4 oz. (100 g.) medium or long grain rice, small packet frozen peas, cayenne pepper.
Dice any pork left from Sunday. Peel onions, simmer in the salted water until just tender (save this stock), drain, dry well. Do this earlier, so rice can be cooked in time. Put onions, tomatoes, mushrooms and pieces of pork on to metal skewers. Brush with oil or melted fat. Cook under grill for 5–6 minutes. Serve on the cooked rice: fry chopped pepper in margarine, add the $\frac{1}{2}$ pint (3 dl.) onion stock, rice. Cook for 10 minutes, add peas and cook for a further 5 minutes. Taste and season well; arrange on a hot dish. Dust with cayenne.

Stuffed Prune Croûtes 4 rounds bread about $\frac{1}{2}$ inch (1 cm.) thick, 1 egg, 3 tablespoons milk, 1 oz. (25 g.) sugar, 2 oz. (50 g.) margarine or butter, 12–16 large prunes, cream cheese.
Remove crusts from bread. Beat egg with milk, sugar. Dip bread into this quickly so it is not too soft. Fry in hot margarine or butter until crisp. Stone prunes (cooked or canned), fill with a little cream cheese. Serve on the hot croûtes.

TUESDAY

Calf's Head with Piquant Sauce 1 calf's head, few large carrots, few onions, 1 turnip, bay leaf, seasoning, chopped parsley, 1 oz. (25 g.) margarine, 1 oz. (25 g.) flour, $\frac{1}{4}$ pint ($1\frac{1}{2}$ dl.) milk, 1–2 gherkins, 1–2 teaspoons capers.
Ask butcher to split the head. Remove white brains and soak in separate basin of cold water. Put head to soak in cold water for 1 hour, then put into large saucepan with fresh water to cover, carrots, onions, turnip, bay leaf, seasoning. Cover, simmer for $2-2\frac{1}{2}$ hours; lift on to a dish. When cool, cut meat into neat pieces, removing skin from tongue. Reheat meat in the stock, then lift on to a hot dish with the vegetables, garnish with chopped parsley. Serve a little strained stock over meat if wished. Make a thick white sauce with margarine, flour, milk, add just over $\frac{1}{4}$ pint ($1\frac{1}{2}$ dl.) stock from cooking the head and strained brains. Simmer for 5 minutes, add diced gherkins and capers, season well.

Almond and Apricot Salad arrange cream or cottage cheese on small lettuce leaves topped with blanched almonds and in a border of drained, cooked or canned apricots.

FRIDAY

Curried Eggs and Prawns 4–5 hard-boiled eggs, 1 onion, $1\frac{1}{2}$ oz. (40 g.) margarine, 1 oz. (25 g.) flour, 2 teaspoons curry powder, $\frac{3}{4}$ pint ($4\frac{1}{2}$ dl.) milk, seasoning, 2–4 oz. (50–100 g.) prawns, boiled rice or creamed potatoes. To garnish: cooked peas, watercress.
Shell eggs. Fry finely chopped onion in margarine for 3 minutes, stir in flour, curry powder. Cook for 2 minutes, gradually stir in milk, bring to boil, add seasoning, eggs and prawns. Simmer for 3 minutes. Arrange in a border of boiled rice or creamed potatoes. Garnish with peas and watercress.

Lemon Shortcake 3 oz. (75 g.) margarine, 4 oz. (100 g.) castor sugar, 1 lemon, 1 egg, 5 oz. (125 g.) self-raising flour, lemon marmalade or lemon curd.
Cream margarine and sugar with grated lemon rind, add egg and flour. Press mixture into two 6-inch (15-cm.) greased and floured sandwich tins. Bake for 15 minutes near top of a moderately hot oven, Gas Mark 5–6, 375–400°F. (190–200°C.). Turn out carefully. Cool, sandwich with lemon marmalade or curd. Sprinkle the lemon juice over the top.

SATURDAY

Stuffed Aubergines 2 large aubergines (eggplants), seasoning, 2 onions, 3 tomatoes, 2 oz. (50 g.) fat, 8 oz. (200 g.) sausagemeat, little chopped parsley, margarine.
Halve aubergines lenthways, remove centre pulp. Season shells well. Chop pulp finely, mix with chopped onions, skinned chopped tomatoes, toss in the fat for a few minutes. Blend with sausagemeat, seasoning, parsley. Press into aubergine halves, put into a greased casserole, top with a little margarine and foil. Bake for 40 minutes in a moderate oven, Gas Mark 5, 375°F. (190°C.).

Hot Rum Soufflé 1 level tablespoon cornflour, $\frac{1}{4}$ pint ($1\frac{1}{2}$ dl.) milk, 1 oz. (25 g.) butter, 2 oz. (50 g.) sugar, 1–2 tablespoons rum, 3 eggs.
Blend cornflour with milk, heat until a thick sauce, stir in butter, sugar, rum. Remove from heat, add egg yolks, then the stiffly beaten egg whites. Bake in a soufflé dish for 25 minutes.

Week 44

The picture on page 42 shows a generous sized sirloin of beef for a Sunday's lunch. The cooking times are mentioned in the recipe below but in greater detail on pages 64 and 86, and Week 32, page 86, gives full instructions for baking Yorkshire puddings.

If you want a picnic meal and are travelling by car you could take the joint of beef and carve it as required, see picture, page 131.

For your shopping list the main meals need:
5–7 eggs, 2¾ pints (generous 1½ litres) milk, 8–11 oz. (200–275 g.) Cheddar or other cooking cheese.
Sunday, Monday and Tuesday need:
Joint of beef, pâté (unless making your own), salt pork or piece of bacon.
Horseradish cream, mincemeat (unless making your own).
Potatoes, carrots, green salad ingredients, cauliflower, lettuce, onions, haricot beans, tomatoes (optional), lemon, cooking apples.
Wednesday, Thursday, Friday and Saturday need:
Smoked haddock, ½ leg or ½ shoulder or best end neck of lamb or piece loin of lamb, bacon rashers.
Sherry, thin cream, ice cream (optional), yoghourt.
French bread.
Potatoes, parsley, peas, carrots, onions, garlic, turnips, cooked beetroots (store carefully), tomatoes, cucumber (optional), lettuce, watercress, rhubarb (apples, bananas, pears, oranges – optional).

Sunday

Roast Beef and Horseradish Puddings joint of beef, fat for cooking, see method. For the batter: 4 oz. (100 g.) plain flour, pinch salt, 1 egg, ½ pint (3 dl.) less 1 tablespoon milk and water, seasoning, 1 level tablespoon horseradish sauce.
Weigh the beef, allow 15–20 minutes per lb. (½ kilo) if cooking in a hot oven, see page 64. Add only the minimum of fat if the joint is very lean. For slower cooking of beef see page 86. Mix all the ingredients for the batter, cook in well heated and greased patty tins for a good 15 minutes. Always cook these towards the top of the oven and raise the heat slightly when warming the tins and for the first few minutes of the cooking time. Serve with cooked carrots, roast potatoes. Picture, page 42.

Hot Peaches Royale arrange 8 halved canned peaches and syrup in an ovenproof dish. Drain a can of raspberries, save juice for Thursday's jelly. Put raspberries into the peaches, top with 1 oz. (25 g.) desiccated coconut mixed with 1 oz. (25 g.) brown sugar. Put in oven when dishing up main course, lower heat to moderate.

Wednesday

Finnan and Egg Kedgeree 6 oz. (150 g.) medium or long grain rice, 1 finnan haddock, 2–3 hard-boiled eggs, 1½ oz. (40 g.) butter or margarine, 3 tablespoons milk. To garnish: parsley. To serve: peas, carrots.
Cook and drain rice. Use 4 oz. (100 g.) for this dish, cover 2 oz. (50 g.) with foil, store for Friday. Cook and flake haddock, shell and chop hard-boiled eggs. Heat butter or margarine, milk, in a saucepan, add rice, fish, eggs, heat gently. Pile on a hot dish, garnish with parsley, serve with peas and carrots.

Rhubarb Compote 3 oz. (75 g.) sugar, ¼ pint (1½ dl.) water, 1 lb. (½ kilo) early rhubarb.
Make a syrup of sugar and water, add rhubarb, cut into neat fingers; heat for few minutes only, so fruit keeps firm. Serve with Sherry Fingers.

Sherry Fingers 3 oz. (75 g.) margarine, 3 oz. (75 g.) sugar, 1 egg, 4 oz. (100 g.) self-raising flour, 2 tablespoons sherry, 1 oz. (25 g.) split blanched almonds.
Cream margarine with sugar, add egg yolk, flour, sherry. Put into a greased 7-inch (18-cm.) sandwich tin, brush with egg white, coat with the almonds. Bake for about 25 minutes in moderate oven, Gas Mark 4-5, 350-375°F. (180–190°C.). Serve hot or cold.

Thursday

Garlic Lamb on Oven Cooked Vegetables 1 lb. (½ kilo) potatoes, 12 oz. (300 g.) onions, seasoning, ½ leg or shoulder or best end of neck of lamb or piece of loin of lamb, 1 garlic clove.
Slice potatoes and onions, put into a meat tin and season well. Slit the skin of lamb and insert the split garlic clove. Cook the meat in a hot oven, Gas Mark 7, 425°F. (220°C.), allowing 20 minutes per lb. (½ kilo) and 20 minutes over.

Walnut Fingers fruit jelly, 2 oz. (50 g.) chopped walnuts, cream or ice cream.
Make up the jelly. Allow to cool, then add chopped walnuts. Pour into a flat dish, allow to set, cut in fingers with a knife dipped into hot water. Serve with cream or ice cream.

MONDAY

Cold Beef slice the cold beef neatly and arrange on a bed of green salad.

Curried Cauliflower cook the cauliflower in the usual way and coat with a creamy white sauce, adding a teaspoon of curry powder to the flour, recipe page 5.

Collegiate Puddings 4 oz. (100 g.) breadcrumbs (or 2 oz. (50 g.) breadcrumbs and 2 oz. (50 g.) flour), ½ teaspoon baking powder, 2 oz. (50 g.) shredded suet, 2–3 oz. (50–75 g.) sugar, 4 oz. (100 g.) dried fruit, ½ teaspoon mixed spice, pinch salt, 2 eggs or 1 egg and milk. To serve: hot custard sauce.
Mix breadcrumbs or breadcrumbs and flour, baking powder, suet, sugar, dried fruit, spice, salt. Bind with eggs or egg and milk. Put into 4 greased cups or 7 castle pudding tins, cover with greased paper, steam for 30–40 minutes. Turn out and serve with hot custard sauce.
Soak 12 oz. (300 g.) to 1 lb. (½ kilo) dried haricot beans in cold water for Tuesday.

TUESDAY

Pâté Fingers serve fingers of pâté on lettuce with wedges of lemon and hot toast and butter.
A bought pâté can be used for this hors d'oeuvre, or there is a recipe on page 68.

Boston Baked Beans 2 large onions, 8 oz. (200 g.) salt pork or cheap bacon, soaked haricot beans, ½ pint (3 dl.) water from soaking beans, seasoning, little black treacle (optional) or 3–4 tomatoes (optional).
Peel and slice onions. Dice pork or bacon, put the onions, pork or bacon, soaked beans, ½ pint (3 dl.) water in which beans were soaked, into a casserole. Season well, cover and cook in a cool oven, Gas Mark 2, 300°F. (150°C.), for approximately 5 hours, stirring from time to time. If desired, a little black treacle may be added to the beans, or, for a tomato flavour, add the skinned, sliced tomatoes. The beans are a course in themselves, but can be served with a green vegetable if required.

Apples Marguerite core and slit the skins of 4 large cooking apples. Put into a greased ovenproof dish, fill the centres with mincemeat, bake for approximately 1½ hours.

FRIDAY

Cheese Pie cook a mixture of sliced potatoes, onions, carrots, turnips and peas in well seasoned water until just tender, add small can sweetcorn then strain. Put some of the vegetables on one side, but toss the rest in ¼ pint (1½ dl.) warmed thin cream and 6–8 oz. (150–200 g.) grated or diced Cheddar cheese. Put into a very hot dish, top with the rest of the vegetables, see picture page 90, a little more grated cheese and brown under a hot grill.
To vary: mix all the vegetables with a cheese sauce, recipe page 5, and top with crumbs and cheese.

Vegetable Salad dice beetroot, tomato, gherkin or cucumber, serve on a bed of lettuce.

Rice Mould 1 pint (6 dl.) custard sauce, 1 level dessertspoon powdered gelatine, 2 tablespoons cold water, 2 oz. (50 g.) cooked rice (from Wednesday), 1 oz. (25 g.) chopped glacé cherries, 1 oz. (25 g.) dried fruit or chopped crystallised peel, evaporated milk.
Make custard sauce and while hot stir gelatine, softened in the cold water, into this. Cool, then add cooked rice, cherries, dried fruit or peel. Put into a mould, allow to set. Serve with evaporated milk.

SATURDAY

Onion Soup 3 large onions, 1–2 oz. (25–50 g.) butter or good beef dripping, 1¼ pints (7½ dl.) beef stock, seasoning, grated cheese. To serve: French bread.
Peel onions and slice very thinly, then cut the slices across. Fry in the butter or dripping for 5 minutes. Add stock and seasoning; simmer for 30 minutes. Put in hot soup cups, top with grated cheese and brown under the grill for 1 minute only. Serve with slices of crusty French bread.

Hot Bacon and Potato Salad 4–6 rashers bacon, cooked potato, chopped parsley, watercress.
Dice bacon, fry lightly, mix with diced hot potato, bacon fat, chopped parsley, and serve in a border of watercress.

Yoghourt and Fruit serve fresh fruit salad, made with sliced apple, bananas, pears and oranges, or canned fruit, with yoghourt.

Week 45

Fried Chicken (Sunday's menu) will be enjoyed by all the family for the quick method of cooking retains the maximum of flavour.

Any bones left should be used in making Monday's sustaining soup. Bones from a joint can also be used to make this soup.

Herrings are some of the most economical and nutritious fish (see Wednesday).

For your shopping list the main meals need:
13–15 eggs (plus those in Christmas pudding), 4¾ pints (nearly 2¾ litres) milk, 4–6 oz. (100–150 g.) Cheddar or other cooking cheese.
Sunday, Monday and Tuesday need:
Young chicken, bacon rashers, stewing steak (store carefully).
Christmas pudding ingredients, anchovy paste, thick or thin cream.
Potatoes, salad ingredients (optional), haricot beans, onions, garlic (optional), tomatoes, carrots, celery, cabbage, apple, lemon, bananas.
Wednesday, Thursday, Friday and Saturday need:
Herrings, rump steak, stewing veal (store carefully).
Oatmeal, thick or thin cream or ice cream.
Potatoes, tomatoes, mushrooms; green vegetable, parsley, onions, cooking apples, lemons, orange.

Sunday

Herb Fried Chicken 1 young chicken, seasoning, good pinch mixed herbs, 1 oz. (25 g.) flour, 1–2 eggs, fine breadcrumbs, fat or oil for frying.
Joint the chicken, put the backbones on one side to use in the soup for tomorrow. Mix seasoning, herbs and flour, coat the chicken in this mixture, then in beaten egg and crumbs. Fry steadily until crisp, brown and tender. This will take up to 15 minutes. Drain on absorbent paper. Put on a hot dish or in a basket, as picture page 130. Serve with hot vegetables or salad. The giblets can be simmered to make a gravy.

Christmas Pudding 3 oz. (75 g.) flour (plain or self-raising), 3 oz. (75 g.) breadcrumbs, 3 oz. (75 g.) shredded suet or melted butter or margarine, 4 oz. (100 g.) chopped crystallised orange peel, 4 oz. (100 g.) sugar (brown or white), 1½ lb. (¾ kilo) mixed dried fruit, 1 medium peeled grated apple, 1 teaspoon mixed spice, 2 tablespoons orange marmalade, grated rind and juice of 1 orange, 3 eggs, ¼ pint (1½ dl.) dry sherry, 2 tablespoons Curaçao.
Mix all the ingredients together. Put into a 3-pint (1¾–2-litre) greased basin, cover well and steam for 5 hours. Remove wet covers and put on dry ones. Serves about 12.
Note. Soak haricot beans overnight in cold water.

Wednesday

Oatmeal Herrings herrings, milk or beaten egg, seasoning, medium or coarse oatmeal (or rolled oats), fat.
Brush cleaned herrings with milk or beaten egg and roll in the seasoned oatmeal (or use rolled oats). Fry in a little hot fat until golden brown, serve with Mustard Sauce.

Mustard Sauce 1 oz. (25 g.) margarine, 1 oz. (25 g.) flour, 2 teaspoons mustard, ½ pint (3 dl.) milk, seasoning.
Heat margarine in a pan, stir in flour, blended with mustard, and cook for 2–3 minutes. Stir in the milk, bring to the boil, stirring well; cook until thickened, add salt and pepper to taste. Less mustard could be used, if wished.

Apple Cinnamon Slices 10 oz. (250 g.) shortcrust pastry, see page 10, 3–4 large apples, brown sugar, powdered cinnamon.
Put 5 oz. (125 g.) pastry away for Friday*, or bake the flan at the same time as slices. Roll out rest of pastry into neat oblong. Put on to a flat baking sheet, bake 'blind' in a hot oven, Gas Mark 7, 425°F. (220°C.), for 10 minutes. Cut peeled apples into wafer-thin slices. Arrange on half-cooked pastry, top with brown sugar, a light dusting of cinnamon, and return to oven for a further 20 minutes, reducing heat if pastry is becoming too brown.

Thursday

Savoury Minute Steaks thin slices rump steak, packet stuffing, fat for frying. To serve: fried tomatoes, mushrooms.
Coat slices of steak with a light layer of packet stuffing and fry for 2–3 minutes. Serve with fried tomatoes, mushrooms, and cream potatoes and a green vegetable.

Soufflé Fritters with Jam Sauce 4 oz. (100 g.) flour, pinch salt, 2 eggs, just over ¼ pint (1½ dl.) milk, fat for frying, sugar, about 4 heaped tablespoons jam, finely grated rind and juice of 1 lemon.
Make a batter with flour, salt, egg yolks and milk, then fold in the stiffly beaten egg whites. Fry in hot fat until crisp and golden brown. Put on a hot dish, dusting lightly with sugar, keep hot in a very low oven. Put jam, lemon rind and juice in a pan and heat for a few minutes – a little water may be added for a thinner sauce. Pour over fritters.

MONDAY

Minestrone Soup bones from meat, 2 pints (1¼ litres) water, seasoning, 2 oz. (50 g.) haricot beans, 1 onion, 1 oz. (25 g.) fat, 1 garlic clove (optional), 1 rasher bacon, 3 tomatoes, 1 carrot, 2 tablespoons chopped celery, 1–2 oz. (25–50 g.) macaroni, 4 oz. (100 g.) finely shredded cabbage, grated cheese.
Simmer saved bones with water, seasoning, soaked beans, for 45 minutes. Strain off stock and beans, put on one side. Fry chopped onion in fat with crushed garlic, chopped bacon, add beans, stock, skinned chopped tomatoes, diced carrot, celery, simmer for a further 45 minutes. Add macaroni and cabbage, cook until both are tender (approximately 15 minutes). Taste and re-season. Put into hot dishes and top with grated cheese.

Anchovy Crisps spread slices of buttered toast with anchovy paste, put together to make toasted sandwiches, top with scrambled, fried or poached egg.

Harlequin Cream make a blancmange with just under 1 pint (6 dl.) milk. Cool slightly, fold in 2–3 tablespoons cream, 1 oz. (25 g.) chopped glacé cherries, 1 oz. (25 g.) chopped dates or sultanas, 1 oz. (25 g.) chopped nuts. Set in glasses or mould. Decorate with chopped nuts.

TUESDAY

Casserole Bombay 1 onion, 1 apple, 1 oz. (25 g.) fat, 1 level tablespoon flour, 2 teaspoons curry powder, ¾ pint (4½ dl.) stock, 1 tablespoon sultanas, 1 tablespoon chutney, few drops lemon juice, pinch sugar, ¾–1 lb. (⅜–½ kilo) diced stewing steak, seasoning. To serve: boiled rice or creamed potatoes, chutney, bananas, carrots.
Fry peeled chopped onion and apple in fat, add flour, curry powder, cook for several minutes. Stir in stock, bring to boil, cook for about 10 minutes, then add sultanas, chutney, lemon juice, sugar and stewing steak. Simmer for 10 minutes, taste and re-season, if liked. Put into casserole, cover tightly; cook for 2 hours in centre of a cool oven, Gas Mark 2, 300°F. (150°C.). Serve with boiled rice or creamed potatoes, chutney, sliced bananas, grated raw carrots. *Note.* More curry powder can be used.

Cheese with Walnut Triangles cut fairly thick slices of bread into triangles, brush with melted margarine and roll in a mixture of chopped walnuts and grated cheese. Put into the oven for about 15 minutes until crisp. Serve with cheese and watercress.

FRIDAY

Salmon Flan 5 oz. (125 g.) shortcrust pastry*, 1 oz. (25 g.) margarine, 1 oz. (25 g.) flour, ⅓ pint (2 dl.) milk, medium can pink salmon, 2 chopped gherkins or little chopped parsley, seasoning. To garnish: parsley, hard-boiled egg.
Roll out pastry, line a 7–8-inch (18–20-cm.) tin or flan ring. Bake 'blind' in a hot oven, Gas Mark 7, 425°F. (220°C.), until crisp and golden brown. Cool. Make a thick sauce of margarine, flour and milk, add salmon and gherkins or parsley, season well. Put the cool filling into the pastry case, garnish with parsley and sliced hard-boiled egg.

Orange and Lemon Pudding 2 oz. (50 g.) margarine, 2–3 oz. (50–75 g.) sugar, 1 orange, 1 lemon, 2 eggs, 2 oz. (50 g.) self-raising flour, milk. To serve: custard.
Cream margarine with sugar, add finely grated orange and lemon rind, then egg yolks and flour. Measure the fruit juices and add enough milk to give ⅜ pint (2¼ dl.), stir this gently into the mixture (if it curdles it does not matter). Fold in stiffly beaten egg whites. Put in a pie dish, stand in another dish of cold water. Put into coolest part of a moderate oven, Gas Mark 4, 350°F. (180°C.), and bake for 40 minutes. Serve with custard.

*recipe page 10; it is suggested that this is made on Wednesday.

SATURDAY

Veal in Creamy Paprika Sauce 1 lb. (½ kilo) diced stewing veal, 2 onions, pinch herbs, seasoning, 1 pint (6 dl.) water plus 1 chicken stock cube *or* 1 pint (6 dl.) stock, 1 oz. (25 g.) flour, 2 teaspoons paprika, ½ pint (3 dl.) milk, 1 oz. (25 g.) margarine. To garnish: chopped parsley.
Simmer veal with thinly sliced onions, herbs, seasoning, in water and stock cube or stock for 1¼ hours. Blend flour and paprika with milk, add to the veal, together with margarine, and stir until the mixture thickens. Taste and re-season, if wished. Garnish with chopped parsley.

Chocolate Custard 3 eggs, 2–3 oz. (50–75 g.) sugar, 1 oz. (25 g.) cocoa, 1 pint (6 dl.) warm milk. To serve: cream or ice cream.
Beat eggs with sugar and cocoa. Add warm milk, strain into a soufflé dish, cover with greased paper. Steam gently for approximately 1¼ hours. Serve hot or cold with cream or ice cream.

Put 2½–3 lb. (1¼–1½ kilos) collar of bacon to soak for following Sunday.

Fresh apricot compote, recipe on page 112

Week 46

Sunday

Cider is an excellent accompaniment to bacon, see Sunday's menu. This particular Cider Sauce is thickened, but if you like to omit the flour you have a refreshing clear liquid to serve with the bacon.

For your shopping list the main meals need:
16–17 eggs, generous 1¼ or 2¼ pints (¾ or generous 1¼ litres) milk – if making custard on Monday, plus little top of milk, 12 oz. (300 g.) cream cheese, 2–3 oz., (50–75 g.) Cheddar cheese.

Sunday, Monday and Tuesday need:
Collar of bacon, minced beef (store carefully).
Cider, apple or redcurrant jelly, digestive biscuits, sherry, tomato juice, thick or thin cream or ice cream (optional).
Potatoes, onions, parsley, tomatoes, mixed vegetables or salad, dessert apples, lemons.·

Wednesday needs:
Calf's or lamb's sweetbreads, bacon rasher, ice cream.
Potatoes, onion, tomatoes (optional).

Thursday, Friday and Saturday need:
White fish, stewing steak, ox kidney.
Rolled oats.
Potatoes, tomatoes, parsley, onion or leek, watercress, celery, cooking apples, rhubarb, dessert apples.

Collar of Bacon in Cider Sauce 2½–3 lb. (1¼–1½ kilos) piece collar bacon, 1 pint (6 dl.) sweet or dry cider, 8 medium onions, pepper, 4 dessert apples, 1 oz. (25 g.) flour, 2 tablespoons apple or redcurrant jelly.
On Saturday put bacon to soak in cold water overnight. If preferred, use a joint of milder cured bacon which does not need soaking. Put bacon in a casserole, add cider, skinned onions, pepper. Cover casserole with lid or foil. Bake for 2¼–2½ hours in very moderate oven, Gas Mark 3, 325°F. (170°C.). Core, but do not peel apples. Add to casserole 1 hour *before* serving, and turn bacon over. Remove skin, arrange bacon on dish with onions and apples. Blend cider with flour, put into pan, add apple or redcurrant jelly, cook steadily, stirring well, until smooth and thickened.

Sultana Cheese Cake 3 oz. (75 g.) crushed digestive biscuit crumbs, 2 oz. (50 g.) butter, 2 oz. (50 g.) castor sugar, 2 eggs, 12 oz. (300 g.) cream cheese, 2 oz. (50 g.) plain flour, 3 oz. (75 g.) sultanas. To decorate: extra sultanas, 1 tablespoon sherry.
Butter 8-inch (20-cm.) shallow ovenproof dish, coat with crumbs. Cream butter, sugar, beat in eggs, cheese, flour, sultanas. Spread in dish, bake for about 1 hour. Decorate with lines of sultanas soaked in the sherry.

Wrap left-over bacon.

Wednesday

Fried Sweetbreads 1 lb. (½ kilo) calf's or lamb's sweetbreads, salt, 1 egg, crisp breadcrumbs, fat for frying.
Put well washed sweetbreads into cold salted water, bring to boil, cook for 15 minutes. Throw away water, allow meat to cool, skin, coat in beaten egg and crumbs. Fry until crisp and golden brown.

Tomato Sauce 1 onion, 1 rasher bacon, 1 oz. (25 g.) fat, medium can tomatoes plus ¼ pint (1½ dl.) water *or* 4 large tomatoes plus ½ pint (3 dl.) water, seasoning, pinch sugar, 1 level tablespoon flour, 2 tablespoons water.
Fry chopped onion and bacon in fat, add tomatoes and water (chop fresh tomatoes); season well. Add pinch sugar, simmer for 30 minutes, sieve, then return to pan together with flour blended with water. Boil until thickened and clear.

Raspberry Melbas can raspberries, 1 teaspoon corn-flour or arrowroot, 2 tablespoons redcurrant or apple jelly, ice cream.
Strain raspberries, blend ¼ pint (1½ dl.) syrup with the cornflour or arrowroot, put into pan with few raspberries and the jelly. Boil until thickened and clear, sieve if wished, then cool. Arrange raspberries round ice cream, coat with sauce.

Thursday

American Fish Pie 1 lb. (½ kilo) white fish, seasoning, 3 tomatoes, 2 eggs, 1 lb. (½ kilo) potatoes, 1 oz. (25 g.) margarine, 1 oz. (25 g.) flour, ½ pint (3 dl.) milk, 1 tablespoon chopped parsley.
Boil fish in salted water, break into large flakes. Skin and slice tomatoes. Hard-boil eggs, shell and slice. Boil and mash potatoes. Make a parsley sauce with margarine, flour, milk, parsley, seasoning. Mix fish with the sauce. Arrange layers of fish and sauce, toma-toes and eggs and potatoes in a pie dish, beginning and ending with potatoes. Bake towards top of a moderate oven, Gas Mark 4, 350°F. (180°C.), for approximately 30 minutes.

Apple Flapjack 2 oz. (50 g.) margarine or fat, 2 oz. (50 g.) sugar, 2 level tablespoons golden syrup, 4 oz. (100 g.) rolled oats, good 1 lb. (½ kilo) apples, little sugar.
Heat margarine or fat, sugar, syrup in saucepan. Stir in oats. Peel and slice apples, put into rather shallow wide dish with little sugar and very little water, press flapjack mixture over top. Bake in centre of oven for 35–40 minutes. Serve hot or cold.

MONDAY

Rice and Steak Loaf 3 oz. (75 g.) medium or round grain rice, 1 oz. (25 g.) margarine, ½ pint (3 dl.) tomato juice, 1 grated onion, seasoning, 12 oz. (300 g.) minced beef, 2 teaspoons chopped parsley, 1 egg.
Cook rice, margarine, tomato juice, onion and seasoning until rice is soft – take care it does not stick towards end of cooking time. Mix thoroughly with beef, parsley, beaten egg. Put into a well greased loaf tin, cover with greased paper or foil, bake for 1 hour in coolest part of a moderate oven, Gas Mark 4–5, 350–375°F. (180–190°C.).

Spiced Upside-down Pudding 5 oz. (125 g.) self-raising flour, mixed spice, 3 oz. (75 g.) margarine, 3 oz. (75 g.) sugar, 1 egg, milk. For the topping: 1 oz. (25 g.) butter or margarine, 1 oz. (25 g.) brown sugar, can pears. To serve: ice cream, cream or custard.
Sieve flour with 1 teaspoon mixed spice, rub in margarine, add sugar, egg and enough milk to make a sticky consistency. Melt butter or margarine in bottom of tin or ovenproof dish, add brown sugar, sprinkling of mixed spice. Arrange pears on this, add 2 teaspoons syrup from can, cover with pudding mixture. Bake in centre of oven for about 1 hour. Turn out, serve with rest of syrup and ice cream, cream or custard.

TUESDAY

Savoury Pinwheels 2 hard-boiled eggs, 3 tomatoes, 3 oz. (75 g.) breadcrumbs, seasoning, 12 oz. (300 g.) bacon left from Sunday, 1 oz. (25 g.) margarine, 1 oz. (25 g.) flour, ¼ pint (1½ dl.) milk. To serve: hot vegetables or salad.
Shell and chop eggs, mix with skinned chopped tomatoes, 1 oz. (25 g.) breadcrumbs, season well. Mince bacon, add thick sauce made with margarine, flour, milk, 2 oz. (50 g.) breadcrumbs and seasoning. Form into an oblong on a floured board; spread with egg and tomato mixture. Roll like a Swiss roll – cut in slices. Either heat for 15 minutes on a greased tin in a hot oven or under the grill. Serve with hot vegetables or with salad.

Pancakes with Lemon Sauce 4 oz. (100 g.) flour, pinch salt, 1–2 eggs, ½ pint (3 dl.) milk or milk and water, oil or fat, 2 lemons, ½ pint (3 dl.) water, 1 level dessertspoon cornflour, 2–3 oz. (50–75 g.) sugar.
Make a thin batter with flour, salt, eggs, milk or milk and water. Fry spoonfuls of mixture in hot oil or fat, until pancakes are crisp and brown on both sides. Keep hot on uncovered dish over hot water or in low oven. Simmer pared rind of lemons in the water for 5 minutes, strain over cornflour blended with lemon juice. Return to pan, cook until thick. Add the sugar.

FRIDAY

Potato Soup 1 onion or leek, 1 oz. (25 g.) fat, 12 oz. (300 g.) peeled potatoes, seasoning, 1½ pints (9 dl.) stock or water and chicken stock cube, top of the milk, chopped watercress.
Fry chopped onion or leek in fat, add chopped potatoes, seasoning, stock or water and stock cube, simmer for 30 minutes. Beat until smooth or sieve, add a little top of the milk, reheat, serve topped with chopped watercress.

Golden Crust Omelettes 2 slice bread, butter, 4 eggs, 2 egg yolks, seasoning, 2 tablespoons water, grated cheese.
Remove crusts from bread, cut in dice, fry until golden brown in hot butter. Beat eggs, egg yolks with seasoning and water, add bread; cook half mixture in hot butter in omelette pan, fill with grated cheese; cook rest of mixture in same way.

Rhubarb Snow 1 lb. (½ kilo) rhubarb, 2–3 oz. (50–75 g.) sugar, 2 egg whites.
Cook rhubarb with sugar and no water until soft. Beat well, fold in stiffly beaten egg whites. Pile into glasses.

SATURDAY

Steak and Kidney Pudding 8–10 oz. (200–250 g.) suet crust pastry, see page 69, 1–1¼ lb. (½–⅝ kilo) diced stewing steak, 4–6 oz. (100–150 g.) diced ox kidney, seasoning, flour, water or stock, pinch mixed herbs (optional).
Make the pastry. Roll out about three-quarters and use this to line a 2 pint (1¼ litre) basin. Coat steak and kidney in well seasoned flour. Put into pastry lined basin. Add enough water or stock to half fill, with seasoning to taste and herbs, if liked. Roll out remainder of pastry and form into a round the size of the top of the basin. Damp the edges of the pastry with water. Press the lid in position; cover the pudding with greased greaseproof paper then foil. Tie into position. Steam for at least 4 hours.
When serving the pudding you can make a slightly thickened gravy to serve with it or you can pour a little extra stock into the pudding.

Cheese, Fresh Fruit serve crisp apples, a sharp cheese like Stilton or Lancashire, and celery.

Week 47

Sunday

The traditional way to thicken the savoury minced beef mixture known as Collops (Thursday) is with oatmeal. If you do not wish to buy this especially use the same weight of flour or rolled oats.

Smoked haddock, because of its definite flavour, is a good choice for a soufflé (Friday's menu).

For your shopping list the main meals need:
12–13 eggs, 2½ pints (nearly 1½ litres) milk, no cheese needed in cooking.

Sunday, Monday, Tuesday and Wednesday need:
Boiling fowl, sausages (store carefully), gammon.
Thick cream, rum or brandy, fine semolina, ground almonds, honey.
Potatoes, onions, carrots, tomatoes, parsley, green vegetable, cabbage, celery, oranges, fresh apricots (optional), plums, cooking apple.

Thursday, Friday and Saturday need:
Smoked haddock, minced beef, lamb cutlets.
Oatmeal (optional – see Introduction), ice cream.
Potatoes, onions, tomatoes, parsley, prunes, rhubarb, dates.

Chicken Ragoût with Savoury Croûtons joint a small boiling fowl, coat in 1 oz. (25 g.) seasoned flour, fry in 2 oz. (50 g.) fat until golden brown. *Put wings and back on one side for Monday.* Lift rest of chicken on a plate. Fry 2 sliced onions, 2 sliced carrots, 2 skinned sliced tomatoes in the fat. Gradually blend in 1 pint (6 dl.) stock, bring to the boil, cook until thickened. Season, add chicken, cover pan and simmer gently for 1½–1¾ hours. To make the croûtons: blend pinch mixed herbs, pinch dry mustard, little chopped parsley with 1 oz. (25 g.) butter. Spread over 2–3 slices toast, dice. Sprinkle on the ragoût just before serving.
Save 2 tablespoons gravy for Monday.

Halva Ring 3 oz. (75 g.) butter, 3 oz. (75 g.) sugar, 1 egg, 3 oranges, 3 oz. (75 g.) fine semolina, 1 level teaspoon baking powder, 3 oz. (75 g.) ground almonds. To serve: cream, oranges.
Cream butter and sugar, add beaten egg, grated rind 1 orange, semolina sieved with baking powder, almonds, 2 tablespoons orange juice. Put into well greased 8-inch (20-cm.) ring tin, bake in centre of moderately hot oven, Gas Mark 5, 375°F. (190°C.), for 50 minutes or until firm. Turn out; while hot, soak with juice from 2 oranges. Serve cold topped with cream and orange segments.

Wednesday

Egg and Gammon Fingers 1 oz. (25 g.) margarine, 1 oz. (25 g.) flour, ¼ pint (1½ dl.) milk, chopped or minced gammon, 3 hard-boiled eggs, 1 oz. (25 g.) breadcrumbs, seasoning, flour or egg and crumbs, fat for frying.
Make a thick white sauce with margarine, flour, milk, add the gammon, chopped hard-boiled eggs, breadcrumbs and seasoning. Form into finger shapes, coat in flour or egg and crumbs, fry until crisp and golden brown. Serve with Winter Coleslaw.

Winter Coleslaw shred ¼–½ small crisp cabbage, mix with a little chopped celery, grated raw carrot, 1 oz. (25 g.) sultanas and mayonnaise.

Cumberland Pudding 4 oz. (100 g.) self-raising flour, ½–1 teaspoon mixed spice, 2 oz. (50 g.) brown sugar, 2 oz. (50 g.) shredded suet, 3 oz. (75 g.) dried fruit, 1 large apple, 1 egg. To serve: rum- or brandy-flavoured custard sauce.
Mix flour, spice, sugar, suet, dried fruit and peeled diced apple. Bind with egg, put into greased basin, cover, steam for 1½–2 hours. Serve with rum- or brandy-flavoured custard sauce.

Thursday

Oatmeal Minced Beef Collops 1–2 onions, 2 tomatoes, 1 oz. (25 g.) fat, ¾ pint (4½ dl.) plus 4 tablespoons brown stock, 1 lb. (½ kilo) minced beef, 1 oz. (25 g.) oatmeal, seasoning, pinch mixed herbs, little chopped parsley. To serve: creamed potatoes or crisp toast.
Fry chopped onions, skinned chopped tomatoes in the fat, add stock and minced beef (saving the 4 tablespoons stock). Cook the beef in the liquid for ¼ hour, stirring well to keep this smooth. Blend oatmeal with 4 tablespoons stock, add to mixture with seasoning, herbs, parsley, simmer for 1 hour. Serve in a border of creamed potatoes or with crisp toast.

Caramel Milk Pudding 4 oz. (100 g.) sugar, 3 tablespoons water, 1 pint (6 dl.) milk, 2–3 oz. (50–75 g.) rice, chopped nuts.
Make a caramel by heating 3 oz. (75 g.) sugar and water until golden brown. Cool, then add milk and remaining sugar and heat gently until caramel is dissolved in the milk. Add rice and simmer very slowly until rice is tender. Serve in a hot dish, topped with chopped nuts.

MONDAY

Sausage and Chicken Pasty back and wings of cooked chicken, 8 oz. (200 g.) sausages, 1 onion, 1 large raw potato, seasoning, 2 tablespoons chicken gravy, 1 lb. (½ kilo) cooked potatoes, melted margarine. To serve: green vegetable.
Remove meat from back and wings of cooked chicken. Skin sausages, cut in slices, mix with chicken, finely chopped onion, diced potato, seasoning and gravy. Mash cooked potatoes. Use half to line a greased pie dish; put in filling, top with potatoes, peaking to look like the top of a pasty. Brush with melted margarine. Bake for 30 minutes in a hot oven, Gas Mark 6–7, 400–425°F. (200–220°C.), until brown. Serve with a green vegetable.

Lemon Apricot Mould small can apricots *or* 8 oz. (200 g.) fresh apricots plus little water and sugar, 1 lemon jelly, just under ¼ pint (1½ dl.) lightly whipped cream.
If using fresh apricots, cook with water and sugar until just soft. Pour off apricot juice, add enough water to give ¾ pint (4½ dl.) and dissolve jelly in this. Allow to cool, then add whipped cream and chopped apricots. Set in mould.

TUESDAY

Roast Gammon with Honey Glaze put 5 slices gammon into a well greased ovenproof dish, top with a little butter. Cook for 20 minutes towards the top of a moderately hot oven, Gas Mark 6, 400°F. (200°C.). Brush 4 of the slices with a little honey, return to the oven for a further 10–15 minutes; put these and the 5th slice (not topped with honey) into a cooler part of the oven. Put the 5th slice of gammon on one side for Wednesday.

Plum Strudel 6 oz. (150 g.) flour, pinch salt, 2 tablespoons oil, 1 egg, water, 8 oz. (200 g.) plums, 1 oz. (25 g.) fried crisp breadcrumbs, 2 oz. (50 g.) sultanas, 1 oz. (25 g.) blanched almonds, ½ oz. (15 g.) margarine, little egg white or milk, icing sugar.
Make a paste of flour, salt, oil and egg and cold water to mix. Roll out wafer thin. Slice stoned plums thinly, mix with breadcrumbs, sultanas, chopped almonds. Brush strudel paste with melted margarine, cover with plum mixture, roll over to make a long wide strip, put on to a lightly greased baking tin. Brush top with a little egg white or milk, bake for approximately 25 minutes in centre of a moderately hot oven. Lower heat to moderate when gammon is taken out and cook for a further 20 minutes. Dust with icing sugar.

FRIDAY

Haddock Soufflé 8 oz. (200 g.) smoked haddock, 1 oz. (25 g.) margarine, 1 oz. (25 g.) flour, ¼ pint (1½ dl.) milk, 3 eggs, seasoning.
Cook haddock until just soft, flake, and save 4 tablespoons stock. Make a thick sauce with margarine, flour, milk and haddock stock, add the fish and beaten egg yolks, then fold in the stiffly beaten egg whites, taste, season. Put into a greased soufflé dish, bake for 30 minutes in centre of a moderately hot oven, Gas Mark 5, 375°F. (190°C.), until well risen and golden. Do not overcook. Serve at once.

Prune Chocolate Bars 4 oz. (100 g.) uncooked prunes, 4 oz. (100 g.) self-raising flour, 1 oz. (25 g.) cocoa, 4 oz. (100 g.) brown sugar, 3 oz. (75 g.) melted butter, 1 egg, ice cream.
Chop prunes into small pieces, add to flour, cocoa, brown sugar, melted butter and egg. Put into a well greased 6–7-inch (15–18-cm.) square sandwich tin. Bake for 20 minutes in centre of oven, cut into fingers. Serve topped with ice cream.

SATURDAY

Lamb Cutlets Parisienne coat the cutlets in a little well seasoned flour and fry until tender, serve with fried tomatoes and *Parisienne Potatoes*, i.e. tiny balls of potato, fried or roasted until golden brown.

Jelly Whip 1 lb. (½ kilo) rhubarb, ¾ pint (4½ dl.) water, 2 oz. (50 g.) chopped dates, sugar, 1 level tablespoon powdered gelatine, 2 tablespoons water, 2 egg whites.
Cook rhubarb with water, dates and sugar to taste until a soft pulp. Add gelatine softened in the water, stir until dissolved. Cool and allow to stiffen slightly, then add stiffly beaten egg whites and pile into a shallow dish. Save egg yolks until Sunday.

Week 48

The Orange Baskets (Wednesday's menu) are a simple, but refreshing dessert. Use a teaspoon or, better still, a grapefruit spoon to remove the pulp. In this way you do not damage the orange cases. If you need to cut the pulp, do this with kitchen scissors so you do not make it too soft and produce too much juice.

For your shopping list the main meals need:
9 eggs, 3 pints (1¾ litres) milk, no cheese used in cooking.
Sunday, Monday and Tuesday need:
Veal fillet, stewing steak, ox kidney, bacon rashers or bacon pieces.
Sherry, sponge cakes, glacé cherries, orange juice.
Potatoes, mushrooms, tomatoes, green pepper, watercress, spinach, bananas, lemon, cooking apples.
Wednesday, Thursday and Friday need:
Lambs' hearts, cod's roe, bacon rashers.
Ice cream, chocolate, Swiss roll.
Potatoes, carrots, peas, mushrooms, large oranges, fresh fruit (grapes).
Saturday needs:
Pork chops.
Thick cream, thin cream (optional), rose hip syrup, crystallised rose petals (optional).
Potatoes, broad beans (optional), dessert apples.

Sunday

Baked Veal and Mushrooms 2 lb. (1 kilo) veal fillet, 2–4 oz. (50–100 g.) chopped mushrooms, 2 oz. (50 g.) breadcrumbs, 2 oz. (50 g.) chopped bacon, 2 oz. (50 g.) melted butter, seasoning.
Split veal fillet through the middle and fill with mushrooms mixed with the breadcrumbs, bacon, melted butter and seasoning. (This rich fat stuffing keeps the veal moist.) Wrap veal in greased foil and bake for 2 hours in a moderately hot oven, Gas Mark 5–6, 375–400°F. (190–200°C.).
Put some of the meat and stuffing on one side for Monday.

Banana Trifle egg yolks from Saturday, 1 extra egg, 1 oz. (25 g.) sugar, 1 pint (6 dl.) milk, little sherry, 4 sponge cakes, jam, bananas, lemon juice, glacé cherries.
Add egg yolks to the extra egg, beat with the sugar and warm milk, cook until a smooth sauce over hot but not boiling water (use a double saucepan) and stir from time to time. Flavour with a little sherry. Split the sponge cakes, fill with jam and mashed bananas, press together again, put into the serving dish. Add the hot sherry-flavoured custard. Allow to cool and decorate with sliced bananas (dipped in lemon juice to prevent them turning brown) and halved glacé cherries.

Wednesday

Braised Hearts and Carrots 4–5 lambs' hearts, 8 oz. (200 g.) carrots, seasoning, 1 oz. (25 g.) flour, 2 oz. (50 g.) fat, ¾ pint (4½ dl.) brown stock. To serve: carrots and peas.
Clean hearts and slice thickly. Peel and slice carrots. Coat the hearts in seasoned flour and fry in fat for 5 minutes, add stock, carrots and seasoning. Lower the heat and simmer for 1¼ hours. Serve in a border of freshly cooked carrots and peas.

Orange Baskets 4 large oranges, ice cream, grated chocolate.
Remove tops from the oranges, then carefully remove the pulp. Pack the pulp back into each orange case and top with ice cream just before serving. Decorate with a handle of orange rind from the tops and a little grated chocolate.

Thursday

Bacon and Cod's Roe if buying uncooked cod's roe, steam for 20 minutes. Skin and then slice thickly. With cooked roe just cut into slices (use fresh *not* smoked roe). Fry rashers of bacon until crisp, then heat roe in the bacon fat.

Potato Hash 1 oz. (25 g.) fat, 8 oz. (200 g.) mashed potato, 1 egg, seasoning.
Make this before cooking bacon and cod's roe. Heat fat in the frying pan. Add mashed potato mixed with the beaten egg and seasoning. Cook gently until the bottom side forms a skin, then fold like an omelette and tip on to a hot dish, keep hot while cooking bacon and roe; or use a second frying pan for this.

Cheese, Fresh Fruit try an unusual cheese, e.g. Port-Salut, and serve this with grapes.

MONDAY

Sage Croquettes veal and stuffing left from Sunday, 8 oz. (200 g.) mashed potato, 2 eggs, good pinch dried sage, seasoning, little sage and onion stuffing (from packet), fat for frying.
Mince veal and stuffing, mix with mashed potato, 1 beaten egg and sage. Season well and form into croquette shapes. Coat with beaten egg and a little dry stuffing and fry until golden brown.

Pepper and Tomato Salad 2–3 firm tomatoes, 1 green pepper, seasoning, oil, vinegar. To serve: watercress.
Slice tomatoes and pepper (discard core and seeds of pepper). Toss in seasoned oil and vinegar and serve on a bed of watercress.

Cherry Balls $\frac{1}{2}$ pint (3 dl.) canned orange juice, 1 pint (6 dl.) water, 3 oz. (75 g.) self-raising flour, $1\frac{1}{2}$ oz. (40 g.) shredded suet, $\frac{1}{2}$ oz. (15 g.) sugar, 2 oz. (50 g.) glacé cherries, water to bind.
Put orange juice, water into a saucepan. Make dumplings with flour, suet, sugar, chopped cherries and water to bind. With lightly floured hands form into small balls and cook for 15 minutes in the hot orange liquid. Serve this liquid as a sauce.

TUESDAY

Steak and Kidney Burgers 8 oz. (200 g.) good quality stewing steak, 2 oz. (50 g.) ox kidney, 1 grated potato, 1 egg, seasoning, tomatoes. To serve: canned spaghetti, creamed spinach.
Put steak and kidney through a mincer or chop very finely. Bind with potato, egg, seasoning, form into flat cakes. Bake for 20 minutes; top with baked tomatoes. Serve with spaghetti and spinach.

Toffee Apple Pudding 1 oz. (25 g.) butter, 2 oz. (50 g.) brown sugar, 12 oz. (300 g.) apples, 2 tablespoons golden syrup, 5 tablespoons water. For the crumble: 2 oz. (50 g.) margarine, 4 oz. (100 g.) flour, 3 oz. (75 g.) sugar.
Grease a pie dish with butter and coat with brown sugar. Fill with the thinly sliced apples, golden syrup and water. Cover with crumble mixture, made by rubbing margarine into flour and adding sugar. Press this down firmly. Bake for 45 minutes in the centre of a moderate oven, Gas Mark 4, 350°F. (180°C.).

FRIDAY

Bean and Mushroom Quiche for the shortcrust pastry: 6 oz. (150 g.) flour, pinch each salt, celery salt, mustard, cayenne pepper, 3 oz. (75 g.) fat. For the filling: 3–4 oz. (75–100 g.) chopped mushrooms, 1 oz. (25 g.) butter, medium can baked beans, 2 eggs, 2–3 rashers bacon.
Sieve flour with seasonings, rub in fat, bind with cold water. Roll out the pastry and line an 8-inch (20-cm.) flan ring or sandwich tin. Fry mushrooms in butter, mix with baked beans, eggs, and the chopped, fried bacon. Bake the pastry case 'blind' for 15 minutes in a hot oven, Gas Mark 7, 425°F. (220°C.), then spoon in the bean mixture, lower the heat to very moderate and cook for a further 20 minutes to set the filling.

Swiss Meringue 4 thin slices jam Swiss roll, 2 eggs, 1 oz. (25 g.) sugar, $\frac{3}{4}$ pint ($4\frac{1}{2}$ dl.) milk, 2 oz. (50 g.) castor sugar.
Put Swiss roll into a pie dish. Beat egg yolks with the 1 oz. (25 g.) sugar, add milk. Strain this over Swiss roll. Bake in centre of very moderate oven for 40 minutes. Whisk egg whites until stiff, fold in castor sugar. Pile over sponge, set for 15–20 minutes. If wishing to serve cold, fold 4 oz. (100 g.) sugar into egg whites, set meringue for 1 hour in very cool oven, Gas Mark $\frac{1}{2}$, 250°F. (130°C.).

SATURDAY

Pork Chops 4 large pork chops, 2–3 dessert apples, little sugar, pinch powdered sage.
Grill or fry the chops, snipping fat so it becomes crisp. Allow 20–25 minutes' cooking time so meat is adequately cooked. Core, but do not peel apples, cut into $\frac{1}{4}$-inch ($\frac{1}{2}$-cm.) rings; 10 minutes before end of cooking time, add apple rings to chops. Brush with a little of the hot pork fat, sprinkle lightly with sugar and a pinch sage. Serve with the pork chops.

Creamed Broad Beans drain cooked or heated canned broad beans and stir into a white sauce made with 1 oz. (25 g.) margarine, etc., see page 5. Add 2–3 tablespoons cream.

Rose Hip Cream $2\frac{1}{2}$ level tablespoons cornflour, $\frac{3}{4}$ pint ($4\frac{1}{2}$ dl.) milk, 1 oz. (25 g.) sugar, nearly $\frac{1}{4}$ pint ($1\frac{1}{2}$ dl.) thin or thick cream, 3 tablespoons rose hip syrup. To decorate: glacé cherries or crystallised rose petals, little whipped cream.
Blend cornflour with $\frac{1}{4}$ pint ($1\frac{1}{2}$ dl.) cold milk, add $\frac{1}{2}$ pint (3 dl.) boiling milk. Return to pan with sugar, cook until thickened, *cool slightly*, stir in cream then rose hip syrup – *never add this to a very hot mixture*, otherwise you lose some of the Vitamin C. Put into individual glasses, leave to set. Decorate with cherries or rose petals and cream.

Herb fried chicken, recipe on page 120

WEEK 49

If you cannot buy cannelloni then make small thin pancakes instead for Saturday's menu. A recipe for pancakes is on page 23. If you want to make your own sponge cake for the dessert on Tuesday, see page 39.

For your shopping list the main meals need:
6–10 eggs*, nearly ½ pint (¼ litre) milk, 4 oz. (100 g.) Cheddar or Parmesan cheese, 4–8 oz. (100–200 g.) cream cheese.
*more if making sponge for Tuesday.

Sunday, Monday and Tuesday need:
Shoulder of lamb.
Thick cream, sponge cake (unless making your own).
Potatoes, onions, red or green pepper, tomatoes, carrots, cucumber and other salad ingredients, cooking apples, lemons, oranges and other fruit for salad, rhubarb.

Wednesday and Thursday need:
Rump or sirloin steaks, bacon rashers, pig's head (store carefully).
Brandy (optional), coffee ice cream, thick cream.
Lentils, potatoes, courgettes, parsley, onions, large tomatoes, green salad ingredients, fresh fruits.

Friday and Saturday need:
Sprats, minced beef.
Cannelloni, concentrated tomato purée, thin cream or yoghourt.
Watercress, lettuce, onions, tomato, grapes, cooking apples, plums (optional).

SUNDAY

Creole Shoulder of Lamb 2 onions, 2 oz. (50 g.) fat, 1 red or green pepper, 4 large tomatoes, seasoning, pinch cayenne pepper, shoulder of lamb. To serve: roast potatoes.
Slice the onions and fry for 5 minutes in the hot fat. Add the sliced pepper (discard core and seeds) and tomatoes with seasoning and a pinch of cayenne pepper. Slit the meat to form a pocket, put in the mixture and skewer the meat or tie it firmly. Roast in a hot oven, Gas Mark 6–7, 400–425°F. (200–220°C.), allowing 20 minutes per lb. (½ kilo) and 20 minutes over. Serve with roast potatoes. Put some left-over meat on one side for Monday.

Lemon Apple Pudding 4–5 oz. (100–125 g.) breadcrumbs, 3 oz. (75 g.) margarine, 2 oz. (50 g.) brown sugar, 2 lemons, 1–1¼ lb. (½–⅝ kilo) apples, granulated sugar to taste, little water.
Toss breadcrumbs in margarine, fry until crisp and golden brown. Add the brown sugar and grated lemon rinds. Cook the peeled sliced apples with granulated sugar, lemon juice and the minimum of water. Arrange lemon crumb mixture and apples in layers in a pie dish, beginning and ending with crumbs. Bake for 20 minutes in a hot oven, then lower heat to moderate, Gas Mark 4, 350°F. (180°C.), when taking the meat out of the oven. Put the pudding in the coolest part of the oven.

WEDNESDAY

Steaks Diane with Courgettes and Creamed Potato Ring 1 lb. (½ kilo) peeled potatoes, seasoning, 1–2 oz. (25–50 g.) margarine, 1 egg, 2 tablespoons top of milk, courgettes, butter, chopped parsley, 1 onion, 4 thin rump or sirloin steaks, Worcestershire sauce, little brandy (optional).
Make potato ring: cook potatoes in boiling salted water, mash, season again, add margarine, egg, top of the milk; mix well. Form into a ring on ovenproof dish, brown in a very moderate oven, Gas Mark 3, 325°F. (170°C.). Meanwhile, cook the courgettes (tiny marrows). Do not peel, just cut off the ends; put into a steamer, season lightly, cook over boiling water for 10–15 minutes, toss in butter and chopped parsley. Fry the finely chopped onion in 2–3 tablespoons butter. Add steaks, cook until tender. Lift into the centre of the potato ring; add to butter remaining in pan little chopped parsley, Worcestershire sauce, little brandy if wished. Heat for 1 minute. Pour over the steaks.

Walnut Sundae arrange coffee ice cream in sundae glasses. Top with whipped cream and chopped walnuts.

Soak 4 oz. (100 g.) lentils for Thursday in enough cold water to cover.

THURSDAY

Lentil Soup 4 oz. (100 g.) lentils, 1 onion, 1 carrot, bacon, stock, seasoning, 1 tablespoon flour, ¼ pint (1½ dl.) milk. To garnish: chopped parsley.
Drain lentils, put into saucepan with chopped onion, chopped carrot, diced bacon. Cover with some stock, add seasoning. Simmer gently for 1¼ hours. Sieve or beat until smooth. Return to pan with flour, blended with milk. Cook until smooth and thick. Garnish with parsley.

Pork Brawn 1 pig's head, seasoning, water, 1 level dessertspoon powdered gelatine.
Wash pig's head very well. Put into a saucepan, add seasoning, water to cover. Simmer for 1½ hours. Remove head, chop meat into neat pieces, return to the stock, simmer for a further hour. Lift meat from pan, put into a basin, dissolve gelatine in ½ pint (3 dl.) hot stock, pour over meat, allow to set.

Stuffed Tomatoes remove centre pulp from 4 firm tomatoes, mix with a hard-boiled egg, little chopped parsley and mayonnaise, pile back into tomato cases. Serve on a bed of green salad.

Fresh Fruit serve fresh-flavoured citrus fruits such as oranges.

MONDAY

Curried Lamb and Rice 2 oz. (50 g.) margarine or fat, 1 onion, 1 apple, 1 tablespoon flour, $\frac{1}{2}$–1 tablespoon curry powder, $\frac{3}{4}$ pint ($4\frac{1}{2}$ dl.) stock, 1–2 oz. (25–50 g.) sultanas, 1 tablespoon chutney, seasoning, pinch sugar, few drops lemon juice or vinegar, left-over lamb from Sunday. To serve: boiled rice.
Heat margarine or fat. Fry finely chopped onion and apple in this. Stir in flour and curry powder, cook for several minutes. Add stock, bring to the boil, cook until slightly thickened. Add sultanas, chutney, seasoning, sugar, lemon juice or vinegar and diced lamb. Simmer gently for 1 hour in a tightly covered pan and serve in a border of boiled rice.

Sunshine Fruit Salad make a syrup of 2 oz. (50 g.) sugar, $\frac{1}{4}$ pint ($1\frac{1}{2}$ dl.) water, add the juice of an orange and lemon. Dice a selection of fruits. Pour the cold syrup over the fruit. Serve with cream if liked.

TUESDAY

Eggs Italienne hard-boiled eggs, cooked spaghetti, grated Parmesan or Cheddar cheese.
Serve hard-boiled eggs on a bed of spaghetti, top with a thick layer of grated cheese. Put for 1 minute under a hot grill.

Spring Salad make a salad with as many of the early vegetables as possible, e.g. grated carrot, sliced early cucumber, etc.

Rhubarb Layer Gâteau make or buy a sponge cake. Split and fill with a layer of thick rhubarb purée and whipped cream. Top with well drained, neat pieces of cooked rhubarb and decorate with cream.
Note. A recipe for a suitable sponge cake is on page 39.

FRIDAY

Devilled Sprats 1–$1\frac{1}{2}$ lb. ($\frac{1}{2}$–$\frac{3}{4}$ kilo) sprats, seasoning, flour, good pinch curry powder, shake cayenne pepper, fat for frying. To serve: watercress, brown bread and butter.
Wash and dry sprats, remove the heads before frying. Coat in seasoned flour to which is added the curry powder and cayenne pepper. Fry the sprats in hot fat for about 8 minutes. Drain and serve with watercress and brown bread and butter.

Cream Cheese and Grape Salad arrange large spoonfuls of cream cheese in the centre of a ring of lettuce leaves and decorate with black and green grapes.

SATURDAY

Cannelloni Milanaise 8 oz. (200 g.) cannelloni, seasoning, 1 oz. (25 g.) fat, 1 onion, 1 tomato, 8 oz. (200 g.) minced beef, $\frac{1}{4}$ pint ($1\frac{1}{2}$ dl.) stock. For the sauce: 1 onion, 1 apple, 1 oz. (25 g.) margarine, small tube or can concentrated tomato purée, 1 teaspoon cornflour, $\frac{1}{2}$ pint (3 dl.) water, pinch sugar.
Boil cannelloni (large pasta tubes) in salted water until tender; drain, cool. Heat fat, fry grated onion, chopped tomato for 2–3 minutes, add minced beef, seasoning, stock; simmer until meat is tender, fill pasta. Put pasta into an ovenproof dish, top with sauce, heat for a short time in a moderately hot oven, Gas Mark 5, 375°F. (190°C.). *To make tomato sauce:* fry grated onion, grated apple, in margarine, add rest of ingredients, season and simmer until thick and smooth.

German Crumb Pudding 4 oz. (100 g.) breadcrumbs, 2 oz. (50 g.) butter, 2 oz. (50 g.) brown sugar, 1 teaspoon mixed spice, 1 lb. ($\frac{1}{2}$ kilo) apples or apples and plums, honey, little water. To serve: thin cream or yoghourt.
Toss crumbs in butter until very crisp, add sugar and half spice, continue to heat until sugar has melted slightly. Cool. Cook prepared fruit with honey, water, rest of spice, until a thick purée; cool. Arrange alternate layers of crumb mixture and fruit in glasses. Top with layer of cream or yoghourt before serving.

Week 50

Sunday

The Fried Chicken and Corn Fritters (Sunday's menu) is a modified Chicken Maryland. If you fry bananas as well as corn fritters you produce this American classic. The picture of Crown Roast, page 139, shows the lightly cooked cauliflower coated with a batter (similar to that used for corn fritters) and fried, but you may prefer to cook the sprigged cauliflower in the usual way and serve it in or round the lamb (Tuesday's menu).

For your shopping list the main meals need:
5 eggs, 1½ pints (nearly 1 litre) milk, 5 oz. (125 g.) Cheddar or other cooking cheese.
Sunday and Monday need:
Joints frying chicken, stewing steak, canned, fresh or frozen sweetcorn, brandy, thick or thin cream, ice cream.
Potatoes, watercress, tomatoes, onions, carrots, parsley, swedes.
Tuesday, Wednesday and Thursday need:
Crown roast of lamb, bacon rashers, boiled bacon or cooked ham, desiccated coconut, plain chocolate.
Potatoes, watercress, carrots, cauliflower, large tomatoes, peas, mixed salad ingredients, mint and parsley, bananas, prunes, dessert pears.
Friday and Saturday need:
Scallops, fillet steaks, sherry (optional), thin cream (optional), thick cream, lemon curd.
Potatoes, lettuce, watercress, mustard and cress, tomatoes, mushrooms, parsley, apples, plums, rhubarb, lemon.

Fried Chicken and Corn Fritters 4 large or 8 small joints frying chicken, 2 egg yolks, 2–3 oz. (50–75 g.) crisp breadcrumbs, fat or oil for frying. For the corn fritters: 4 oz. (100 g.) flour, pinch salt, 1 egg, ¼ pint (1½ dl.) milk, small can sweetcorn or cooked sweetcorn. To garnish: watercress, tomatoes.
Coat chicken well with beaten egg yolks and crumbs. Fry for 15–20 minutes. Or brown outside of chicken in hot fat or oil, then bake in a hot oven, Gas Mark 6, 400°F. (200°C.), for 20–25 minutes. To make the fritters: make a thick batter with the flour, salt, egg, milk, add the well drained sweetcorn. Fry spoonfuls of the mixture in hot fat or oil until crisp and golden brown. Garnish chicken with the fritters, watercress and tomatoes.

Coffee Brandy Mousse 1 level tablespoon powdered gelatine (or enough to set 1 pint (6 dl.)), just over ¾ pint (4½ dl.) strong *sweetened* coffee, 1 tablespoon brandy, 2 egg whites. To serve: cream.
Soften the gelatine in a little cold coffee. Add to very hot coffee and stir well until dissolved. Cool until the mixture begins to stiffen slightly, add the brandy and fold in the stiffly beaten egg whites. Pour into a dish. Serve with cream.

Wednesday

Salad Platter of Spring Lamb cut rest of crown roast into cutlets. Arrange on a bed of mixed salad. Coat any vegetables left from Tuesday in mayonnaise, top with a mixture of mint and parsley.

Devils on Horseback 8 large prunes, 4 rashers bacon, buttered toast.
If the prunes are quite tender after soaking, do not cook; otherwise simmer until just tender. Stone, and wrap each prune in a half rasher bacon. Secure with wooden cocktail sticks. Grill until bacon is crisp, then serve on fingers of hot buttered toast.

Thursday

Ham and Rice Mornay 3 oz. (75 g.) long grain rice, seasoning, 4–6 oz. (100–150 g.) boiled bacon or cooked ham. For the cheese sauce: 1 oz. (25 g.) margarine, 1 oz. (25 g.) flour, ½ pint (3 dl.) milk, 3 oz. (75 g.) grated cheese. For the topping; grated cheese, breadcrumbs.
Boil rice in salted water; strain. Mix rice with diced bacon or ham. Put half rice and ham mixture into a greased dish. Cover with a layer of cheese sauce, made with the margarine, flour, milk, cheese and seasoning; top with more rice and ham, the rest of the sauce, a sprinkling of grated cheese, seasoning and breadcrumbs. Heat in a hot oven, Gas Mark 6, 400°F. (200°C.), for 25 minutes.

Chocolate Pears 4 ripe dessert pears, 4 oz. (100 g.) plain chocolate, 2 tablespoons water or milk.
Peel and core the pears. Stand upright in a shallow dish. Coat with hot chocolate sauce, made by melting the chocolate with the water or milk in a basin over hot water.

MONDAY

Sea Pie with Mashed Swedes 1–1¼ lb. (½–⅝ kilo) stewing steak, seasoning, 1 oz. (25 g.) flour, 2 oz. (50 g.) fat, 2 onions, 4 carrots, 1 pint (6 dl.) stock, pinch mixed herbs. For the pastry: 4 oz. (100 g.) self-raising flour, pinch salt and pepper, 2 oz. (50 g.) shredded suet, 2 teaspoons chopped parsley, water to bind.
Coat diced steak in seasoned flour, melt fat in a large saucepan, fry meat until golden brown, add sliced onions, sliced carrots, cook for 2–3 minutes. Gradually stir in stock, bring to the boil, stirring well, add seasoning, herbs. Lower heat, cover pan, allow mixture to simmer steadily for 1¾ hours. Sieve flour with salt, pepper. Add suet, parsley, water to bind. Roll or flatten suet crust to a round the size of the pan. Ensure there is plenty of gravy in the pan, put round of pastry on top, cook steadily for 25 minutes. Cut pastry into neat pieces, arrange on dish with meat and vegetables.

Mashed Swedes cook swedes until tender, mash, add margarine and pinch grated nutmeg.

Mandarin Orange Sundae drain the syrup from a can of mandarin oranges. Put this into a pan with 3–4 tablespoons orange marmalade. Heat until thickened slightly. Cool. Top ice cream with mandarin oranges and sauce.

TUESDAY

Crown Roast Lamb with Vegetable Stuffing ask the butcher to make a crown roast of loin of lamb. You will need to buy at least 10 chops for this, so it can be formed into a round. Roast in a hot oven, Gas Mark 7, 425°F. (220°C.), allowing 20 minutes per lb. (½ kilo) and 20 minutes over; the heat can be reduced to moderately hot after about 30 minutes, or allow 35 minutes per lb. (½ kilo) and 35 minutes over in a moderate oven, Gas Mark 4, 350°F. (180°C.). Protect the ends of the bones with foil to prevent them from burning. When cooked, fill the centre with watercress and cooked carrots. Remove the foil and cover the ends of the bones with cutlet frills. Garnish with cauliflower or cauliflower fritters and tomatoes, topped with cooked peas.
Save some meat for Wednesday.

Coconut Baked Bananas bananas, butter or margarine, sugar, desiccated coconut.
Allow 2 small bananas per person, coat well in melted butter or margarine, then roll in mixture of equal quantities of sugar and coconut. Put into a greased dish and place in centre of a moderately hot oven, Gas Mark 5–6, 375–400°F. (190–200°C.), when removing meat. Put 8 large prunes to soak in a little cold water for Wednesday.

FRIDAY

Creamed Scallops with Green Salad 8 medium scallops, ½ pint (3 dl.) milk, pinch salt, 1 tablespoon cornflour, 3 tablespoons top of the milk, 1 oz. (25 g.) butter, 1 tablespoon cream and/or 1 tablespoon sherry, seasoning, lettuce, watercress, mustard and cress, oil, vinegar.
Simmer scallops in milk, adding salt. After 10 minutes, when scallops should be tender, add cornflour blended with top of the milk, and butter, to the milk. Simmer very gently, stirring all the time, until sauce is smooth and thick. Add cream and/or sherry; taste and season if wished. Toss shredded lettuce, sprigs watercress, mustard and cress, in well seasoned oil and vinegar.

Mixed Fruit Brigade Pudding stale bread, margarine, apples, plums, rhubarb [1 lb. (½ kilo) fruit in all], water, 2–3 tablespoons golden syrup, 2 oz. (50 g.) currants, 2 oz. (50 g.) breadcrumbs.
Cut bread into ¼-inch (½-cm.) slices. Remove crusts, divide bread into fingers. Coat in a little melted margarine, line bottom and sides of a basin with some of these. Cook equal quantities of each fruit with little water, no sugar. Mix with syrup, currants, breadcrumbs. Fill basin with this, cover with more bread fingers, coated in margarine, steam for 1¼ hours.

SATURDAY

Tournedos Chasseur 4 fillet steaks, melted butter, 3–4 tomatoes, 2–4 oz. (50–100 g.) mushrooms, 1–2 oz. (25–50 g.) butter or margarine, seasoning, 2 tablespoons stock, fried bread.
Tie steaks into neat rounds. Brush with melted butter, grill until tender — the time depends on personal taste. While steaks are cooking, fry skinned sliced tomatoes, sliced mushrooms in the melted butter or margarine. Season well, add stock to give a moist mixture. Arrange the tournedos on rounds of crisp fried bread, top with the tomato mixture.

Sauté Potatoes slice boiled potatoes, fry in hot fat until golden brown, top with chopped parsley.

Crumb Lemon Gâteau 2 eggs, 3 oz. (75 g.) castor sugar, grated rind of 1 lemon, 3 oz. (75 g.) crisp bread-crumbs (raspings), 1 tablespoon lemon juice, lemon curd, cream.
Whisk eggs with sugar and lemon rind until thick and creamy. Fold in breadcrumbs and lemon juice. Divide the mixture between two 6–7-inch (15–18-cm.) well greased and floured cake tins, bake for about 12 minutes towards top of a moderately hot oven, Gas Mark 5–6, 375–400°F. (190–200°C.). Turn out, sandwich together with lemon curd and cream. A mixture of thick and thin cream gives a lighter filling.

WEEK 51

SUNDAY

The steak pie, with its flavour of mushrooms and onions, can be cooked the day before then reheated gently on Sunday.

One of the oldest traditional recipes is suggested for the main dish on Saturday, i.e. Faggots with Pease Pudding.

For your shopping list the main meals need:
16 eggs, generous 2 pints (1¼ litres) milk, minimum 8 oz. (200 g.) Lancashire cheese, 6 oz. (150 g.) Cheddar cheese.

Sunday and Monday need:
Stewing steak, bacon rashers, sausages (store carefully). Potatoes, small onions, button mushrooms, tomatoes, cooking apples, dates (optional), lemon.

Tuesday, Wednesday and Thursday need:
Calves' or lambs' liver, cooked ham, cooked tongue (store carefully).
Crystallised or preserved ginger.
Potatoes, onions, mushrooms, tomatoes, chicory, red pepper, green peppers, cabbage, carrots, celery, dessert apple.

Friday and Saturday need:
Cutlets white fish, belly of pork, pigs' liver, pig's kidney.
Ice cream, walnuts.
Potatoes, split peas, onions, bunch mixed herbs, tomatoes, lemon, grapefruit, dates, dried figs.

Steak, Mushroom and Onion Pie 1¼ lb. (⅝ kilo) steak, seasoning, 1 oz. (25 g.) flour, 1 oz. (25 g.) fat, ¾ pint (4½ dl.) brown stock, 8 small onions, 2 oz. (50 g.) button mushrooms, 6 oz. (150 g.) flaky pastry*, recipe page 137.
*make double quantity if desired, i.e. ½ for Monday.
Cut steak into neat pieces, coat in the seasoned flour, fry in fat until golden. Stir in stock, bring to the boil, cook until thickened. Add onions, simmer for 1½ hours. Lift meat, onions and about ¼ pint (1½ dl.) stock into a pie dish. Add mushrooms, cover with the flaky pastry. Bake for 25 minutes in centre of a hot oven, Gas Mark 7–8, 425–450°F. (220–230°C.), then lower heat to very moderate for a further 25 minutes.

Pineapple Delight medium can pineapple – slices or cubes, 1 tablespoon cornflour, 2 eggs, 2 oz. (50 g.) sugar.
Strain off juice from pineapple, add enough water to make ½ pint (3 dl.) Blend with the cornflour, stir over a gentle heat until thickened and smooth, add a little sugar if wished. Remove from the heat, add the beaten egg yolks and chopped pineapple. Put into a pie dish, top with a meringue. *To make a meringue:* whisk the egg whites, fold in the sugar. Set in a very moderate oven, Gas Mark 3, 325°F. (170°C.), for about 20–25 minutes, serve hot.
To serve cold: use 4 oz. (100 g.) sugar for the meringue, dry out in very cool oven for 1 hour.

WEDNESDAY

Baked Green Peppers with Egg and Onion Stuffing
4 medium green peppers, seasoning, little fat, 3 onions, 2 oz. (50 g.) breadcrumbs, pinch sage, 3 eggs.
Remove tops from peppers; cut away core and seeds. Simmer shells in boiling salted water for 10 minutes. Meanwhile, chop slices of pepper removed from the top, fry in a little hot fat with chopped onions for 5 minutes. Add breadcrumbs, sage, seasoning and beaten eggs. Spoon mixture into the well drained pepper shells, put into a greased dish, cover with greased paper, bake for about 35–45 minutes in a cool oven, Gas Mark 2, 300°F. (150°C.), until the egg filling is set.

Baked Caramel Custard 3 oz. (75 g.) sugar, 6 tablespoons water, 1 pint (6 dl.) warm milk, 2 whole eggs plus 2 egg yolks.
Make a caramel sauce with sugar and 3 tablespoons water. When brown, add another 3 tablespoons water to make a thinner sauce. Coat an ovenproof mould, soufflé dish or tin with this. Make a custard by pouring milk over eggs and egg yolks (save 2 whites for Thursday). Strain into the caramel-lined mould or tin. Stand in another container of water and bake in the coolest part of the oven for 1½ hours. If wished, beat a little sugar with eggs before adding milk.

THURSDAY

Meat and Cheese Platter ham, Cheddar cheese, tongue, Lancashire cheese. For the coleslaw: ¼–½ a firm cabbage, 2 raw carrots, 1 eating apple, little chopped celery, mayonnaise.
Arrange slices of ham, Cheddar cheese, tongue, Lancashire cheese, on a bed of coleslaw. To make this, shred the cabbage very finely, mix with grated carrots, diced apple, chopped celery and mayonnaise.

Fruit Puffs 1 egg yolk, 4 oz. (100 g.) self-raising flour, good ¼ pint (1½ dl.) milk and water, 4–6 oz. (100–150 g.) dried fruit, 3 egg whites, fat for frying. To serve: golden syrup.
Beat egg yolk into flour. Add milk and water, dried fruit and stiffly beaten egg whites. Drop spoonfuls of this fluffy batter into hot fat, fry until crisp and golden brown. Serve with hot golden syrup.

MONDAY

Bacon, Sausage and Tomato grill or fry rashers of bacon, sausages and tomatoes. The sausages have a delicious flavour if skinned and brushed with milk, then coated in flour to which a very good pinch of mustard is added.

Lancashire Apple Pie put sliced apples, sugar to taste, a few sultanas or chopped dates and a little water into a pie dish. Top with 6 oz. (150 g.) flaky pastry, recipe below, or shortcrust pastry, see page 10. Bake in the centre of a hot to very hot oven for 20–25 minutes then lower heat to very moderate for another 20 minutes. Serve with fingers of Lancashire cheese.

Flaky Pastry 6 oz. (150 g.) plain flour, pinch salt, 4½ oz. (115 g.) margarine or butter (or a mixture of fats), squeeze lemon juice, water to mix.
Sieve flour and salt. Rub in one-third of the fat. Add lemon juice and water to make an elastic dough. Roll out to an oblong. Cover two-thirds of the dough with half the fat. Fold in three, turn, seal ends, depress pastry at regular intervals, then roll out again and repeat with remaining fat. Keep cool.

TUESDAY

Liver Risotto 1 onion, 2 oz. (50 g.) mushrooms, 2 tablespoons oil, 3 oz. (75 g.) long grain or Italian rice, 1 pint (6 dl.) chicken stock, seasoning, pinch garlic salt, 8–12 oz. (200–300 g.) calves' or lambs' liver. To serve: grilled tomatoes, grated cheese.
Fry finely chopped onion, sliced mushrooms, in oil. Add rice, toss in oil for 3 minutes, add stock, seasoning, garlic salt. Simmer for 15 minutes, add the diced liver. Cook until liver is tender. Serve in a border of grilled tomatoes, top with grated cheese.

Chicory and Pepper Salad slice 2 heads chicory and 1 red pepper, with seeds and core removed. Toss in oil and vinegar.

Ginger Cream 1 lemon jelly, ½ pint (3 dl.) water, ½ pint (3 dl.) evaporated milk, 2–4 oz. (50–100 g.) chopped crystallised or preserved ginger.
Make up jelly with the water. Cool slightly, add the whipped evaporated milk and chopped ginger. Serve in glasses.

FRIDAY

Fish Medallions with Hollandaise Sauce 4 cutlets white fish, seasoning, few strips lemon rind. For the sauce: 2 egg yolks, seasoning, pinch dry mustard, 1 tablespoon lemon juice, 1–2 oz. (25–50 g.) butter. To garnish: gherkin rings, tomato.
Poach cutlets in a little seasoned water, adding strips lemon rind, until they are just soft. Drain, put on to a hot dish, top with Hollandaise sauce and an attractive garnish of gherkin rings and tiny shapes of tomato. To make sauce: put egg yolks, seasonings, lemon juice, into a basin over hot, but not boiling, water. Whisk until thick and creamy, then *gradually* beat in butter – do this very slowly.

Grapefruit Alaska 2 grapefruit, sugar, ice cream. For the meringue: 2–4 oz. (50–100 g.) sugar, 2 egg whites. Halve grapefruit, remove pulp, pack back again into the grapefruit cases with a very little sugar. Top with a spoonful of ice cream, then with meringue, made by folding sugar into stiffly beaten egg whites. Brown for 3 minutes only in a very hot oven, Gas Mark 9–10, 475–500°F. (240–250°C.).
Put 12 oz. (300 g.) split peas to soak in cold water for Saturday.

SATURDAY

Faggots with Pease Pudding 4–6 oz. (100–150 g.) belly of pork, 12 oz. (300 g.) pigs' liver, 1 pig's kidney, 1 onion, seasoning, 2 oz. (50 g.) breadcrumbs, pinch sage, pinch thyme, 1 egg. For the pease pudding: 12 oz. (300 g.) split peas, 1 onion, bunch herbs, 2 eggs, 2 oz. (50 g.) butter, seasoning.
Simmer diced pork, liver, kidney, onion in salted water for 45 minutes. Strain; mince, mix with crumbs, sage, thyme, seasoning, 1 egg. Put into a greased tin, mark in squares, cover with greased foil, cook for 1 hour in a moderately hot oven, Gas Mark 5–6, 375–400°F. (190°–200°C.). To make the pease pudding: simmer soaked split peas in fresh salted water with onion and herbs for 2½ hours. Strain, sieve, add eggs, butter, seasoning. Put into a greased basin, cover and cook over a pan of simmering water for 1 hour.

Oriental Fingers 4 oz. (100 g.) margarine, 4 oz. (100 g.) brown sugar, 1 tablespoon golden syrup, 1 egg, 4 oz. (100 g.) self-raising flour, 8 oz. (200 g.) chopped dates, 4 oz. (100 g.) chopped figs, 4 oz. (100 g.) chopped walnuts. To serve: custard or sweet white sauce.
Cream margarine, sugar, golden syrup, add egg, flour, dates, figs, walnuts. Press into a greased dish, bake for 25 minutes in centre of a moderately hot oven until golden brown in colour. Cut into fingers, serve hot with custard or sweet white sauce, page 5.

Roast duckling, recipe on page 30

Week 52

The easy-to-make dressing for the Pork Salad (Monday's meal) gives an entirely new flavour. The fruit flan (Thursday) could be made with shortcrust or sweet shortcrust pastry, but the richer fleur pastry (often called biscuit or flan pastry) gives a better result. The egg white left over could be added to the 2 whites for Friday's dessert, in which case increase the sugar slightly.

You may be able to buy marzipan (or sweetmeat) eggs for the Easter Pavlova. If not make marzipan as page 104, form into eggs and tint with culinary colourings.

For your shopping list the main meals need:
13 eggs*, generous 2 pints (1¼ litres) milk, 2–3 oz. (50–75 g.) Cheddar or other cooking cheese.
*More if making marzipan.
Sunday, Monday, Tuesday, Wednesday and Thursday need:
Loin pork, boiling chicken (store carefully — remove giblets from body of bird), middle or scrag end neck of mutton or lamb, ice cream (optional), thick cream. Potatoes, spring onions (optional), mixed salad ingredients, peas, aubergines, parsley, onions, carrots, cooking apples, lemon, fruit for pancakes and flan.
Friday and Saturday need:
Slices (cutlets) turbot, shrimps (or prawns), sausagemeat, minced beef (store carefully), biscuit crumbs, thick cream, marzipan Easter eggs or make marzipan as page 104, new potatoes, parsley, tomatoes, chives and/or spring onions, lettuce, lemon.

Sunday

Glazed Roast Pork with Raisin Stuffing 4 oz. (100 g.) raisins, 4 tablespoons water, 2 oz. (50 g.) breadcrumbs, 2 apples, seasoning, pinch sage, piece loin of pork, oil, little honey.
Make stuffing: put raisins in a saucepan with water, heat for a few minutes to plump the raisins. Mix with breadcrumbs, grated apples, seasoning, sage. Put into a dish and bake for 30 minutes. Brush pork with oil and seasoning. Roast in a hot oven, Gas Mark 7, 425°F. (220°C.), allowing 25 minutes per lb. (½ kilo) and 25 minutes over. Remove from oven ½ hour before pork is cooked, brush with a little melted honey to give a sweet taste to the crackling. Return to the oven.

Almond Crumble large can pineapple, 1½ oz. (40 g.) margarine, 3 oz. (75 g.) flour, 2 oz. (50 g.) sugar, 1 oz. (25 g.) blanched chopped almonds.
Put aside 3 tablespoons pineapple syrup and 2 tablespoons pineapple for Monday. Put rest of pineapple and little syrup into a pie dish. Rub margarine into flour, add sugar and almonds. Press this mixture over pineapple, brown towards the top of the oven for 25 minutes. Reduce temperature to moderate, Gas Mark 5, 375°F. (190°C.), when taking meat out of oven.

Wednesday

Irish Stew 1¼–1½ lb. (⅝–¾ kilo) middle or scrag end of neck of mutton or lamb, 2 large sliced potatoes, 8–12 oz. (200–300 g.) sliced onions, seasoning, 1 lb. (½ kilo) peeled whole potatoes. To garnish: chopped parsley.
Put meat into a saucepan with sliced potatoes, sliced onions. Cover with water, season, simmer for 1¼ hours. Add whole potatoes, simmer for a further 30 minutes. Serve garnished with chopped parsley.

Glazed Carrots boil carrots, strain, then toss in melted margarine and chopped parsley until shiny.

Fruit Pancakes 4 oz. (100 g.) flour, pinch salt, 1 egg, ½ pint (3 dl.) milk, fat for frying, thick fruit purée.
Make pancake batter as page 23, with flour, salt, egg and milk. Cook pancakes and fill with a large spoonful of fruit purée just before serving.

Thursday

Chicken Creams left-over chicken from Tuesday, 1 oz. (25 g.) margarine, 1 oz. (25 g.) flour, ¼ pint (1½ dl.) milk, 2 eggs, 2 tablespoons breadcrumbs, seasoning.
Chop or mince chicken, mix with a thick sauce made with margarine, flour, milk, add eggs, breadcrumbs. Season well, put into small moulds, steam for 30 minutes and serve with *Parsley Cream Potatoes*. To make these blend cooked mashed potatoes with a generous amount of butter, milk or thin cream and chopped parsley.

Fruit Cream Flan for the fleur pastry: 3 oz. (75 g.) butter or margarine, 2 oz. (50 g.) sugar, 5 oz. (125 g.) plain flour, egg yolk, water. For the filling: ¼ pint (1½ dl.) thick cream, little sugar, 1 lb. (½ kilo) cooked or canned fruit, 1½ teaspoons arrowroot.
Cream the butter or margarine and sugar, add the flour, egg yolk, then enough water to make a firm rolling consistency. Knead well, roll out. Line an 8-inch (20-cm.) flan ring, bake 'blind' as page 10, in a moderately hot oven. Cool. Fill with sweetened whipped cream then *well drained* fruit. Blend ⅓ pint (2 dl.) fruit syrup with the arrowroot. Boil until thick and clear, cool slightly, brush or spread over fruit.
To vary: Cranberry Apple Flan: fill flan with thick sweetened apple purée instead of cream, then cranberry sauce, see picture page 139, and recipe page 5.

Cranberry apple flan, recipe on this page   Crown roast, recipe on page 135

MONDAY

Chinese Pork Salad pineapple from Sunday, 1 tablespoon chopped spring onions *or* 1 chopped pickled onion, 1 tablespoon mustard pickle, pineapple syrup from Sunday, few drops lemon juice, left-over pork. To serve: mixed salad.
Chop pineapple, mix with spring onions or pickled onion, mustard pickle, pineapple syrup, lemon juice, to give a 'sweet-sour' taste. Slice the pork, top with this mixture and serve on a bed of mixed salad.

Golden Topped Sponge 3–4 tablespoons golden syrup, 3 oz. (75 g.) margarine, 3 oz. (75 g.) castor sugar, 2 eggs, 4 oz. (100 g.) self-raising flour, 1 tablespoon milk. To serve: golden syrup.
Put syrup into a greased basin. Top with sponge mixture made by creaming margarine and sugar, adding eggs, flour, milk. Cover basin, steam for $1\frac{1}{4}$–$1\frac{1}{2}$ hours, turn out and serve with extra golden syrup.

TUESDAY

Steamed Chicken with Egg and Liver Sauce 1 boiling chicken, little margarine or butter, seasoning. For the sauce: 1 oz. (25 g.) margarine, 1 oz. (25 g.) flour, $\frac{1}{2}$ pint (3 dl.) milk, 1 hard-boiled egg. To serve: cooked peas.
Put chicken into a steamer, rubbing the breast with margarine or butter. Put giblets into water below the steamer. Season chicken and steam – allow 30 minutes per lb. ($\frac{1}{2}$ kilo) and 30 minutes over. Make a sauce with margarine, flour, milk. Add seasoning, chopped cooked liver, chopped hard-boiled egg. Arrange jointed chicken on a hot dish, coat with the sauce and garnish with peas. Keep left-over chicken in a cool place.

Aubergines au Gratin instead of cooked potatoes serve aubergines. Slice 2 aubergines thinly, coat in a very little seasoned flour and fry in hot fat until tender. Put in a heatproof dish, top with a little melted margarine and grated Cheddar cheese. Brown under a hot grill, top with chopped parsley, see picture page 123.

Pear Milk Jelly dissolve a lemon jelly in the hot syrup from a can of pears, *cool*. Add enough milk to make up to 1 pint (6 dl.). Chop half the pears, add to the jelly. Put into a shallow serving dish. Allow to set, then top with sliced pears. Serve with cream or ice cream.

FRIDAY

Stuffed Baked Turbot with Shrimp Sauce 4 slices turbot, 1 tablespoon chopped parsley, 1 oz. (25 g.) melted margarine, 1 oz. (25 g.) chopped shrimps, 2 egg yolks, 2 oz. (50 g.) breadcrumbs, seasoning. For the sauce: 1 oz. (25 g.) margarine, 1 oz. (25 g.) flour, $\frac{1}{2}$ pint (3 dl.) milk, 1 tablespoon lemon juice, 2 oz. (50 g.) shrimps.
Arrange turbot in a greased dish. Top with stuffing made by mixing parsley, margarine, shrimps, egg yolks and breadcrumbs. Season well, cover with greased foil. Bake for 25 minutes in a moderately hot oven, Gas Mark 6, 400°F. (200°C.). Make a sauce with margarine, flour, milk. Add lemon juice, shrimps, seasoning. Heat, *but do not boil.*

Frosted Apricot Crunch medium can apricots, 2 egg whites, 1 oz. (25 g.) sugar, 2 oz. (50 g.) crisp biscuit crumbs. To serve: cream.
Rub apricots through a sieve, add to syrup from can, put in freezing tray, then into ice-making compartment of refrigerator; chill for 20 minutes until fairly thick. Fold in stiffly beaten egg whites, sugar, biscuit crumbs. Return to freezing tray, chill until firm. Serve with cream. If you have no refrigerator, add a level dessertspoon powdered gelatine to the hot apricot purée, allow to cool, then fold in crumbs and egg whites and allow to set.

SATURDAY

Chutneyed Galantine mix 8 oz. (200 g.) sausagemeat with 1 lb. ($\frac{1}{2}$ kilo) minced raw beef, 2 tablespoons chutney, pinch mixed herbs, 2 skinned chopped tomatoes, 2 egg yolks, seasoning. Put into a greased loaf tin, coated with crisp breadcrumbs, cover with greased foil, bake in centre of a moderate oven, Gas Mark 5, 375°F. (190°C.), for 1 hour. Serve with:
Potato Salad: boil new potatoes until just soft, skin while warm. Mix with chopped chives and/or spring onion and mayonnaise. Serve on a bed of lettuce, garnish with chopped parsley.

Easter Pavlova 4 egg whites, $\frac{1}{2}$ teaspoon vinegar, 1 level dessertspoon cornflour, 8 oz. (200 g.) castor sugar, 2 egg yolks, 2 oz. (50 g.) sugar, grated rind and juice 1 lemon, $\frac{1}{4}$ pint ($1\frac{1}{2}$ dl.) whipped cream. To decorate: marzipan Easter eggs.
Whip egg whites until really stiff. Add vinegar slowly to whisked whites. Blend cornflour with castor sugar, gradually beat half into egg whites, fold in the rest. Form into a flan shape on oiled paper, dry out for $2\frac{1}{2}$–3 hours in a very cool oven, Gas Mark 0–$\frac{1}{4}$, 200–225°F. (98–110°C.). Beat egg yolks, sugar, lemon rind and juice over hot water until very thick and creamy. Continue beating as mixture cools, fold into whipped cream and fill Pavlova case. Decorate with marzipan Easter eggs.

Index